FRONTMAN

SURVIVING THE ROCK STAR MYTH

FRONTMAN

SURVIVING THE ROCK STAR MYTH

RICHARD BARONE

Backbeat
Books

An Imprint of Hal Leonard Corporation

New York

Published in 2007 by
Backbeat Books
An Imprint of Hal Leonard Corporation
19 West 21st Street, New York, NY 10010

Printed in the United States of America

While every effort has been made to trace the owners of the copyright material reproduced herein, the publishers would like to apologize for any omissions and will be pleased to incorporate missing acknowledgments in any future editions.

Book design by Snow Creative Services
Jacket photography and endsheets copyright © Mick Rock, 2007

Library of Congress Cataloging-in-Publication Data
Barone, Richard.
   Frontman : surviving the rock star myth / by Richard Barone. — 1st ed.
      p. cm.
   Includes index.
   ISBN-13: 978-0-87930-912-1
   ISBN-10: 0-87930-912-1
   1. Barone, Richard. 2. Rock musicians—United States—Biography. I. Title.
ML420.B177A3 2007
782.42166092—dc22
[B]

                                                        2007019002

www.backbeatbooks.com

For Josephine Barone:

Guardian angel, guide, mother, and superstar

"Mythology begins where madness starts. A person who is truly gripped by a calling, by a dedication, by a belief, by a zeal, will sacrifice his security, will sacrifice even his life, will sacrifice personal relationships, will sacrifice prestige, and will think nothing of personal development; he will give himself entirely to his myth. . . ."

—Joseph Campbell

CONTENTS

FOREWORD
BY TONY VISCONTI

That charismatic guy (or girl) who sings lead, the one that makes the fans swoon, could be a soloist but prefers to stand with his mates shoulder to shoulder and split the share of the proceeds equally—including the fans who claw their way to the dressing room. The frontman is what we pay good money to see/hear/swoon over. The frontman is the big draw and probably the most irrational member of the band. His whims, flashes of genius, tantrums, and sudden flights of fancy are the sparks that ignite the band's engine. Without him the band is just a rhythm section (but don't tell them).

The frontman is usually the writer or cowriter of the songs, most often the lyricist. As a record producer, I have worked with their puffed-out chests for decades and witnessed them at their most vulnerable moments—no, not in the boudoir—behind a microphone in a darkened recording studio. In that most hallowed place, they must make the listener see/hear/swoon without the visual stimulus of a live performance—not an easy task by any means. In this trial by microphone, they scream for more vocal, more reverb, more effects, more wine, more candles, and (for the sixtieth time) just one more take. When they hear their vocal played back, they say they hate it. Yet when it is time for the final audio mix, they want their vocal to be the loudest element of the recording. But I give them everything, caress every whim, and take every suggestion seriously, because the frontman is the visionary, the young dude that carries the news. Without the frontman, the rest of us would be out of work.

The frontman eventually goes solo and it is inevitable. Maybe it's because of "musical differences" (the most given excuse for the band's breakup); Bowie exterminated the Spiders and Morrissey now stands aloof from the Smiths. Let's face it, frontmen are stars and stars have massive egos. Richard Barone is a frontman, and a star, but disarming and urbane. He continues to make glorious solo albums and I have had the pleasure of producing one of them. Richard Barone is now an author who writes about one subject he knows well.

See what it's like to see the business of music . . . through the eyes of a frontman.

Tony Visconti

May 2007

Tony Visconti is hailed by many as one of the greatest producers of all time. Synonymous with groundbreaking music, he has worked with the most dynamic and influential names in pop, including T.Rex, David Bowie, U2, and Morrissey. His best-selling book, Tony Visconti: The Autobiography; Bowie, Bolan and the Brooklyn Boy, *was recently published by HarperCollins U.K.*

INTRODUCTION

What everybody wants to believe in most is the fantasy. . . .
The parties that last for days, the sex, untold riches, and endless
supplies of drugs. Nobody noticed that, at the height of Beatlemania,
John Lennon screamed, "Help! I need somebody!"

When I considered the fates of so many, why, I wondered, was I let off
with just a warning? This book is my version of how it all happened.
Any inaccuracies or misinterpretations are mine alone.

R. B.
New York City
March 21, 2007

CHAPTER 1

THE LITTLEST DJ

HOW TO HAVE YOUR OWN RADIO SHOW AT AGE SEVEN

Florida sticks out like a sore thumb. Long before the 2000 election debacle, anthrax, and endless other anomalies, the Sunshine State jutted out from the mainland like a UFO landing strip, welcoming all aliens into its orange groves and shopping malls with open arms. Being born in Florida carries with it certain responsibilities. Most important, an embracing of both astronaut and outcast, sunshine and storm warnings, Disney characters and drug lords. . . .

The state always seemed like an outpost to me—far removed from the media centers of New York and Hollywood. Except for news coverage of the occasional hurricane, and the arrests of rock icons like Jim Morrison and Janis Joplin, my state was far from the media mainstream. Tampa, my hometown, in particular, was not best known for its nightlife, either. Mick Jagger and Keith Richards memorialized the pursuit of pleasure in the Tampa Bay area in the title of the anthem they wrote there: "(I Can't Get No) Satisfaction."

There was a flat little park near our house, just a few trees, patchy lawn, and sidewalk paths, that my dad always called "Little New York." He would walk with me there, telling me about the *real* New York City, where his brother, my uncle Peter, lived. Somehow I knew instinctively that was where I wanted to be. Just like Ricky Ricardo, named "Ricky" like me, fronting his band in a New York nightclub, in the reruns of *I Love Lucy* I watched every morning on the black-and-white television screen in front on my playpen.

Mom would carefully show me the autographed publicity photos of movie stars she kept in a special scrapbook. She would point out her favorites, stars she had written to when she was a girl. They all seemed so perfect, unattainable, and, though of another era, timeless in their own way. Gazing up at the sky at night, I would look for them—and try to comprehend what made them "stars."

I was obsessed with Top 40 AM radio, and walked around with a transistor radio pressed against my ear by day and under my pillow at night. Songs like "Set Me Free" by the Kinks and "Time of the Season" by the Zombies filled me, and I'm sure countless other curious youths, with the mysteries of love, sex, and adolescence. It was this music that made me the hopeless romantic I would someday become, believing that "Love Is All Around" and "All You Need Is Love." Always listening for the perfect pop song, I kept the weekly Top 40 countdown playlists next to my bed, noting each song I heard in the dark with a little check mark and a description of the tune. I could differentiate between the different types of reverbs and echoes used, and mostly, I was intrigued by how these records created their own little worlds, inviting me in for their three minutes or so. I would live inside those songs. That was where I wanted to live.

In the daytime, when my asthma didn't keep me housebound, I would play DJ, alone in the backyard—a green tweed portable turntable and stack of 45s, with the Florida sun beating down on my Technicolor childhood. I had an old 45 of Paul Anka's "Put Your Head on My Shoulder," and when I learned he was making records at fifteen, I wanted to start even younger. Mom and Dad would watch Dean Martin and other Rat Packers on television, and from their reaction I learned what entertainment was, and would sometimes put on my own "shows" for them and my grandmother.

One Sunday when I was seven, Mom and Dad and my little sister, Maria (my older brother, Anthony, was off as usual with his own friends), packed into the Chevrolet Impala for a family outing to Tampa's particularly unglamorous Municipal Beach. There, my favorite radio station was broadcasting live. I knew this from my constant radio-listening, and the station's constant plugging of their live Sunday show, *Beach Party*. After staking our claim to a little patch of beach, laying down a massive beach towel and a big silver ice chest filled with cans of TAB and cold cuts, I walked in search of the broadcast site. The day, the summer sun, and the sand were all white-hot. Behind a long, dual turntable console emblazoned with the call letters W-A-L-T, each letter framed by a pastel pink diamond shape, my favorite DJ, Marv Ray, was spinning tunes. This was too good to be true. I watched and listened, both live and on the ever-present radio pressed to my ear. I mustered up enough nerve to step up and talk to him.

It's possible Marv wears a toupee, I thought. Something about him seemed visually wrong—perhaps I had imagined a much younger man, or someone more like one of the handsome movie stars in my mother's scrapbook, or, *at least* like a rock star. I waited until he put on a record, then walked up in my swim trunks, looked up at my him, and blurted, "I could do that!"

Like with everything else I've gotten myself into, good and bad, it all began with a blurt.

"I could be a DJ."

"Okay, son," he spoke, softer than I'd expected, pulling his head-phone off one ear. "I'll put you on right after the next commercial."

Now I got nervous. What would I say? Why did I do this? Will I stutter? Not that I had ever stuttered before, but what if I started, right then, on the air?

Marv was busy cueing up the next record, and on the phone to the station. I almost decided to run away when he wasn't looking. The muffled little waves of Tampa Bay were crashing in the background, and the particular sound of children shrieking at the beach echoed in the distance. I never seemed to be the one shrieking in the distance like that, never just having fun. That was always for other kids. Even now, I was hard at work, trying to figure out how to get on the radio.

Before I knew it, Marv was casually talking to me, asking me where I was from, how old I was, what grade I was in, did I have a girlfriend (*"No!"*). . . . And I answered calmly, truthfully (I think), and probably a little cockily.

Then I realized we had been on the air the whole time.

Aiming the microphone toward me, he told me to announce the next record.

"You're listening to *Beach Party*, coming to you live from Tampa Municipal Beach, on W-A-L-T Eleven Ten. Now here's Donovan . . . Mel-low Yel-low!"

"And that's Ricky Barone, the Littlest DJ," Marv added over the familiar hi-hat intro of the record.

Marv was again back on the phone with the station. The listener phones there had lit up, he told me. I assume his producer told him to keep me around, because he asked me to announce the next record, and the next, until I was on the air for the remainder of his show.

I was a hit. Marv asked me to come back the following week, and "The Littlest DJ" was on the air with *Beach Party* every Sunday for the rest of the summer. Spinning records, announcing, doing the commercials . . . and going home each Sunday with a stack of promo 45s to fuel my pop passion for the next week. A dream came true. It only takes one to prove to you that it can happen.

With Brian Wilson and the Beach Boys harmonizing on the turntable, beachcombing boys and girls would come up to me, and listeners would call in with requests. I had my personal favorites, of course, and played them as often as permitted by the station. Besides the Beatles and other British groups, I was attracted to the hits of Nancy Sinatra, especially her songs with Lee Hazelwood. And, ever since I heard that Paul McCartney had said that Peggy Lee was the Beatles' favorite American singer, I always kept an ear out for her and would play "Fever" as a golden oldie. But it was chiming guitar pop that was my passion. Shining pop moments.

Even then, I was aware of "guilty pleasures"—records that existed solely for their ephemeral rush or catchy hooks—and played them on my segment of the show with zeal. That is, I knew the Monkees were "fakes," actors on a TV show, but that didn't stop me from playing their songs. And that Petula Clark singles, like "Don't Sleep in the Subway," produced by Tony Hatch, were undeniable pop confections. Could I ever have dreamed that a decade later I would be sitting on a hotel room bed in Miami with Monkee Davy Jones, strumming an acoustic guitar, singing Beatles songs together all night? Or, how could

I imagine that, even further down the line, I would be standing in the wings of the legendary Hollywood Bowl stage with Petula Clark herself, as she insinuated I was giving preferential treatment to a certain young female singer on a show—because I was, *ahem*, having an affair with her? I don't think so. I mean, I was still only seven years old.

I learned to never assume your fears are justified. There is a special calm in the center of your worst fears. From the first time I was on the radio, I felt at home there. Funny, because I was secretly a shy boy. I was mildly aware that my voice was being heard by tens of thousands of people in their homes, in their cars, or on the beach. But the second the red light came on, I felt wrapped within a protective cocoon, the calm center of the storm, the safe eye of the hurricane. And most importantly, I felt loved . . . even if by strangers.

When I returned to elementary school in September, I didn't make a big deal about being on the radio all summer. I had seen it as a job to be done and that I was the one to do it. Other than lusting over Marv Ray's bright-red 1963 Ford Thunderbird convertible, I wasn't too caught up in the trappings of celebrity. Yet.

Possibly the most important thing the episode contributed to my life was an intimate exposure to the mystical art of the hit single, what makes a record snap, crackle, and pop on the radio. I was fortunate that the mid-'60s is when I walked into the story. It was the beginning of a peak period in the art of recording, when just the right elements of adventurism, technology, and songcraft came together to create a body of work that still inspires today. Records that sound as good on our iPods as they did on those little transistor radios.

Of course, no era can ever be repeated. You can't step in the same river twice, etc. That is the nature of all things. But this goes beyond nostalgia, because even listeners born long after the era still gravitate toward this music. We would be wise to consider what made those records great, and how they led to the pop music that followed. Maybe it was because the emphasis wasn't on repeating past successes, but genuinely creating something new. Another contributing factor was specialization: there were arrangers, musicians, songwriters, producers, and singers. Now, instead of doing one thing well, an artist is driven to do all of these himself, and the results are watered down. The art of arranging, especially, is being lost.

When I think now of all those unrealized marketing opportunities! "The Littlest DJ" school lunchboxes, notebooks, portable turntables. . . The possibilities were endless! Why, oh why didn't someone think of it then? I could be making a killing with my stash on eBay today! Instead, I left WALT armed only with the experience of having been on the other side of the curtain. Now anything was possible. And, by the time fall arrived, I was back in the third grade, and "The Littlest DJ" was already a memory.

Now the need to own and play a guitar was becoming unbearable. Mom and Dad, either through supreme intuition or my constant whining, understood—or succumbed—and got me a quite amazing axe: a used Sears Silvertone electric guitar. It was a bit battered and beat-up, in glorious black punctuated with oversized silver flakes, white sides, and contained in a matching red felt-lined case housing its own amplifier, which hummed softly. Inside the amp, a few vacuum tubes glowed brightly and even generated enough heat to warm my bedroom on the rare cold Florida night. Actually, the guitar was made for Sears by Danelectro and featured their legendary "lipstick pickup." (Apparently, the company purchased an overrun of chrome lipstick tubes from a cosmetic company, and used them to house their electric guitar pickups.) Now a collector's item, then an entry-level guitar that I could barely hold, much less play. But, boy, was it cool!

I couldn't for the life of me figure out how to get any kind of legitimate sound from the instrument. The six strings on that Silvertone were as mysterious to me as the string theory of quantum gravity. Again, either parental intuition or their own self-defense from my atonal explorations led to a solution, and soon a sweet-faced, sixteen-year-old Italian boy named Manuel was recruited to come over once a week and give me lessons. The chords he played and attempted to teach me were unbelievably rich—his thick fingers slid from one smooth jazz chord to another, and though I listened and watched with deep appreciation and admiration, I remained unmoved.

Because I wanted to *rock*.

Manuel's lessons gave me the basics, though: applying pressure with my left hand's chubby fingers on the strings along the fretboard resulted in note selection, while my right hand's strumming or picking resulted in rhythm or articulation. Got it. That's all I needed to know.

I took a few group classes at a nearby recreation center, to which I was dutifully driven by my dad. I was the only kid in the class with an *electric* guitar! But mostly I started the process of teaching myself. I got a few Mel Bay books, and sat alone with the Silvertone beast at home, playing along with Beatles and Donovan records.

The guitar would be the undercurrent and thread for the rest of my school years and, yes, like the string theory of space-time continuum, connect my past to the present day. I have rarely gone a day without playing a guitar.

Learn what you need to know. That's my humble advice. Some of my favorite artists have used limited palettes. The Ramones and Kraftwerk, for instance. Others, like the Beatles and countless artists, increased their palettes when necessary, i.e., when their songwriting evolved and required more shadings. Not to say that studying music theory is unimportant. Of course, I recommend it. Without that knowledge, you are limiting yourself. But you don't need to be a virtuoso to start with, or even become one. That's not necessarily what music is about, and the thought (and resulting fear of failure) can stifle you, or stop you completely. Most of the greats learn as they go, studying from the inside. With whatever you're doing—and I don't mean just music—learn what you *need* to know, then dive in. It's really about your passion: if you "follow your bliss," as Joseph Campbell and the B-52's said, you will find a way to make it work. It's like learning to swim: you'll splash around and struggle a bit, then you will learn to survive.

Of course, I can't swim.

But that's another story.

CHAPTER 2

SEX FLAG

HOW TO WREAK HAVOC THROUGHOUT YOUR SCHOOL YEARS AND WHY

It was in fourth grade that I learned about sex. Seated behind me in class that year was girl whose name I shall never forget: Barbara Bladen. I had heard rumors of some of the things she would tell me about from my teammates in the Little League dugout. My brother was the coach, my dad was the manager of the team, and I played third base, where my mind could wander into the outfield until something was batted my way. "You gotta be kidding," was my usual response to any dugout sex talk. "Why would anyone want to do *that*?" But in hushed tones from behind her desk, pushed up close to mine, Barbara explained everything like Masters and Johnson, and it all made sense. A prepubescent Dr. Ruth. I am still indebted to her.

Not to say that I *acted* on anything she taught me, but I remember thinking, "Wow—what a great concept!" Besides, it explained the lyrics of at least 99 percent of the pop songs I listened to and had announced on the radio. ("Wild Thing," "Light My Fire," "Let's Spend the Night Together"... bingo.) I couldn't wait to tell the world.

As a member of the Safety Patrol, one of my duties, besides serving as a crossing guard for fellow students on a tiny side street with virtually no vehicular traffic, was to raise the American flag. Every morning, I would carefully unfold the Stars and Stripes and send it up the flagpole between the two royal palms in front of the B. C. Graham Elementary School building.

One morning, I made my own flag.

I found a large rectangular swath of bright blue fabric in the main hallway of the school and, sitting on the steps with a fat Magic Marker, wrote on it three letters in the biggest, boldest lettering possible:

S E X

As a few fellow Patrol officers watched in giggling amusement, I attached it to the chain and sent it clanging ceremoniously up the flagpole. We all saluted and went to class as the bell rang.

The next bells ringing were the principal's office phones, ringing off the hook with calls from angry parents in neighboring homes. The search for the culprit began—and ended just as quickly. Everyone knew it was me.

I was surprised to find myself in a tremendous amount of trouble. Scared beyond belief, but defiantly cocky, I was pulled from class and sent to the office. My parents were called in the next day (my father, a steelworker, having to take a rare day off from work), and I was paddled by the principal, hard. Those were the days of corporal punishment in public schools. Of course, I was suspended from the Safety Patrol and later, when I was finally allowed to return to active duty, I did so halfheartedly. My spirit was temporarily crushed.

At home, the incident was never discussed. A dog-eared paperback entitled *What to Tell Your Children About Sex* was simply left on my bed. I remember thinking, "Why don't they just *tell* me about it? What's the big deal?" Anyway, I studied the book with great interest.

I had had no idea that waving my sex flag would cause such a commotion. I was only expressing myself. I hadn't yet considered that I might already be using sex to reach out for love. And certainly I hadn't considered that there could be anything wrong with sex. Now that I was aware of it, in fact, sex seemed to be everywhere: in every song, in every movie, in every commercial. How could it be wrong?

So I learned then what Madonna later failed to clarify in her 1989 hit, "Express Yourself": It might not always be socially acceptable. But that doesn't mean don't do it.

This had not occurred to me. At home and at school I had been encouraged to express myself quite freely up until that point. I felt both crushed and exhilarated, proud (to be a rebel) and embarrassed. It was my parents' disapproval and disappointment that was hard to take. Finding ways to express myself fully *without severe punishment* was my new goal.

I got into more trouble, though. And, yes, usually it was sexual. I think I knew too much about sex for my age . . . probably more than I know now, if that's possible. But I knew I could get away with so much more if I played in a band. Rock bands got away with everything. They were *expected* to get into trouble.

Once and for all, I knew I had to be a musician. Regardless of how well I did scholastically, which was pretty well, my primary concern was how I would be able to use the knowledge from every subject in school in my music career: poetry (music is metaphor), literature (without literary references, you are nothing), art (let your music be visual), history (you had better know what's gone down before), photography (image, baby), phys. ed. (music is energy, music is physical), and music (duh).

Math, also . . . music *is* mathematical. But I wasn't so great at math.

Whatever the class was, I had the intention of applying the resulting knowledge to writing, recording, and performing music. I didn't tell anyone about this. This was my secret: Music was now my reason for doing everything I did. Later, matters of the heart and the libido would enter the picture but, even then, music was in on the act. I mean, it is common knowledge that rock stars get all the action. The power is primordial. Musician, producer, and neuroscientist Daniel J. Levitin, in his book, *This Is Your Brain on Music*, quotes Charles Darwin's *Descent of Man*: "I conclude that musical notes and rhythm were first acquired by the male or female progenitors of mankind for the sake of charming the opposite sex."

Love, of course, is another thing altogether. I began more and more to believe in the idealized notion of love that exists only pop songs. And, even rock stars have trouble finding it. I got deeper into playing my guitar—privately, of course, in my bedroom.

Sometime in the fourth or fifth grade I was given my first tape recorder. It was a little, grey-and-cream Norelco mini reel-to-reel recorder, with two tiny two-and-a-half-inch plastic reels of quarter-inch tape. I recorded everything I heard: my grandmother's stories of her village in Sicily, birthday parties, the prompted barking of our impossibly cute, miniature poodle, and most of all, my guitars: the Silvertone and my new acoustic. I tried placing the mic in every conceivable position, distance, and location in relation to the guitar. I was particularly intrigued by the sound of the mic placed in a vase, an empty water pitcher, or at the end of a plastic tube or hose. Sometimes I taped the mic to the instrument itself, to pick up the vibration and create distortion. Anything to shape the sound. I would zoom home from school to watch *Astro Boy* cartoons and mess around with the tape recorder in front of the TV, intoxicated by the smell of 3M Scotch Brand recording tape. The obsession was isolating, though—I found myself mostly alone, recording my own voice or trying to figure out the harmonies of the Beatles' "Nowhere Man" ("sitting in his nowhere land"), then contemplating the lyrics and the irony. When I got to junior high, I finally began to meet other musicians.

Thanks to a Supreme Court decision, George Washington Jr. High now had a large black population, unlike the mostly white elementary school I had attended. Soon I was digging the heavy funk of James Brown and all the various shades of R&B, alongside the Beatles' *Abbey Road* and *White Album*. In gym class there seemed to be time to talk about music (and, incidentally, bisexuality, but more about that later). There, I met Melvin, a bass player and fellow seventh-grader with a big afro. After a few conversations about the nature of funk music and the importance of the bass guitar to it, I started a quest for my own bass.

Still, and always, a Beatles nut, I wanted a Hofner violin-shaped bass like the one McCartney used on their early records. I didn't consider that its woofy and imprecise tone really wasn't at all the sound I was looking for at that moment; it was what I had set my sights on. I soon found a violin-shaped "Phantom" bass in an audio equipment mail order catalog, and saved up $49.95 (plus shipping). It was the most garish, artificial-looking sunburst I have ever seen—before or since—with a skull and crossbones emblazoned on its hideous oversized headstock. Disgusting, yes, but I took to those four fat strings with much more ease and confidence than I did to six. Mainly, the idea of not playing chords, but playing fat, driving notes on single strings appealed to me. I would practice landing on "the one," listening to James Brown arrangements and Motown hits, over and over, to understand how to "decorate the clock" as Don Van Vliet, aka Captain Beefheart, would say.

I wasn't particularly comfortable with telling fellow students or teachers of my plans to be a musician or recording artist, or God forbid, to dare mention I was going be a *rock star*. I wanted to play that card close to my chest, and be one of the boys. So, when anyone, student or teacher, asked me what I wanted to be when I got out of school, I'd say, "A male prostitute," without skipping a beat. That always shut them up.

I met a couple of other guys who played guitar and bass, too. One talked about Les Paul guitars worshipfully, and got me interested. I remember clipping a full-page, black-and-white Gibson ad from a scholastic magazine, showing a Les Paul Special, that I hung up in my locker at school and lusted over, like a pin-up in a soldier's barracks. I had a friend since second grade, William, who was a drummer, and I suggested—since a drum kit is not as mobile as a guitar—that we all meet at his place after school to jam. I didn't play, but recorded the group with my new mono cassette recorder. As loose and loud as they were, the synergy of musicians playing together in the contained space of William's parents' living room was magical to me. I started noticing the sound variances in the room, finding the best spot to place the one mic for recording. After a few of these sessions, though, William's parents had had enough and pulled the plug. Considering the racket, the broken glassware, and the general mess we made, it was a predictable end to that short-lived combo.

By the end of junior high, I had graduated to a full-size, Akai stereo quarter-inch, reel-to-reel tape deck from Radio Shack. My first real, almost-semi-pro tape recorder! I had heard the phrase "sound-on-sound" in school, and, locating the erase head, I promptly cut its connecting wires so I could begin doing some primitive overdubbing. Of course, without Simul-Sync I was working in the dark: I could not listen to the tracks I had already laid down. I had to line the tape up to where I wanted to begin and just play or sing, hoping it was aligned with the previously recorded basic track. More often than not, it wasn't. So, these experiments often ended up in a form that could be regarded as, shall we say, avant-garde. I filled endless reels with these lo-fi excursions. Sometimes, actual songs would emerge, but the *sound* was what I was most concerned with.

The summer before I started high school, my parents gathered us into the Impala and took my sister and me on a cross-country drive from Tampa to California. This was my first experience of life outside Florida. We drove for a week and stopped in every state along the way. The real world—and things did seem more real. The deserts were real, the cities were real. In comparison, everything back home seemed like an imitation of life, like Disney World's Main Street, USA. Too clean. The real world was dirty, and not always pretty. Some of the farms were abandoned, with untended crops burnt by the sun. There were poor people in shacks along the highway. And sometimes there was roadkill in the emergency lane. That 4,000-mile road trip was a turning point, putting the whole country in perspective. The experience shaped the way I later saw music and . . . well, everything. A larger scale, the big picture. Everything changed.

I got slimmer, and even got new glasses for the trip, consciously altering my appearance for the first time. I traded in my nerdy, black plastic frames for minimal, gold wire rims with tinted, octagonal lenses. At fourteen, I was already preparing to be photographed for an album cover, beginning a lifelong endeavor.

We spent most of that summer with my aunt Marie, in San Francisco, who happened to live on *Florida* Street in the Mission District. I couldn't seem to completely get away from Florida, even there. With new friends Nick and Mike, I played baseball in the street and smashed my very first, and only, window, which felt great. Needless to say, it was a rite of passage. I even had to pay for it with my own money.

I fell in love with the sounds, sights, and smells of San Francisco. Playing chess on the stoop after dinner, as the sky got darker and the city lights came on. The Golden Gate Bridge! Mountains! Hippies! The potential danger of earthquakes! I knew it would be hard to go back to boring Tampa at the end of the summer. I had gotten letters from my friends—they seemed so far away. One pal wrote about smoking pot, the spiritual experiences (with illustrations) he had had while sniffing glue, and quoted the last verse of the Rolling Stones' "Ruby Tuesday": "Lose your dreams / And you will lose your mind / ain't life unkind?"

We got back home in the fall, just before school was about to begin. Just as I thought I would, I saw things differently. Tampa seemed smaller and flatter. Hillsborough High, though, was a big school—a grand, gothic building with a clock tower and stained glass windows— with lots of traditions begging to be broken. Looking more like an Ivy League college than a high school, it had been built at a time when high school was the end of the education line for many, if not most. There were some tense moments early in the school year, with minor racial incidents and rioting . . . the result of frazzled nerves caused by the cross-town busing of students. We would be sent home early, and some days were lost entirely. Growing pains, I think, as the populations adjusted to integration. But soon, things leveled off.

I made friends quickly. Most had cars, and lunchtime was escape time. Returning to classes after lunch was unofficially optional. My friends would often stumble back from lunch in a mild, sedated stupor, eight-track tapes of Pink Floyd, Led Zeppelin, or my favorite, John Lennon's first solo album, *Plastic Ono Band*, blasting from the backseat and door speakers of their Chevrolet Camaros. The bass rumbled and vibrated hypnotically—I often became distracted during conversations, as I listened more intently to the stereo images, the balance of the mixes, and how much low-end the car's sound system could handle, than to the casual fast food banter.

My feelings about drugs were complex. On one hand, I was curious, but I had a fear of burning out too young. I was seeing it happen around me all the time. I certainly didn't want to burn out *before* I became a *rock star*!

My new friends were a creative bunch: Sherri, a fellow Beatles nut and guitar player who had a big, red, semi-hollow Silvertone with a hefty Bigsby tailpiece; Julian, a filmmaker; Marla, a wild child and soulmate, who would become my first roommate and bandmate; and

Jean, fellow traveler and lifelong friend. We encouraged each other to take our work—and our lives—to the logical extreme conclusions.

We all need all the encouragement we can get, after all. An artist lays so much on the line, and sticks his neck out so far. There are so many land mines to set off, so many banana peels to slip on. It helps when someone is there to dismantle the bomb, catch you when you fall, or celebrate with you when you remain standing.

Even though I was only in high school and the stakes were low, I was developing a way of working—a way of collaborating. What I have always been interested in is to deliver the best that I can deliver, while bringing out the best in my collaborators. A lot of what makes this happen is credited to the chemistry between people, but I believe this chemistry can be created. The two main active ingredients are:

LOVE + TRUST

It's hard to write or record a song with someone you don't love in some way, and nearly impossible to write with someone you don't trust. You may be able to get away with faking it, but the results are rarely as good. I nearly always fall in love with artists I work with, and I feel something mutual in return. Not a romantic love, but to me, going to a recording session is like going on a date. I dress for it and I must not be the first or only one to feel this way—the phrase "recording date" has been used for decades!

My first year of high school was also the year when I knew *for certain* that I dug guys, though I always really knew. When I was fourteen, I met someone at an after-school meeting for a club we were both members of. I had noticed other guys before, but this was different: I wanted to be with him all the time. How could I tell him? Did he have a girlfriend? What if I liked his girlfriend, too? What would become of me? I couldn't sleep that night. My mind raced with possibilities. I was tongue-tied. I couldn't adequately express myself. Silence came so much more easily to me than words. All of my questions and emotions came out in songs, then and later.

I flew a Falcon, I flew a Thunderbird
I threw everything away
There was a pasture, someone was chanting
I couldn't listen anyway
And in the future, if there is time left
Then I will show you how I feel
Too many scared guys
Too many scared guys
I want to kiss you, but I'll go away
Let me go—away . . .

The glam rock revolution did not make much of a dent in Florida, home of the strictly T-shirt-and-faded-denim-clad, Allman Brother's scene. But that was cool—it made the glam rockers *ours*. The New York Dolls, David Bowie, Lou Reed . . . and, most of all, Marc Bolan, where my rock 'n' roll heart and my teenage sexual ambiguity collided in the sweetest possible way.

Bolan, his name and image synonymous with his group, T.Rex (after the group's first few acoustic albums, only Marc's photo appeared on the front covers), was the quintessential rock star. Aggressive, sensitive, masculine, feminine, acoustic, electric, confident, and vulnerable—his poetic, abstract, suggestive lyrics came just at the right time for me, hungry for a post-Beatles role model. Hyper-popular in England and around the world in the early '70s, but somehow less so in the more Doobie Brothers–dominated U.S. (except for the massive hit, "Bang a Gong (Get it On)") the actual sound of the recordings knocked me over the head. The tunes were so precisely arranged and recorded, yet with an appealing bit of looseness and spontaneity. Brilliant. The producer's name was Italian, like mine, and in my mind he began to symbolize everything that I thought a producer should be. For the next several years, his name appeared on the vast majority of my favorite records. It was uncanny. I had found my producer: Tony Visconti. I would just have to wait two decades or so before I would actually get to work with him.

I got to see T.Rex in concert at the Convention Center in Tampa, where they were opening for Three Dog Night. It was one of the loudest blasts of boogie I had yet or have since heard, but Bolan was the epitome of rock star charisma. Wailing on backup vocals was the beautiful and soulful Gloria Jones, whose record "Heartbeat" I had played on the radio. My sister, Maria, caught a tambourine thrown by Marc, during "Get It On," and I placed a silver star ring by the purple Mary Jane–shoed feet of the star, which he bent to pick up and place on his finger. Immediately following the set, Sherri and I raced to their hotel (a roadie told us it was the Hawaiian Village on Dale Mabry Highway), where we found ourselves face to face with Marc's primary sideman, the percussionist Mickey Finn. We had a long conversation in the parking lot about the nature of fame—how odd it was for T.Rex to be superstars in some countries and not in others. Over and over, Mickey told us to "go knock on Marc's door, he'd love to meet you." Intuitively, we chose not to.

I finally got a real bass around this time, a white small-bodied Fender MusicMaster (like a Mustang, but *without* the racing stripe, and with a simpler, single pickup configuration). It was perfect for copping the punchy, pop basslines on the current wave of Brit Pop records. I also acquired, through my trademark pleading, the mowing of lawns, and doing other miscellaneous odd jobs, a huge Fender Bassman 50 amp rig, which would rattle my poor mother's house like a freight train barreling through my bedroom. To this day I am amazed that she or my dad didn't complain more. It was incredibly *loud*, and they were incredibly tolerant. But I did start to get a better handle on my playing, especially simplifying my parts, and found that, more often than not, *simple is better.*

That doesn't just go for bass playing, either.

In *The Rise and Fall of Ziggy Stardust and the Spiders from Mars*, David Bowie portrayed the archetypal frontman drama. As the composite character based on several of his contemporaries (including Bolan, whose magnified image was projected as a backdrop during live performances), the still widely unknown Bowie stepped out and himself *became* "the special man" who "took it all too far." He proclaimed his bisexuality with flaming red spiked hair, wild costumes, and radical makeup. With handfuls of pharmaceuticals, he came dangerously close to fulfilling the album's prophetic outcome by nearly becoming a "Rock 'n' Roll Suicide" himself.

I started to take my own appearance to extremes, growing my hair quite long, then short, wearing a combination of baggy '40s vintage and glam-inspired clothing, and even occasional eye makeup. At one point, I shaved off my McCartneyesque eyebrows, as Bowie had done, perfectly captured in Mick Rock's brilliant *Ziggy* photographs: inspirational images of the mythical power of rock and roll in the present tense. I noted his photo credits on my favorite LP jackets and knew I wanted him to photograph me one day. Years later, Rock would confide in me that while we has being carted off for quadruple-bypass heart surgery, he was singing *Ziggy's* "Rock 'n' Roll Suicide" at the top of his lungs. The road to excess, it seems, is contagion.

For all that, I wasn't particularly flamboyant or outrageous. I still longed to be one of the boys, too. I went to our school football games and other events with a different set of friends. I wanted it all. I wanted everybody to love me. I learned to fly my sex flag at half-mast.

I was a member of the yearbook staff, along with Sherri and other close friends, which gave us almost unlimited power. (On a surreal note, the yearbook advisor, Mrs. Ann Cook, was the "Gerber Baby," whose face appeared on every jar of Gerber Baby Food. She still looked exactly the same.) Joining the staff was a strategic move: I knew teachers and students alike wanted to be well represented in the yearbook, and wouldn't want to risk upsetting us. So, teachers would practically give us carte blanche to do whatever we wanted, and students were amenable. We could have gotten away with murder.

Getting to class ridiculously late was okay—we could always say we were on a photo shoot for the yearbook. We had unlimited hall passes and other paper credentials, which were often used to roll joints when the yearbook office ran out of rolling papers. For a final report project in the mythology class we never attended, Sherri and I reenacted the Trojan War by sitting at opposite ends of a table and firing unwrapped Trojan condoms at each other. We each received an A for the course. By the time I was a senior and was named yearbook editor, we ran the school. At the state convention of yearbook staffs, we won top honors, though the school was disgraced publicly for the seventeen wine bottles found under my hotel room bed.

The minute I graduated high school, I moved in with Marla. I was working as a sacristan at Sacred Heart Catholic Church downtown, a Jesuit parish with a staff of several very intellectual priests, the kind the Church used to banish for their progressive thinking. Jesuit priests often have a second, secular area of expertise, such as science, journalism, or engineering. One of the priests I worked with, for instance, had designed the intricate and groundbreaking baggage-handling system at Chicago's O'Hare Airport. These priests taught me to celebrate Jewish holidays, like Passover, because Jesus did. They encouraged me to visit churches of all faiths to learn about them, too. Each Sunday, I visited another denomination's church after attending my own—Pentecostals, spirit-filled Baptists, Holy Rollers—houses of worship where gospel music would reach the kind of fever pitch that could make the Catholic statues blush and the stained glass shatter.

My duties at the church varied, but included being an altar boy when needed, and neatly laying out the priests' vestments on the big dressing table. Though I didn't have an especially religious upbringing, I loved the Mass, memorizing it in its entirety and reciting it secretly in Latin with another altar boy. The voicings of Gregorian chants filled me with awe. Though I was conflicted about Catholicism, I did *not* make a sex flag to wave in place of the Vatican's in front of the church. Some lessons, apparently, had been learned in elementary school.

Our apartment was located along a spooky curve in the Hillsborough River, at the end of a dark, narrow, one-lane road called Hamilton Heath, in a strange part of Tampa called Sulfur Springs. The entire area had once been submerged in a major flood caused by Hurricane Donna in the early 1960s, and now seemed stuck in that era. A creepy, musty vibe permeated the big house and surrounding area. The top floor of the château-shaped house had been converted into two apartments, with Sherri and Julian taking the one next door. Their living room was dominated by a gigantic New York Dolls poster, ours by images of Marc Bolan. It was magical, yet I felt uneasy there. I set up my tape recorder in my bedroom, but made very few recordings. Unexplainable occurrences kept me on edge—like the violent gusts of wind gushing through the apartment when there was no wind elsewhere.

Then, one early evening, as Marla and I were going out for the night, we simultaneously witnessed a shadowy apparition of a lady in a big dress, as if from another era. She held the edge of her dress up as she walked down our stairs. Damn! That was a ghost. When we told our landlords the next day, they laughed and told us the house was haunted. "Didn't you know that?" they asked, without surprise or irony. They told us that, decades before, a woman had been killed in the room that was now my bedroom. "She was murdered by her son. She's never really left." That was too much for Marla. We went to see a Fellini film that night, and during the intermission, she disappeared. She left with a few essentials to hitchhike to Colorado.

Not willing to remain at 25 Hamilton Heath alone, I moved back in with my parents for a while—my tail only slightly between my legs—and prepared to start college.

My friend Julian had joined the Navy and was stationed at the base in Guam. On his first trip back to Tampa, the gang was going to meet him at Tampa International, glammed-out and ready for a night with our sailor pal on leave, when trouble struck. Stopping at a 7-Eleven convenience store on the way, I picked up a twenty-five-cent Almond Joy candy bar. I asked Sherri to pay for it when she paid for her own stuff. I unwrapped it and was leaving the store eating it when two plainclothes policemen grabbed me. I was arrested, frisked vigorously, handcuffed, and thrown into the back of the unmarked car before the others had even emerged from the store. They never saw what happened. I was just suddenly gone, like Marla from the Fellini film. I was taken to the Tampa Police Department, booked, photographed, fingerprinted, and put into a holding cell. With my friend arriving at the airport any minute, I was sitting on a jail cell floor, surrounded by a bunch of drunk and violent redneck outlaws.

I heard the inevitable cliché, "What are you in for?" making the rounds. They asked me last. I demurred. Finally, when asked again and again, I yelled, "For stealing a fucking Almond Joy bar!" They glared, noticed my outfit: clunky platforms, pleated baggy pants with a thin silver belt, and makeup. . . . I thought I was done for. I kicked and pushed in a maze of thick tattooed arms, rough hands, and wild whiskey grins, until a guard came by.

That moment became a metaphor for my entire time in Tampa: I knew I had to get out of there soon, or I wouldn't get out alive. Luckily, my posse finally found me at 5:00 A.M. or so, and put up the $100 bail just in time.

Sometime later, I had my day in court, representing myself, and putting Sherri on the witness stand. I presented the case seriously, bringing an Almond Joy bar as an exhibit, which generated a wave of laughter from everyone in the courtroom. The arresting officers hung their heads when I described precisely how thoroughly I had been handcuffed and frisked. I was found innocent in a torrent of laughter, and took a quick bow as I left the courtroom. A decade later, I was at a Tampa Waffle House when a cop came over to me and said, "Man, aren't you the guy who was in on that candy bar rap?" The legend lived. I have never eaten another Almond Joy bar since.

The University of South Florida occupies a sprawling campus, ten or so miles from the center of Tampa. With a huge enrollment it was easy to get lost in its sheer size. And, with low, unremarkable buildings scattered far apart connected by massive flat areas of mowed nothingness and narrow sidewalks, it was, to me, not a creative environment. As a freshman I took all the required courses, but settled on majoring in mass communication, studying cinematography with an emphasis on documentary filmmaking.

Except for viewing an astonishing number of great, classic films and documentaries, including the excellent *Lonely Boy*, a portrait of the teenage idol Paul Anka on tour, I found my classes a snooze. For my final in the life-drawing class, I turned in a charcoal rendering of a full frontal nude of myself, after weeks of classes of drawing the female form exclusively. The instructor was visibly shaken; it is too easy to shock in a small town. In a drama class, during a particularly bland discussion on the plays of Ionesco and the Theatre of the Absurd, I stood up to comment that the inane discussion *itself* was absurd. Amidst the laughter, the professor ostracized me. The boringly academic music courses, too, left me flat. I wanted to go to New York University to study film.

But mostly, I just wanted to get out of there—out of town.

The most interesting aspect of going to USF was the hip, off-campus record store, School Kids Records. I started working there when, one day while I was browsing, the owner asked if I would mind the cash register while he ran out for a minute—a minute that became an hour. I worked there part-time, off and on, for the next year or so. On the bathroom door at the store was a brilliant life-size painting of Captain Beefheart, from the *Trout Mask Replica* album cover. This "school" is where I received my real education. Here, I studied the latest imports (distributed by a clever New Jersey distributor called JEM Records) and illegal bootleg recordings (the FBI confiscated LPs more than once while I worked there), discovered obscure artists and even learned which labels were doing what—and how effectively they were at doing it. I carefully read liner notes to learn the musicians' names and who produced, who engineered, and who mastered the records that appealed to me. Besides the British bands, I was particularly interested in the post–New York Dolls scene, then emerging in New York, which I read about in *Hit Parader* and *Creem* magazines. Debut albums by the Ramones, Richard Hell and the Voidoids, Patti Smith, and Television were soon in my collection. I was on fire with these new sounds and visual styles. In particular, the first Ramones album, which I found in the cutout bin for $1.99, was a watershed album I played over and over.

Dance music was coming into the picture now, too, and I gravitated to certain artists just like I did to glam and punk. James Brown's new, heavier funk sound (including the records he produced for his own label, People Records), as well as Melvin Van Peebles, Millie Jackson, and early Donna Summer were some of my favorites.

With Marla (returned from her Homeric hitchhiking odyssey) on bass and Dorsey (my co-worker at the record store) on drums, we started a band, Snails. I sat with Marla in my bedroom at my parents' house for hours, as she mastered the two- or three-note bass lines of the Velvet Underground's "I'm Waiting for the Man" and "White Light/White Heat." Our band's name referred to our song tempos (fast). Also, the fact that snails are hermaphrodites intrigued us to no end.

I had now switched back to playing guitar, having recently purchased a black Gibson model L6-S ("El Success," I called it) which I played through my Fender Bassman 50 amp. The single cutaway solid body was reminiscent of a Les Paul, which slightly relieved my longtime lust. Everything went through my newly acquired Echoplex tape delay unit, causing another local musician friend, Tim Scott, later of the Rockats, to remark that our sound was "all echo." Our first live show was in the Rathskeller pub at the University of Tampa. Marla and I took turns on lead vocals. Just before going on, I was afraid I would be nervous, afraid I would have stage fright, the same way I'd felt before I went on the radio for the first time, a decade ago. Once we were playing, though, something like a switch went off in my head, and I felt completely at ease.

Marla had gotten a job in a tiny, ramshackle recording studio on the edge of nowhere, called Recnac, which made it easy for us to book ourselves in and lay down some tracks, especially after-hours. The studio had a simple mixing console, and two TEAC A3340 four-track tape machines with Simul-Sync (finally!) to record and mix down to. Now I could finally start making some *records*, I thought. Our first recording was "Poodle Party," which was inspired by a ridiculous snapshot of the family pet wearing a birthday party hat. The song had an overdriven guitar sloppily playing a Brill Building-type chord progression in a very T.Rex style, and an overdubbed group of friends singing along and making party sounds. Using all the mic placement techniques I had accumulated, we came up with some nice, though admittedly rough, sounds.

Inspired by the pop of Sparks, T.Rex, the early Beatles, as well as the experimentation of Captain Beefheart and, of course, the Velvets, we were encouraged by what was just starting to happen in New York City. Though unintentional, we became the first punk band in Tampa.

And the tunes kept coming. But now what?

CHAPTER 3

TINY TIM

LEARNING THE TRUE MEANING OF FAME

Sometimes I felt Florida was one big UFO landing zone. I mean, there were so many UFOs in the skies that summer of 1976 that the novelty wore off. Like shooting stars, they started with a flash, then continued on in their bizarre trajectories. Once, on a typically aimless drive down a pitch-black highway north of Tampa, Sherri and I saw a mothership. We were driving in my red 1975 Chevy Monza with David Bowie's *Station to Station* cranked up on the cassette deck, when three lights appeared in the sky ahead, like low stars above the horizon. Just as we realized those lights were moving . . . *toward us,* they suddenly went dark. Like the one car ahead of us, we pulled into the emergency lane to watch as one of these giant dark stars glided slowly and silently past, slightly above the trees on our right. It was about the size of a K-Mart and had no lights or visible markings, black against the empty black Florida sky. I distinctly remember thinking it felt like negative space, even though I wasn't sure what that meant. Sherri jumped up and down screaming, "Take me with you! Take me with you!" (I wasn't quite so sure I wanted that, so I stood by and watched quietly.) The male driver from the car ahead came over and asked excitedly, "Man! Did you see that?" Whether it was a group hallucination, a figment of bored, Ziggy-Stardusted Florida imaginations, a weather balloon from nearby MacDill Air Force Base, or a true close encounter, the local newspapers reported sightings that night, and my eyes were red for a week.

Another kind of alien made Florida their landing zone in the late '70s: former '60s pop superstars glided through town like invisible UFOs, playing the local rock clubs, third-rate discos, dives, and hotel bars, on their way down to Miami. Fabian, Herman's Hermits, Steppenwolf . . . a hit parade of pop's past. I made it a point to see them all—to try to understand what bit of magic they had, what had given them their flash of brilliance, and to see if they had any left. Of these, Tiny Tim was special.

For one thing, Tiny Tim was not merely a flash in the pan. Born Herbert Khaury, he had bravely developed his persona over a decade or so in Greenwich Village before he hit the big time in 1968. His appearances on the smash TV show *Rowan & Martin's Laugh-In*, his Top 20 hit, "Tip-Toe Thru the Tulips," and his 1969 wedding to Miss Vicki on *The Tonight Show* made him a household name. He was a complex man of extreme contradictions. Seeming frivolous, he was actually a serious musicologist, carrying with him a shopping bag full of sheet music that dated from the earliest recorded music on Edison cylinders right up to the latest chart hits. He had an encyclopedic knowledge of the history of American popular music, and was a truly gifted song stylist with a surprising vocal range. Visually, his long hair, trademark ukulele, and flower power tendencies belied his political and religious conservatism, while his falsetto and feminine demeanor both demonstrated and concealed his love for women. Imagine a man riding the New York City subway system in the late 1950s with wild shoulder-length hair and white face makeup, carrying a ukulele in a crumpled shopping bag. There had never been a pop star quite like him. And, in our jaded, post-MTV, reality show–saturated, everybody's-in-showbiz-and-who-gives-a-fuck world of prepackaged oddballs, it is impossible that there can ever be another.

I didn't know much about him when I read in the *Tampa Tribune* that he was performing at a roadside TraveLodge motel on the north edge of town—but I was intrigued. Tiny Tim was a bona fide celebrity, so Sherri, Marla, and I made the pilgrimage.

We waited in the spartan, fluorescent-lit motel lobby, hoping to meet the star when the show was over. We could hear the small crowd roaring with laughter inside the lounge, as Tiny sang his encore,

"You're a Grand Old Flag" (Tiny was a patriot, and it was our nation's bicentennial year, after all). Next, larger than life, Tiny Tim appeared in the lobby. Wearing his famously mismatched suit and a frilly tuxedo shirt with oversized cufflinks, he seemed genuinely pleased to meet us, and we spoke for a while, snapping some Polaroids. When he realized we had not seen the show, he invited us to his room where he would perform it for us.

At first I was a little taken aback by his offer. Then, as we spoke more, it seemed completely natural. As unnatural as Tiny Tim may have appeared to be, he was a natural—a natural performer, and naturally gracious. We went to his room, and he ordered a couple of six packs. When we had downed those and ordered more, the bar was out of his favorite domestic, Old Milwaukee, and we had to change brands. Tiny was very concerned about mixing "the spirits of the brews," but we did. The man loved his beer.

Like a wizard possessed, he proceeded to play us an expansive range of songs by artists from Henry Burr to Bob Dylan, making the unlikely connections, and told us endless stories of New York, Lenny Bruce, and the Greenwich Village folk scene of the late '50s and early '60s. Stories about the Page 3 club in the West Village, where "the girls . . . liked each other" and Tiny was the emcee, introducing the other performers and chatting with the girls. "Magnificent beauties, with a very . . . fantastic . . . power," he whispered to us. He would write songs for them and have trophies made for them (the first for an eighteen-year-old who called herself Miss Snooky). "It was *won-der-ful*! Until, you know, the police closed it down," he would say, referring to those pre-Stonewall days. His stories of New York were told with a kind of passion and an awe for a city that I had never experienced, a passion and drive for music and the music industry that inspires me still. Who knew? I wanted more. We stayed until the harsh Florida sun came up over the asphalt parking lot.

I told Tiny about my aspirations to be a record producer and that I had already started by producing my own group with Marla, the Snails. So, as we left, I asked if we could come back the next night and if I could bring a tape recorder to record his songs and stories. He seemed excited by that as we all said goodbye.

The next day I borrowed a stereo cassette deck from Scott, the owner of the record store. From the studio, I borrowed a proper set of studio headphones and an extra mic (I had a Shure Unisphere B stage mic that I used to record Tiny's voice), and, from a 7-Eleven convenience store along the way, I bought a bunch of cheap Norelco blank cassettes. That evening, Sherri, Marla, and I made the drive back the TraveLodge, again arriving just as Tiny's late show was ending. We brought him some gifts: red henna for his hair, some sheet music from Sherri's mother's collection, and a large lapel pin—a miniature bunch of plastic bananas, referring to a song he sang for us, "I've Never Seen a Straight Banana."

Setting up in his motel room, I positioned the two mics to provide the most extreme possible separation between Tiny's voice and his ukulele. Tiny sat on his bed, still in his stage outfit. I brought out my 35mm camera and snapped a few black-and-white images of the session. I wore the big KOSS studio headphones the entire time, manually trying to keep the levels balanced as Tiny and his uke moved in and out of mic range. We interacted with him and even sang along at times, while I mixed the performance live to tape. (Miss) Sherri and (Miss) Marla charmed him to no end, making him giggle, perhaps as the girls of the Page 3 had a decade and a half before. Certainly, Tiny Tim seemed to like young girls. The phone in his room rang often, usually his manager in the next room, probably complaining that Tiny was staying up way too late, wasting time with these kids, making way too much noise, and laughing way too much. It was understandable if his manager complained. We were very loud. And Tiny was very happy.

Even more than the night before, when the record light came on, Tiny Tim came alive with humor and history. The stories were astonishing, and he told them with the passion of a mad televangelist; and the songs bounced from decade to decade: from Neil Sedaka's "Laughter in the Rain" (sung entirely in falsetto with rain and thunder sound effects done vocally) to "At Seventeen" by Janis Ian (done entirely sobbing, in mock tears) to a World War I soldier's song he once sang for Lenny Bruce in the hospital ("I don't want to get well, I don't want to get well, I'm in love with a beautiful nurse . . . ").

He told stories of Bruce's daughter, who, at ten years old was too shy to sing in public, until he heckled her ("Army training," he called it). And it was Army training for me, too. Tiny had sensed my own shyness and was already trying to break me out of it. He told of us of his obsession with the actress Tuesday Weld, whom he said he started "chasing" when she was sixteen. "You must believe in your dreams, not in your fears," he repeated several times, looking hard at me. Through my headphones, Tiny Tim's amplified words rang true—it was an unexpectedly emotional moment. I started to believe in my dreams then and there. When Tiny had finally hit the big time in 1968, he told us, Warren Beatty introduced him to the star who he had dreamed of for seven years. At that Hollywood party, accompanied by his own ukulele, he sang to Tuesday Weld the love song he had written for her years before, "Dear Tuesday." She was horrified, yet, *he* was somehow satisfied. "It can happen in *your lives*!" he would say. "We are going to make a hit record and all go to California together!" He looked for the fear in my eyes. Would I ever be ready to leave Florida for good? I wondered.

It had not been all tulips for Tiny. He hadn't had another hit like "Tip-Toe," and after a trio of albums on Reprise, he was dropped by the label, and the public. It was now eight years down the long road, and his child bride, Miss Vicki, whom he married in front of the second largest television audience in the '60s (the first being the moon landing), had recently and very publicly divorced him, taking him for everything, including their daughter, Tulip. In the next few months, matters would only get worse. This was one of roughest years yet for Tiny, yet he was always so thankful . . . and that was a kind of success in itself.

A simple but true lesson from Tiny Tim: be thankful.

It's so easy to be blind to blessings when things go awry, and just as easy to take everything for granted when you are successful. I once bumped into a close friend and colleague of mine whose current record was at the top of the charts—the biggest success of his life, and he was miserable. "Now we have to extend the goddamned tour," he complained. My friend wasn't the only person I have seen this pattern in. It seems that sometimes success can heighten resentments—with your colleagues, lovers, fans, and the world at large.

Nothing good comes from being miserable, unless perhaps you are a blues singer or in a Goth band.

It was hard for us to say goodbye to Tiny Tim when his TraveLodge run ended. But he told us he would be back later in the summer, playing nearby, in St. Petersburg. I suggested that we go into the studio at that time and make a proper recording of "the banana song," which he was convinced would be his big comeback hit. "We'll all be in California before Christmas!" he promised again.

So, Tiny went back on the road, and I went back to school and the studio, where we continued recording more Snails tracks: "Shopping Mall Queen," "Turn Your House into a Donut Shop," and covers of the Velvet Underground's "White Light/White Heat" and Larry Williams's "Slow Down" (another snail joke). Things were different now, though. After our conversations with Tiny, it seemed all the more possible to put records out, have hits, and make dreams come true. What had been a vague improbability now seemed tangible and within reach. The feeling was intense and real and, in some ways, has stayed with me all these years.

It's like the fire of religious faith: faith in the probability of success. Once you feel that fire for an instant, you can use it for a lifetime. I also had learned that fame can isolate you by lifting you up in a tidal wave of good fortune, then leave you high and dry. The clichés ring true: who are your friends? Your family? What happens when the fans that adored you ignore you? I discovered these questions and their answers though Tiny Tim.

When Tiny returned to Florida, his sweet Miss Vicki was everywhere. On every newsstand, that is. In *Oui* magazine, nude and spread-eagled, fondling a framed 8 × 10 photo of her ex-husband. Tiny himself was always impeccably polite, overly well-mannered, and most important, apparently asexual. That is, when he spoke of love, it was in the most idealized, almost spiritual sense. "I'm just thanking the good Lord for the beauty," he would quip. That's why it was such a shock to see his ex-wife in such scandalous poses. It was a tough summer for Tiny. We never mentioned the magazine spread, but it was obvious we knew. Everyone did. And perhaps my friends and I provided a diversion for

Tiny that summer. Once, he and I were out in my car and stopped in to a convenience store. We both glanced down and there she was, Miss Vicki staring at us from the magazine rack, right at the checkout counter. Neither of us said a word.

I thought about how brave Herbert Khaury was for inventing Tiny Tim and for living the character twenty-four hours a day. First, walking the streets and riding the subways as an *unknown* freak, then as a famous one, aware always of the snickers and whispers. The day we were set to go into the studio, Tiny and I were left alone in his motel room for a minute while the girls got ready. In the harsh light of mid day, he stopped at the mirror as he gathered his shopping bag and ukulele—he touched his face, feeling the strands of his long, stringy, recently hennaed hair. I could see my own teenage reflection in the mirror next to his. "Ah, youth . . . where have you gone?" he said to himself in his soft, low baritone, looking at himself at middle age as if for the first time.

The traffic that day was heavy, partially due to us—making it a longer than usual drive to the studio in Tampa from St. Pete. Tiny was actually not so tiny any more, having put on more than a few pounds, and it was a tight fit getting him into the bucket passenger seat of my compact car. With Marla in the backseat, Tiny sat in the front, playing his ukulele, singing in full voice to warm up his vocal chords, and eating paprika-spiced popcorn from an enormous black Hefty trash bag. He said the popcorn was good for his voice. As he sang and played, he was clearly visible to those in other cars, who of course all recognized him. I mean, there was only one Tiny Tim and the whole world knew him, still. Cars were honking, drivers were cheering, and several traffic jams were created by rubbernecking drivers. I realized that, in some ways at least, fame is eternal.

The studio had become a second home to me by this point, so I was not nervous about bringing Tiny Tim in to record some tracks. I felt ready. Yet I could feel immediately that the vibe in the studio was not the same as it had been the motel room, where his performances for us were continuations of his club show. There, he was charged and ready. Now, after a long drive from St. Pete, scrunched in a bucket seat in broad daylight, and walking into this funky little four-track recording studio in Tampa (a serious comedown from his sessions at the major studios of New York and Los Angeles), it was up to me to create environment that would allow him to catch fire. Even in the best of circumstances, the recording studio is always somewhat intimidating, and a lot of comforting and encouragement are required for the artist to relax. All the technical aspects must be smooth-running and nearly invisible. Since Tiny Tim was the first artist I'd brought to the studio, other than my own group, I wasn't completely aware of this.

That's when I learned that *producing* is not the same as *recording*, and I learned fast. Though some producers do both, for me, it is important to separate the functions of producing and engineering. The role of record producer is akin to that of film director. While it was unnecessary to actually direct Tiny, I did attempt to provide a relaxed and creative environment for him to record "I've Never Seen a Straight Banana" and to improvise songs and stories as he had done at the TraveLodge. Once the engineer and I established the basic sound of Tiny's voice and ukulele, I stayed in the live room with Marla as his audience.

That seemed to do the trick, and we were now on track, tracking. Basically, at that point, I just let the tape roll. We did several takes of "Banana," and I asked him to sing "Dear Tuesday." Once we got those down, I asked him to improvise as he had done at the hotel, and he conjured up another charmingly brilliant collage of songs and stories. After the session, we drove Tiny back to St. Petersburg for his evening show and continued to hang out with him during his Florida stay.

I had wanted my recordings to capture the "true" Tiny Tim: the musicologist, the pop music fan, interpreter, and singer who had a tremendous talent for finding obscure gems that complimented his persona. Simply, my goal was to portray the Tiny *we* knew on tape, in the purest way possible.

But often that is not what the music industry wants, or *thinks* it wants. The owners of the recording studio somehow got to Tiny privately and, through a series of shady-seeming transactions, arranged for him to record a song they and their friends had suddenly written for him, "Tip-Toe Disco," to cash in on the new disco craze. Exactly the opposite of what I was trying to do for Tiny. A single was quickly pressed and released on a quickly created local label, and just as quickly never heard from again.

That was also a lesson, but I don't know what to call it. "Look Out for Sharks," maybe. But even if you see them coming, there is usually no stopping them. So, like a shark yourself, you just have to keep moving . . . or die.

The disco single threw me off a little, but I was now focused on polishing up the Snails tracks and thinking about finding a record label for my own group. Not being his manager or representative, I didn't even know how to shop my Tiny Tim project to a label. So even though he had wanted me to make a single out of "the banana song," I put the project on the backburner for a while. Once I get my own deal, I thought, I can complete Tiny's album and release it on the same label. Just a teenager in Tampa, I had no clue, no contacts, and no clout. I put the reels on the shelf.

I sent some of the Snails tunes as demos to magazines, such as *BOMP!,* for reviews and got some good ones. I was surprised to see references to the all-girl Runaways (with Joan Jett). Probably because Marla sang lead on some of the songs, critics made that generalization. We sounded *nothing* like the Runaways. Sometimes we were said to be influenced by a New York group we hadn't heard yet, the Talking Heads. But that was only because Marla was a female bass player, as was their Tina Weymouth. We sounded *nothing* like the Talking Heads. So, it became obvious that writers always need a point of reference. A category. A style. A pigeonhole. I wanted my category, style, and pigeonhole to be the artist who didn't fit into any one category, style, or pigeonhole. Like Tiny Tim, I wanted to find influences from *all* the decades and genres, and use them to create something new. Disclaimer: I cannot claim that this dictum was an easy road to success, though. Quite the contrary.

The first record label I chose to submit the Snails demos to was Clive Davis's Arista Records in New York, mostly because they had signed proto-punk Patti Smith (soon to break her neck falling off a Tampa stage), and her debut album, *Horses*, was one of my favorites. They *had* to be cool to sign her, I reasoned, ignoring the fact that they had had far bigger successes with mainstream artists like Barry Manilow and the country rock group the Outlaws, who were also from Tampa. Hmmm ... maybe I thought that was something in our favor . . . .

I compiled eight or ten of our songs onto a Maxell 7″ reel of tape. Two mistakes already: (1) I sent them too many songs at one time; and (2) I should have sent them an easier-to-handle cassette rather than a cumbersome reel.

A few weeks later, the rejection letter came in the mail to my parents' house, on embossed Arista stationery from Stu Fine at A & R. "No commercial potential" was his classic response, and frankly, for the marketplace at that time and for that particular label, Stu may have been dull and shortsighted, but probably right. I mean, just a quick glance at two of the titles, "Poodle Party" and "Turn Your House into a Donut Shop," is enough to make the accountants run for cover. A few years later though, when New Wave exploded, and groups like DEVO, the Cars, not to mention the Fabulous Poodles. . . . You know what I mean. The world was simply not yet ready for the Snails in 1976. I finally bumped into Stu Fine on a New York City subway, in the mid-'80s, when my band was number one on college radio and had been for four weeks. He introduced himself and congratulated me, never making the connection that I was that kid from Florida. Then I told him about it. A shining showbiz moment on the number 1 train.

I never sent out another Snails demo to a record label. I decided I needed to go to New York for a quick visit—a few weeks—and check out the scene. I could stay with my uncle Peter and aunt Anna on funky Eighth Avenue at 21st Street. I could bring the Snails tapes with me and shop for a deal in person.

Dressed in a midnight blue Nino Cerruti tailored suit, I boarded the Amtrak train from Tampa to New York at the old Union Station. Some found it odd that I would go to New York by train: as a boy, I was obsessed with commercial aviation. I knew all the planes and airlines and loved the idea of air travel. And it would have been even cheaper than a train ticket. Maybe I had a fear of flying, but I didn't want to crash before I got a record deal. And the train was so . . . romantic.

Riding the rails gave me a good sense of where I was going. Flying is a bit like taking an elevator: you can't really get a feel for where you're going. On the train, every mile traveled is witnessed and experienced. Landscape changes.

Even the smell of the air changed as the train passed through different cities and states. Anticipation mounted. As we approached the north, you could sense the pace quickening, the energy intensifying. You could see and feel the machinery of industry all around. Producing for mass consumption. Supplying the big cities. Goods and services. Supply and demand. The skies were a little grayer with factory air and the colors of commerce. Florida got smaller and smaller, fading into the distance.

New York in the '70s was a city in transition. In the throes of financial failure, the city had asked the federal government for aid. "Ford to City: Drop Dead" was the famous *New York Daily News* headline that announced the president's response at mid-decade. And yet a creative renaissance was erupting. Dance music, fueled and fired by the success of the glittering Studio 54, was saturating the charts and television, and a bit further underground, the punk scene centered around a dump called CBGB was ripping and rewrapping rock 'n' roll for a whole new generation. Irreverence ruled. Besides the muggings, the dark, dirty streets of New York were the spawning grounds of a genuine movement. The Brits took the cue and did a good job of packaging punk. But clearly it would not have happened without the initial call to arms of the Ramones and the new Bowery boys—and girls.

I soaked in the scene. Eventually, I realized that I might have been an annoyance to my uncle and aunt, coming in late from nights out to Max's Kansas City and CBGB, so I checked into the Hotel Chelsea, around the corner on 23rd Street. As the setting for Andy Warhol's film, *Chelsea Girls*, I knew something of its colorful past, but probably would not have imagined its future notoriety as the site of Sid Vicious's death. At about a hundred dollars a week, my charming balconied room with its little kitchenette was innocent enough.

At this point I was falling in love with the city and understood what Tiny Tim had been talking about. This is where I wanted to live. But not quite yet. It seemed too much to handle. Where would I stay? How could I make money? I needed time to think. So after a few weeks, I headed back to Tampa.

Getting back into the Central Florida groove, the one thought on my mind was how I could get back to New York City—to live—and soon. I started hanging out with my friend from high school, Jean, who had also recently been to New York and also wanted to go back. After the summer of Tiny Tim and his polite prefixes, Jean became *Miss* Jean. We shared an interest in James Dean, the Sex Pistols, and Carlsberg Elephant Malt Ale, among other things. We would drive around Tampa, drunk and bored to destruction, hitting speed bumps at high speeds and trying to race trains, recording all of our adventures on cassette, like radio dramas.

My hair was now quite spiked and hennaed bright red. A few weeks before, Bob Denver, star of *Gilligan's Island* (whom I met with Jean and my friend Eric, after Bob's dinner theater performance in Woody Allen's *Play It Again, Sam*) lightly stroked my spikey top, his sheepdog eyes gazing at me from below his gray bangs, suggestively asking, "How . . . do you . . . keep it *up* like that?"

That winter was the first time in over fifty years that it snowed in Tampa. Lightly . . . the result was more like a light frost . . . but still, free-floating flakes of snow fell from the Florida skies through the palm trees one night, as I once again drove to nowhere. I took it as a sign: hell freezes over; time to go.

Another night we parked Jean's blue Ford Pinto at the "Little New York" park, the one my father used to walk me to as a kid. While downing Elephant Malts and making one of our taped dramas, two guys in a pickup truck across the park started firing at us with shotguns, thinking we had witnessed their drug deal. With our punkish coifs, we were an easy mark. Suddenly, we were in a high-speed chase through the deserted streets of my childhood neighborhood. Not a cop to be found. They kept shooting at our rear tires, gaining on us, as we remembered the news reports of Pintos being prone to explosion when hit from behind. Luckily we knew the streets pretty well and finally lost our stalkers with some tricky maneuvering. Hearts beating wildly, we knew if we didn't get out of Tampa soon, one or both of us would end up dead.

Later that week, we heard the Monkees were in town, performing at Big Daddy's Disco. There was no debate as to what we would do that evening. One thing about Tampa in late '70s: there still wasn't much competition for nightlife. On that night, the Monkees were the only game in town.

But, they were the game I would have played anyway. Like Tiny Tim, they were of that certain breed of overexposed '60s superstars who, in the public's perception, had gone stale. By that, I just mean they may have exceeded their intended shelf life, like decade-old bread. As the story goes, the music industry (and impresario, Don Kirshner, in particular) had dealt them a bad hand when they had decided to become a "real" band and replaced them with an animated group, the Archies. No matter. The Littlest DJ would always have a special place in his heart for them.

On this tour, it was just Davy Jones and Mickey Dolenz fronting, with a backing band. As I tried to enter the disco I was stopped, not just to check my ID but because I was wearing black high-top Converse sneakers. Sneakers were not allowed. A few smiles later, and the big bouncer at the door smiled back and let me slide. Ahhh . . . must remember how I did that, I thought. This will come in handy getting me past those velvet ropes at Studio 54.

Miss Jean and I, joined by my sister, Maria, found our places near the front of the stage as the show began. Davy looked pretty cool, Mickey, too, and the backing band looked . . . vaguely familiar. I couldn't stop staring at the guitarist and the keyboardist . . . I *knew* these guys, but I didn't know how.

Then it occurred to me. While I was in New York, I had picked up an album called *Live at CBGB*, which featured several of the bands that played there. "These guys are the Laughing Dogs," I said to Jean, and

I told her about the album. "We've got to go backstage after the show and say hello."

A friendly bunch of talented guys from Brooklyn, the Laughing Dogs were visibly knocked out that anyone knew who they were. We talked with them in the dressing room, then went to their hotel where they introduced us to Davy. Mickey, recently married, was on an "extended honeymoon," we were told, so he had disappeared with his bride. More Polaroids. Davy. Laughing Dogs. New girlfriends on the bed. "Hey, what are you guys doing tomorrow? We're heading down to Miami—why don't you come with us?" they asked.

We left early the next morning in Miss Jean's Pinto, making the six-hour trek to Miami Beach. We checked into a fleabag motel, but it didn't matter. We went straight to the hotel where our new friends were staying.

After the show in Miami, we hung out all night with Davy Jones, who by now clearly had his eye on Miss Jean. We sat on his hotel room bed, and he sang and played Beatles songs all night on his acoustic guitar, perfectly.... As he smiled softly at Jean, I imagined he was wondering if I was her boyfriend. Looking at this charming Brit in his mid-thirties, it was interesting to think about showbiz careers, and career life spans in general. I mean, if fame or success comes early, how long can you sustain it? What do you do after? No matter what you do, will you always seem like a has-been? Will you always seem old? He was probably younger than Gwen Stefani is as I write this, at the top of her game. Yet for the Monkees, it had long been over.

I asked myself how it must feel to have once been on the top of the world, on the top of the charts, on the cover of every teen magazine—pampered in the poshest palaces—then be perpetually exiled to the purgatory of third and fourth rate hotels and venues . . . for all eternity.

As the sun came up, Davy sang "Daydream Believer" to Jean.

> Cheer up sleepy Jean
> Oh, what can it mean
> To a daydream believer
> And a homecoming queen?

The next morning we had a big breakfast with Davy and the Laughing Dogs in their hotel restaurant. I told the band how much Jean and I both loved New York and that we were hoping to get back there as soon as we could. That's when the cute bass player, Ronnie, suggested we sublet rooms in their Brooklyn loft. The band was going to be on tour with Davy and Mickey for most of the year anyway: "Why don't you stay at our place?"

Heralding trumpets. Fanfare! I had visions of Luke Skywalker blasting out of Mos Eisley Space Port in the *Millennium Falcon* with Obi Wan and Han Solo. Chewbacca roared!

> I flew a Falcon
> I flew a Thunderbird
> I threw everything away . . .

Escape. Finally.
The next day Miss Jean and I began selling everything we owned.

CHAPTER 4

I ONLY TOOK WHAT I NEEDED

HOW TO MAKE THE MOVE

At some point, regardless of your age, you have to stop planning what you will do in "the future." You will suddenly realize that the future exists in every second. Just like going on the radio or going onstage, you'll find that the fear of making a big change is usually unfounded. It's a big scary shadow . . . of a teddy bear. Everyone will tell you not to look back and maybe they're right. But I looked back a lot . . . to see Florida getting smaller and smaller with each mile I traveled. Detachment is not a dirty word. . . .

It was the strangest thing, but I had absolutely no regrets or hesitations about leaving everything behind. I didn't for a moment think about missing anyone or anything. As if wearing blinders, I was focused only on making the move. I might have been in denial, but it helped kick me the hell out.

This may not be the same for you, and it certainly came as a surprise to me.

To say "I sold everything I owned" is a little misleading. I didn't have much to sell. My big Fender bass amp rig . . . and my car . . . easy. Both sold quickly. I had read somewhere that it was best to sell a car in the rain, because the raindrops would camouflage any imperfections and dents, the paint finish would look all shiny, and the dealer wouldn't want to be out in the rain too long looking for flaws. Well, my Chevy Monza was in perfect condition anyway and not much more than a year old. But to be on the safe side, I did choose a rainy day to drive it to a used car lot on Florida Avenue, and sold it on the spot. Took what they gave me for it. Didn't matter. It was enough.

I didn't have any furniture, just my weights (yes, weights, for lifting), a few thousand vinyl record albums and singles, lots of Beatles bootleg albums and memorabilia, and tons of books. Most of the stuff I left in my childhood bedroom, knowing that I would have all my albums shipped north when I was settled. I bought what seemed at the time like a big steamer trunk at the Army Navy store (where my mom also bought me a great Schott Perfecto black leather motorcycle jacket, just like the ones the Ramones wore), and I stuffed the trunk with what I thought I needed to get me by. I remember how dwarfed that trunk looked when I got it to New York. I would carry my Gibson L6-S in its case onto the train. I felt like real a musician. Too bad I didn't know I should detune the strings to decrease tension on the neck during travel. But even that mistake would lead to a magic moment with one of my heroes. . . .

One little trunk and one guitar. I took only what I needed.

A few days before leaving Tampa, I remember talking with my friend Tim Scott, telling him I was concerned about finding musicians to work with in New York. His response was typically cynical: "It's easy. Just join an existing band and take it over." Oh, I could *never* do that, I thought, as he smiled.

Jean made her preparations, too. She sold her Pinto, and on a sunny fall day we met at Tampa's old Union Station, our families present to see us board the Amtrak local to New York City. Already, I felt filled with the energy of our destination . . . even before we found our coach seats. When we did, the first thing we did was turn on the little cassette player we brought along, and started playing the one song we would play over and over for the entire twenty-four-hour trip: Iggy Pop's "The Passenger." Inspired by Jim Morrison, the Florida boy turned frontman . . . rock star . . . over and over again . . . *Lust for Life* . . . pulling out of Tampa, then looking out the train windows and watching the towns and our pasts blur by. . . .

> Oh, the passenger
> How, how he rides
> Oh, the passenger

He rides and he rides
He looks through his window
What does he see?
He sees the sign and hollow sky
He sees the stars come out tonight
He sees the city's ripped backsides
He sees the winding ocean drive
And everything was made for you and me
All of it was made for you and me
'Cause it just belongs to you and me
So let's take a ride
and see what's mine.

Arriving in New York was different this time, for both Jean and me. Instead of being greeted at Penn Station by relatives, we were now entirely on our own. Hailing our first cab, with all our belongings, the swirling symphony of sights and sounds and smells, and the instant shift into high gear, created a dreamlike state of culture shock . . . far more this time for me than the last time I entered the belly of the beast, a year before. Because this time I knew I wasn't just visiting. The city digested us whole. And its stomach rumbled.

We chose, at the suggestion of the cabby, to spend our first night at the quite nice Hotel Empire at glitzy Lincoln Center. It was a sleepless night, as we could feel the throbbing city all around us. Then, the next day, we moved downtown to the rather shabby George Washington Hotel on Lexington and 23rd. An SRO—single room occupancy or standing room only—either phrase applied. Our rooms had barely enough floor space for one to stand and answer the nonexistent phone. I saw my first junkie collapse and remain in front of the elevator in the lobby as people walked past. Rumor had it that movie queen Veronica Lake, one of the stars in my mother's scrapbook, had sadly spent her last days working as a counter waitress in the drab coffee shop downstairs. This was not exactly the Plaza.

But it was only for a week or so until we could move into our new home, our mystical, shining palace in Emerald City . . . the Laughing Dogs' loft in Brooklyn.

The loft *was* remarkable. Remarkably funky. In an AIR building (Artist in Residence, and so marked above the otherwise nondescript door of the building), 351 Jay Street was on the cusp of Brooklyn

Heights, i.e., almost nice. But our block, and the building, was on the rough side, i.e., not nice. A labyrinth of rusted metal gates and pipes. Dark and industrial. Decades of dust. The elevator was of the freight variety, a rickety, rackety cage with a big up-or-down lever instead of buttons, stopping with a shuddering clunk. The loft's floors were uneven, splintery planks of wood, the bathroom was outside of the loft in the drafty hall. The big factorylike glass windows did nothing to keep out the cold, and one of our roommates was a shady-looking drug dealer with a man-eating German shepherd for protection.

It was heaven.

It was heaven to me, because the Laughing Dogs had built a sound-proof recording/rehearsal studio in the dead center of the loft, with a decent array of guitar amps (including a particularly nice, hot-wired 1966 Fender Deluxe Reverb from their Monkees tour), mics, drum kit, a Hammond B-3 organ, and the old familiar favorite TEAC A3340 four-track, reel-to-reel recorder. I spent most of my time in there, collecting bits of song ideas, seeing how far I could—and learning how far I *should*—take them. Having unlimited access to a studio, the task now was to learn when to *stop* adding things to a recording. My new approach was far more stripped-down than the recordings I had done with the Snails in Tampa. How to make few instruments do the job of many . . . how to simplify the drum beat (since I was the one playing drums on my recordings, there was not much choice but to keep it simple!) . . . how to get the sounds that could stand on their own, and, most important, how to focus on creating songs and arrangements solid and interesting enough to stand up to scrutiny in their minimalism. While not saying I achieved it, that approach to composing and recording became my new interest, my "style," and it would be for the next few years. Until I would go overdub crazy again, in what would be an explosion of mid-'80s overindulgence. Lessons can be forgotten. Don't forget that.

My personal space in the loft was literally a hole in the wall. Three bedrooms of normal size, with normal doors, had been partitioned. But somehow I was designated to sleep in a bizarre sort of storage bin, where the bass player Ronnie used to sleep. It was a rectangular cubby-hole, about eight-feet long and maybe at best three-and-a-half-feet high, and about eight or nine feet off the ground. Located above the refrigerator in the kitchen, I had to climb a ladder to get in. A curtain closed me in. But I could peek out, and from my vantage point, I could instantly discern everything that was going on in the loft.

I liked it. I started drawing or writing on the wall up there . . . mostly inspired by those I missed from back home. Because as much as I didn't admit it, I did feel a terrible loneliness at times. The denial defense mechanism that had allowed me to get out of Tampa was fading . . . it had served its purpose. Now, there were many and much that I missed. Heaven, I found, can be the loneliest place on earth.

By the time I left that little cubbyhole in the wall, there was a mural that few saw, which was my diary of despair. Ornate but primitive, like cave paintings graffitied on the bathroom walls of the Sistine Chapel. Mostly late at night, I was feeling a new kind of loneliness. A kind that happens when you are surrounded by people and stimuli all the time, but find yourself isolated.

> Lonely sidewalks that lead nowhere
> Lonely footsteps up the stairs
> Lonely eyes that look right through
> The lonely lights of the avenue. . . .
> Noboody knows me,
> Knows the way I feel
> Nobody sees that I'm
> Even here. . . .

As if on autopilot, I forged ahead and ignored those feelings. I plunged deeper into New York, into music, into the filthy hole on the Bowery called CBGB, where Jean and I went almost every night.

To see the new superstars, the Ramones, Richard Hell, and the others in such close proximity, just hanging out at the bar, was mind boggling at first, and of course, the sonic onslaught of the Ramones was, well, ear-boggling. To pee standing next to Dee Dee Ramone in the obscenely dirty, graffiti-splattered men's room was awe-inspiring. Miss Jean reported to me that the walls in the women's bathroom had explicitly—favorable—writing, concerning Dee Dee's endowment and prowess, written by his girlfriend.

The sound in the venue was stunning—the low end was so tight and fat. And it was so *loud*, without distorting. The low stage added to feeling that we were all in this scene together, like you had just stepped into a music video with the group. The fact that MTV was still a few years away made it better. I mean, this wasn't staged, baby. This was real. Nobody complained about the filth, the uneven floors, the broken chairs and bottles. With just a long row of neon beer signs to guide us, it was—like the Laughing Dogs' loft—heaven. I was so charged up to find my own band.

Even groups I had never heard of, who I saw play at CBGB, sounded fantastic to me. I felt, saw, and heard the influences I shared with them. It had all come together in a kind of movement. The Suicide Commandos (from Minneapolis), with their Dennis the Menace lead singer, Steve Almaas. Postmodern, metal art-rockers TV Toy, and a young and obscure little group from New Jersey called Fast Car, led by brothers John and James Mastro, still in high school. The night I saw them, I went backstage to introduce myself.

The twenty-four-hour train ride from Tampa had destroyed my Gibson L6-S. By not reducing the tension on the strings, the constant vibration of the train had weakened the neck to the point where the guitar would not stay in tune. Experts in the Laughing Dogs camp agreed, it was time to trade it in. I was pointed in the direction of 48th Street, the street where all the musical instrument stores were. (Boy, how I liked that about Manhattan: there was a street where all the musical instrument stores were!)

Narrow, the store I walked into looked almost like a pawnshop, with a counter like a bank-teller window and most of the instruments behind bulletproof plexiglass or chain link fencing. Standing there, not particularly tall but as large as fame itself, looking at a clear lucite guitar, was Lou Reed. In awe, but knowing it was okay, I said, "Hi," and smiled. Shook his hand. He mumbled and smiled back a little grimly. I told him I was trading in my Gibson, and he seemed unfazed. Just as this verbal exchange was taking place, I spotted a guitar on the wall, a vintage Rickenbacker 340, with a lovely, aged natural finish and trademark white two-tiered teardrop pickguard, three pickups, and stylized "R" tailpiece. Lou noticed me eyeing the guitar, looked at me up and down to size me up, and suggested I try it. Instant love. Lou smiled and said good-bye. Adding a few hundred bucks that I didn't have to the trade-in, I went home with a 1965 Rickenbacker, in a long silver plush-lined case.

A few days later I was cleaning the guitar and removed the pick guard to get inside. My heart almost stopped. Inside the instrument, written in a simple handwriting similar to my own, was written the name *Richard*.

During the day, I wrote songs fast and furious: "Boy Crazy," "Giant T.V.," "Double Date," "Seven Digits," "Don't Be Shy." The guitar seemed to have these songs already inside it, they came so fast. It was alchemy. I believe, in fact, that instruments can write songs. It happened again, years later, when I finally got my first Les Paul, a single cutaway, TV yellow "Special" with P-90s pickups from the Gibson Custom Shop. I took it right out of the box and a song appeared ("Guru").

In general, I feel that the best songs exist already, and one merely has to reach into the air and pluck them like orchids or butterflies in a lush garden.

November turned into December, and into one of the coldest and snowiest New York winters on record. By February, the snow was knee-deep in Astor Place. I remember thinking that when President Ford said to the city, "Drop dead," it must have affected how many snow plows they could afford to buy. My Florida blood could barely stand the cold sometimes, the wind icy and painful on my face. Yet I never had second thoughts, and as much I missed the sunny beach where I had once disc jockeyed on Sunday afternoons, I never once regretted the move.

I would walk the few blocks surrounding our loft, down Montague Street, past Saint Ann's Church. I walked toward the beautiful Promenade of Brooklyn Heights, with its truly majestic view of Manhattan . . . taking in the breathtaking twin towers of the World Trade Center and their reflections on the water. From that angle, the island looked like the great mothership at the end of *Close Encounters of the Third Kind* . . . but upside down.

I walked the streets of Manhattan, a quick F train ride away. Everyone looked so busy; everyone was headed to work. Everyone was making money. Everyone was headed to or going from nine-to-fives. It was like a Talking Heads song.

I looked for trends. An occasional punk. An occasional gay clone dude. I remember thinking, "I can *stand out* here. It's easier than I thought: everyone is so busy . . . too busy to be different. *I'll* be different."

Meanwhile, the Laughing Dogs had gotten signed to Columbia Records and started recording their first album. I watched the label-shopping and signing process carefully, listened to all their talk about lawyers, managers, and agents, hoping that the corporate major-label world would not squash their unique humor and musicality. I was excited to visit them in a real New York recording studio and was lucky that they were recording at Plaza Sound while it was still in operation.

Situated high atop Radio City Music Hall, the Rockettes rehearsed on the same floor, and the studio had been the location of many legendary big band radio broadcasts in the 1940s. Impressive in size, design and details (the floors were rubberized), the acoustics were, to my young ears, stunning. The Ramones had recorded their debut album there, and in general, the studio seemed to have become a favorite of the new wave of punk bands.

The engineer on the Laughing Dogs sessions, Rob Freeman, had recorded and mixed that first Ramones album (still one of my all time faves. Anyone who doesn't agree shall be beaten with a baseball bat!). The first time I spoke with Freeman, I asked him if he would remix the four-track Snails recordings I had brought with me from Florida: I had hopes of creating an indie release of a Snails EP. He did, beautifully, at his home studio. But the Snails EP was not to be—the tapes and the graphics are still in a file folder in my kitchen cabinet, waiting to this day—because before long I had another band to deal with.

There was an ad in the *Village Voice*. "Seeking guitarist/vocalist, into Velvet Underground, Eno, Television. . . . " Answering it, the first and only time I did that, produced a visitation to the loft by an amusing quartet. In retrospect, that gathering had the feeling of preschool-ers meeting in a playground and becoming friends. The whole scene, even in that dusty, dimly lit loft, was bathed in the same kind of pure, sunshiny, yellow light of the field behind B. C. Graham Elementary School, or the nuns' convent where I had attended kindergarten, where boys want you to come and play and you don't *think* of saying no. We had a conversation that was like rolling around in the soft grass. Where nothing is evil and you and your playmates have everything in common.

But these were not the future Bongos. Well, one of them was. An astute music fan named Jim Vantyne; Glenn Morrow, a just-graduated NYU student; Glenn's roommate, an aspiring journalist named Steve Mirkin; and a bass player named Rob Norris (who, it was whispered, had played in one of the last incarnations of the Velvets themselves) were the diplomats who came to check me out. A mysterious drum-mer, named Frank, who I was told (by a wily Glenn Morrow, who knew this would get my attention) resembled "a surfer," was back home in New Jersey, presumably waiting to hear the field report. Glenn, Rob, and Frank had been playing Glenn's epic, yet Talking Heads–influ-enced songs and were looking for a lead guitarist and vocalist to round things out. Jim Vantyne was their creative guru: gay and friendly, slightly campy with a wide "howdy, sailor" smile, and, I later learned, an unabashed obsession with Nancy Sinatra. We talked for a couple of hours about bands, songs, and sensibilities.

They rehearsed in a strange land called *Morristown, New Jersey*. Would I come out and rehearse with them on Sunday?

It was all so exotic to me. Another state! It could just as well have been Ohio, or even Idaho for that matter. It seemed so improbable.

Of course I said yes.

The New Jersey Transit trains were old and rattley with thatched wicker seats. My Rickenbacker, in its silver case (strings detuned), went above me in the luggage rack. Looking out the window I witnessed extreme industrial wastelands . . . meadows with electric-green chemi-cal wastewaters, and tall silos with red tongues of flames on top, licking the gray skies. I felt like an alien. This whole area was like the gigantic utility closet for New York City. Then, a litany of little stations with names like Convent Station and Brick Church came into view.

My mind buzzed and sang with all the songs I had been writing and all the ones I knew I would be writing now . . . and with the sound of my guitar . . . it's trebly buzz. Daydreaming. . . . How would it *feel* to be on a New York stage? To sign to a big record company like Columbia or RCA? To go on tour and to hear my songs on the radio?

And, as the train went fast through another tunnel, its lights flickering off for a second or two, I wondered where the hell I was going.

A voice in my head, sounding like Tiny Tim: "You must believe in your dreams. . . ."

Once in Morristown, what had seemed improbable now seemed inevitable. We jammed and rocked with Glenn's songs. They seemed herky-jerky, with too many changes for my taste. Completely against my new minimalist tendencies. The themes were grand and Springsteenesque: about breadwinners, workers, electricians. The lyrics were literal and without mystery and Glenn's singing was *expressionistic*—like David Byrne's. But no matter. I was in the right ballpark and ready to play ball.

I liked Glenn. More important, I loved Rob's and Frank's playing. It was organic and strong. Artistic yet primal. And although I didn't think Frank looked much like the surfer I was promised (except for his longish hair), he *was* easy on the eyes, and I did think we would become fast friends—at least, I knew I wanted us to. I wanted to play music with both of them.

I came back home to Brooklyn, high with the possibilities—my mind like an Escher painting with the complexities of Glenn's songs. But, I thought, playing through these changes smoothly and with *feeling* would improve my chops. I had played the boys one or two of my own songs, and they seemed to have gone over well.

During the week I practiced, I wrote new songs, I recorded. I couldn't wait until the next Sunday to go back to Morristown and play with the band again. Each week sounded better.

With their Columbia Records deal, the Laughing Dogs were able to replace all of their gear, so, from them I purchased the sweet Fender Deluxe amp I had my eye on. It always had a good amount of a very pleasing distortion, which complemented the otherwise super-clean sound of my Rickenbacker. This helped me forge my own sound from a guitar more known for chime and jangle than bite and dirt.

As winter started winding down, I had my first experience of changing seasons. In Florida, seasons are an abstract concept—something hinted at in calendars, meditated on by poets, and sung about in pop songs. I had never felt such a drastic shift before and it was invigorating. Thawing out, Brooklyn Heights went from beautiful to gorgeous as the entire borough emerged from the gray winter months in full bloom. The sunlight melted the last few vestiges of dirty snow banks and cast a golden glow on even the most industrial buildings.

Manhattan was a new place, too. Like a beautiful lover in the morning, awakening. I knew I was falling hopelessly in love with New York City.

As spring arrived, I needed to make some money. My savings started to run low and, and one day I went up 59th Street to sell the gold coin and watch chain that my great uncle had given to me as a boy. I looked again at all those people going to their nine-to-fives. I knew I needed a job. I was still feeling lonely; I knew I would have to break out of my shyness and meet new people. For now, though, I went back into the loft's studio and wrote to myself:

> Answer pay phones,
> don't be shy.
> Don't be brittle,
> don't be shy. . . .

After Jean and I had lived in the Heights for about six months, falling into a lovely routine of shopping for groceries and making communal vegetarian stir-fries with tofu, things began to fall apart. The Laughing Dogs were planning to tour again and had decided to sell their loft. It was time to vacate. After six months, I had grown to love the loft and the neighborhood, but I always knew it was a temporary thing. That was when I first heard of Hoboken.

When I told Glenn I was looking for a new place to live, he suggested we become roommates. His was moving out. Glenn had a lease on a rent-controlled, three-bedroom apartment just across the Hudson River in New Jersey, for eighty-eight dollars a month. Eighty-eight dollars a month. Total. We'd split it. Forty-four dollars each.

Sounded like a deal to me.

Hoboken. The very name conjured up a kind of time warp. A time when towns had names like, well, Hoboken. . . . A time of *On the Waterfront* (the classic Brando film, with its "I could'a been a contender" line, was shot there), and, of course, the town's golden boy and favorite son, Sinatra. A special subway, PATH, connects Manhattan to Hoboken, Jersey City, and other New Jersey locales through its tunnels beneath the Hudson River. A PATH ride at the end of the '70s was only thirty cents. Thirty cents. This is not a typo.

A mile square city—and it *was* a time warp of a town. Mostly mom-and-pop stores, all on one main street . . . clothing stores with window displays of fashions from twenty years prior on mannequins from the 1950s, seen through protective sheets of yellow plastic gel. Such a far cry from New York City just across the river. Hoboken was a tiny town—in the shadow of the center of the universe. Like a small moon of Jupiter, it was quaint, quiet, and strangely lovable. I had found a new little cubbyhole-in-the-wall-of-a-town to call my own.

Hoboken's miracle mile had ninety-seven taverns—all connected by an intricate system of underground tunnels built during Prohibition. You could always get a drink in Hoboken, as I would soon find out.

It was actually an ideal roommate situation, because Glenn was never in the apartment. His sweet girlfriend, Lisa, lived next door, and Glenn had basically moved in with her. Fire escapes facing the courtyard connected the two buildings, allowing him to pop over from her fifth-floor walkup to our sixth, without walking downstairs. It was sometimes disconcerting to see his tall, shadowy form coming in through the kitchen window late at night, but I grew used to it.

Being on the top floor, the easy-to-reach rooftop became a favorite hangout, from which the entire skyline of Manhattan was visible in sharp detail. The West Side piers, the Empire State Building, the top of the Chrysler Building, and the ever-present red neon RCA logo atop their building in midtown.

A peculiar aroma permeated the town of Hoboken. Like coffee ... but harsher. The apartment at 1118 Hudson Street was directly across from the Maxwell House Coffee factory. The scent in question emanated from the factory every Monday, when the caffeine was extracted from coffee to produce Sanka. The air on those days was noticeably caffeinated, to the point where you could sense the entire town buzzing. Coca-Cola trucks would arrive on those days to retrieve the extracted caffeine, presumably to add it to Coke.

My little bedroom faced the factory, with its famous neon sign, once the largest in the world, with coffee pouring and the motto, "Good to the Last Drop."

Glenn had furnished the apartment with odds and ends, mostly found on the Hoboken sidewalks. I had a little twin mattress on the floor, a bookshelf, and a little bright orange night table. There was a bare lightbulb hanging in the center of the room, and a gigantic black-and-white foam-core-mounted image of soul singer Bill Withers, which sometimes was used as the door to my room, when I wanted privacy. In what had been the dining room, I set up nothing but my black Fender amp. I plugged it in, and leaned my Rickenbacker against it.

Jean had moved in with a friend, to Manhattan's Upper East Side, and I was envious. I mean, I hadn't come all this way to live in a town even smaller than the one I left. I also knew that this was where I needed to be. How did I know?

It felt right.

It didn't look right. It didn't smell right, but. . . .

It was home for now and, for now, all emphasis was on the band. After the inevitable name search, we came up with the most nondescript name we could think of. The letter "a." Yes, the band was called a.

Andy Warhol's first (and only) novel was called *a*. When I visited New York the previous year, my first stop had been Warhol's Factory at 860 Broadway, at Union Square. The bulletproof entrance to his floor held his famous stuffed dog and a framed segment of his famous cow wallpaper. The receptionist, Brigid Polk, took me downstairs for a soda, then up to meet Andy, who gave a personally signed and decorated copy of his then-current book, *The Philosophy of Andy Warhol (From A to B and Back Again)*. Yet those were not the reasons for calling the group "a."

It was the utter simplicity. We simply couldn't come up with anything more basic.

We rehearsed for a few weeks, and as soon as we had enough songs worked out, we booked ourselves at the Show Place in Dover, New Jersey. In the afternoons, it was a strip club frequented by truckers, by night, a hard rockin' club where occasionally, semi-big name groups, passing through on their way across the country, would stop to play. A nice, big stage and a superb sound system, the Show Place gave us a great chance to explore all the possibilities of live performance. I didn't tell the others how few times I had actually performed with a band onstage. The Snails had only played a handful of times, and that was it. In this new and alien environment of northern Jersey, I felt especially uninhibited, although I wondered how this hard rock crowd would like us.

"Ladies and gentlemen: a."

A . . . *what?*

The crowd shuffled. We played. They liked.

istening. The first thing I learned onstage with the group was the importance of *listening*. I found, still believe, and am absolutely sure that at least 50 percent of performing music with others is about listening—listening to what the others are playing and listening to how the music reacts in the room, in the space you're playing. Just ask jazz players about listening. Like actors who appear not to really listen to the other actors in a scene seem phony, so musicians who don't *really* listen to the other players sound wooden, cardboard, disengaged, or—worse—boring. Music played with others is a dialogue. I am reminded of this every time I pick up a guitar and play with others.

We were actually quite good. Frank's drumming was powerful and sometimes unexpectedly Keith Moon–like, sometimes Ringo-esque, and he could swing. Rob's bass was a towering anchor that filled the center. I focused on my guitar playing mostly, with some singing. The audience reaction was good. Even some of the strippers who lingered after their afternoon shows seemed to like us. We were encouraged. We played a few more shows: a high school event in Glen Ridge, New Jersey, and at NYU. Once, we went into a recording studio to cut some demos, and the engineer offered me cocaine. I hesitantly tried a line, after everyone else did, and felt a slight stimulating effect. Didn't think too much of it: I was already naturally wired.

Just around the corner from the apartment in Hoboken was a newly renovated tavern, one of the aforementioned ninety-seven in fourteen blocks. This one happened to be the closest, and had new, young owners. I wondered if we could play there. They didn't have live music, and they didn't have a stage or a sound system. But none of that seemed to matter.

Named after the looming coffee factory a block away, Maxwell's was recently reopened by the new owners, and seemed brighter than most of the other bars, with big storefront corner windows, and unlike the other dark, smoke-filled taverns in town, there were hanging plants in the window. Clean and polished. It was slowly beginning to attract an almost preppy crowd, some students from Hoboken's Stevens Tech, and as the '80s were now nearly upon us, dreaded *yuppies.*

We did play a show or two in the bar's front room, our backs to the windows, passersby looking in, their hands cupped around their eyes against the glass to see. Fun nights.

But as bands do, "a" soon disbanded. The factors causing the breakup were classic: musical and personal differences. I mean, hear this now: those are *always* the reasons. In a band, what else is there, really? Music and personalities, right? For all our similarities, there *were* profound creative and personal differences.

But out of the ashes, just as I had desired and predicted, Frank and I had become good friends. Good enough friends that we were physically ejected from nearly every one of the ninety-seven bars in Hoboken. For a time, we were inseparable. We would talk for hours over, unbelievably, *twenty-five-cent beers* at the Elysian bar on Tenth Street, or take amphetamines (in the form of wicked black beauties) and play on the swings in the playground in the middle of town, speeding our brains out. One night in Manhattan, we got drunk and slept in the garden at Grace Church in the Village, huddled together in the cold, in the bushes where no one could see us.

We started to dress alike, wearing vintage '50s and '60s shirts and baggy pants from thrift stores, and Frank buzzed his longish hair to a kind of crew cut. Once he told me he had had a dream about me: that I was an alien who landed in a UFO. I remembered my own extraterrestrial experiences in Tampa, but didn't mention them. I might have admitted, though, how often I *felt* like an alien.

Frank and I must have had some kind of aura around us when we were together, because we seemed to get special treatment everywhere. Doors would open for us, we'd get the best tables in restaurants, smiles from passersby. . . . Once, we spontaneously stopped in to the Empire State Building. It was a beautiful, clear day, and we wanted to see the view from the top. The line of tourists was daunting. But suddenly we were whisked to the front of the line, and personally escorted by a security guard, straight up to the observation deck. I thought we were being arrested! From up there, we looked at the skyline and all the cars and people below. Everything shimmered. I glanced back toward Brooklyn, and we both looked across the Hudson to Hoboken, then uptown, past the RCA building and toward Central Park, without a word.

In my head, high above Manhattan, Iggy sang, "All of it is yours and mine. . . . "

We listened to a lot of music. We'd talk about the Beatles and listen closely to their harmonies. Frank would talk about ABBA and the virtues of their vocal arrangements, which until then had escaped me, and the Mamas and the Papas.

One night in Morristown, we were in Frank's bedroom with the lights out, and on the stereo was the Flamin' Groovies' song, "Shake Some Action," which we listened to over and over. The song, the feeling, the sound of the guitar on that song. . . . At some level, on some plane of consciousness, the Bongos were conceived on that night.

CHAPTER 5

DRUMS ALONG THE HUDSON

HOW TO INVENT A POP MECCA

With the '80s moments away, New Wave sensibilities were already looming on the horizon, like the first light of a Day-Glo sunrise. Following a nasty hostage crisis in the Middle East, a new president was elected and the general tone of the country was shifting. To *what* exactly, was hard to tell. But a change could be felt.

It was on this cusp of the '80s that the B-52's emerged. I had heard and read about this group from Athens, Georgia, whose local indie release of "Rock Lobster" had sold a then-astonishing five thousand copies. When the group came up to New York to play CBGB, Rob, Frank, and I made the scene, ending up right in the front row, facing a very animated Fred Schneider. The muscular dance/rock drumbeats laid down by Keith Strickland were exactly to my liking, as were guitarist Ricky Wilson's stylized open tunings and scratchy rhythms—on guitars clearly missing their middle strings. To Fred's right, Kate Pierson sounded at once like the soprano on the *Star Trek* theme and a bewigged Yoko Ono. On Fred's left, Ricky's younger sister Cindy sat on the floor, playing bongos.

The sweaty frenzy they created was unlike the punk groups . . . this was . . . well . . . New Wave, baby. Music for the new decade. Fun, rather than angry . . . but still somehow subversive.

At this point, Rob and Frank had both moved to Hoboken, too, and, for a while, we all lived together at 1118 Hudson Street. Glenn, who was now writing for the excellent and influential *New York Rocker*, was rarely there at all, having moved in next door with girlfriend Lisa. After "a's" untimely demise, Rob was quick to find a spot in another group, the punk/rockabilly Zantees. But that didn't stop Frank and I from wanting him to play with us, too. When together, we continued our endless batting around of potential band names. We were close to calling ourselves the Supreme Pontiffs (to commemorate the new pope), or the Portable Grandmothers (a nod to the two elderly ladies who served us breakfast at a tiny Hoboken lunch counter called Schnackenberg's). These were only two among hundreds of names being verbally thrown out, like baseballs from an automatic pitching machine. Tea Cup Poodles . . . Miniature Horse Farm.

But it was that image of Cindy Wilson sitting on the stage banging those little drums that propelled Frank to suggest, "How about *the Bongos*?"

There was a kind of shimmering silence, as the name hung in the air for a while, and then fell gently to earth.

Yes.

Seeing another Jersey group we had read about, the Feelies, at the trendy dance/rock club Hurrah (their opening act was the British, soon-to-be-hit-making Squeeze) was a kick in the (baggy) pants. They had crossed the Velvets with the Stooges, added lots of percussion and exploding fuzz box solos, and come up with something unique. I adore that group still.

The Laughing Dogs' first album had been released by Columbia, but made little impact. An alarm went off in my mind, to beware of big labels. Major labels seem to have a way of taking bands by the hand and walking them into oncoming traffic. Easy to get lost or killed. Much like the situation now, with alternative means of distribution and marketing music, the emerging indie scene was a far more promising route.

The Bongos had a few rehearsals and started playing shows in New Jersey, returning to the Show Place strip joint in Dover. The songs were short, and the sound was instant and spontaneous. Frank had gotten a job as the cook at Maxwell's, where he helped develop their menu, making the tavern a viable restaurant. Through Frank, we asked one of the owners, Steve Fallon, if we could rehearse in the unused storage room behind the kitchen. This became our rehearsal home (along with the Hoboken Circus School, a trapeze academy, run by Russians in a huge Washington Street loft). Later, we asked Fallon if we could invite friends to hang out and see us play in the backroom. He agreed, they did, and a legendary rock venue was born. Soon, admission was being charged, and the room would be packed. We could feel the buzz.

Apparently, so could the Hoboken Fire Department, which attempted to close the club down because of overcrowding. Rob's little Cerwin Vega rehearsal PA with its red cloth speaker grills made its home in that backroom at Maxwell's and, for most of the club's heyday, it was the sound system everyone played through, from R.E.M. and New Order to the Bongos. But I'm getting ahead of myself again. . . .

Steve Fallon was a music fan of vision and exquisite taste, and likeable, despite his annoying habit of always greeting me with "Hi, *faggot*." To my mind, the sound we made was a kind of Buddy Holly meets Donna Summer, through a fuzzy filter of '60s psychedelic garage pop and *Revolver*-era Beatles.

> A room of voices is calling me—
> Three decades questioning
> Me.

A big, fat kick drum beat you could dance to, and punchy, symmetrical bass lines. The guitar parts were strummy and accented, with fuzzy, sustained solos, nods to Robert Fripp and Tom Verlaine and, of course, the Feelies. By keeping the Rickenbacker's toggle switch in the middle pickup position and turning the pickup blend knob more toward the left (emphasizing the pickup nearest the neck) I was able to produce a smoother, more Les Paul–like tone than one would normally create with a Rick. The treble pickup gave me the jangle when I needed it. I played through my hot-wired, overdriven Fender Deluxe amp, and for solos I stomped a DOD overdrive pedal (painted white so no one would know the brand I used), adding a further layer of thick, sustained fuzz.

Suddenly, songs were everywhere . . . like random thoughts flying by during meditation, which meant I had to grab them and write them down fast. I fell into a zone where everything I saw, heard, or felt was potential material for a tune. I was finding them everywhere I looked.

A lot of this was out of necessity: we needed material! But *what better motivation than necessity?*

If you're a songwriter, my advice is to *let yourself fall into this zone,* and stay there as long as possible! Obvious, but worth emphasizing here. The truth is, songs do lurk all around us, waiting to be uncovered, and you simply need to be in the most open state of mind at the right time, to receive them. It's so easy to forget when, for instance, the false condition of writer's block clouds one's vision.

Rob, interested in all things spiritual, was studying the Kabbalah and Jewish mysticism. An illustrated poster of the Tree of Life dominated the wall of his bedroom. He had the only television set in the apartment, a little black-and-white portable, and when he was away at his girlfriend's place back in Morristown, I would sit cross-legged on his mattress on the floor, strumming my Rickenbacker. Watching the TV with the sound off, to trigger my subconscious mind, and with the Tree of Life on the wall overhead, a song would emerge:

> A cable
> Reaches up to heaven
> Unleavened
> Bread comes down from heaven
> You, you know I'm right,
> I'll tell you
> You, you know I'm right.

On the bed next to me lay my first-grade *Think and Do* workbook, brought back on my last trip to Tampa, with the familiar *Fun with Dick and Jane* characters:

> Oh, Sally,
> Let's look for baby Moses
> Oh, Sally
> Can you guess what this is, Sally?
> You, you know I'm right,
> I'll tell you
> You, you know I'm right.

What is most interesting to me, then and now, are songs that come from the subconscious. If a song lyric or poem can come from there, the meaning is understood on some level, no matter how abstract the actual words may seem. For me, having the TV on, or washing dishes or cooking, occupies my conscious mind, the gatekeeper, and allows the subconscious to sneak in. Most of my best ideas come when I'm doing anything other than thinking about having a great idea.

E minor was the favorite chord of my Rickenbacker. The guitar seemed to resonate best with it—I could feel the vibration in its neck and body. One thing I liked was playing minor chords under a major-sounding melody. For instance, a cheerful tune or lyric set against a sad minor chord progression, or vice versa. I nearly always used a drop-D tuning (the low E string tuned to D). By the time we recorded our first album, I was often tuning *both* E strings down to D (you can hear this on "Clay Midgets," "Burning Bush," "Speaking Sands," and others on *Drums Along the Hudson.)*

Sometimes, if the words seemed too narrative or predictable or *revealing*, I would tear or cut the lyric page into strips and rearrange them, a technique William Burroughs often used.

Regardless how stylized or reconstructed they were, in my mind the lyrics were literal expressions of real feelings. In fact, the result of cutting up and rearranging of words was usually even more revealing than I originally intended.

A visit to a Steak 'n' Shake drive-in restaurant in Tampa gave me the verse of "Glow in the Dark." The sign directly in front of each parked car was "Flash Lights When Ready"; "to Order" was implied. But my dirty mind wandered and I added, "That's what she said to me / Some assembly required / That's what I said to her."

I had just read *Naked Lunch* and *The Wild Boys*, when Rob and I suddenly found ourselves in the Tribeca building where Burroughs occasionally wrote. A telescope mounted on its rooftop, to spy into neighbors' windows, inspired "Telephoto Lens."

> Telephoto lens
> Alone in a city
> Making distant friends
> Tonight. . . .

Being a long-time fan of Brian Eno, I had wanted to try to mix some electronic element into our sound. Our friend Dennis Kelley half of a duo called WKGB, happened to own and play an EMS Synthi 1 "brief-case" synthesizer, just like the one Eno had played with Roxy Music and on Bowie's *Low* and *Heroes* albums. Dennis, tall, with an impossi-bly curly near-afro, brilliantly added textures and melodic parts to our new songs and, on stage, would take an output signal from my guitar that he would treat and further distort, using the Synthi's patch bay and joystick. Dennis can be heard on "Telephoto Lens" and "Glow in the Dark." But, after few live shows, his schedule with WKGB demanded all of his time. So, for the Bongos, it was back to being a trio.

I finally got a job at a small health food store across the street from Macy's in Herald Square. I would pop vitamin supplements all day, take unnatural amounts of natural stimulants, and bring various health foods back home for Rob. A *mostly* healthy time. After work, I would party with a co-worker, Alverna, and her young boyfriends. Quite a bit older and quite hip in that distinctly New York way, Alverna claimed to have appeared in some of Andy Warhol's films and probably did, though she never mentioned any titles. One night at a hustler bar at 53rd Street and Third Avenue called Cowboy, she introduced me to the *real* Leon Shermer, Al Pacino's transsexual girlfriend in *Dog Day Afternoon*. We'd hit the velvet-roped disco scene late into the night. Back at the health food store the next day, Alverna would keep the party going by shoving amyl nitrate under my nose while I was trying to take care of customers, nearly causing me to black out more than once.

> Pearl Harbour
> Was waiting
> For something to happen
> Something happened in the night.
>
> I'm nineteen
> She's forty
> I'm stationed, she's rationed
> Tourists don't put up a fight
>
> The Nina,
> the Pinta,
> the Santa Maria
> Ships that passed us in the night."

The store manager, a rather mean-faced, macho Latino, would grab my ass every time I climbed the ladder in the basement storeroom. Eventually, after several times declining his advances, I was fired—for not wearing a tie. Jobless again.

Through Dennis Kelley, the Bongos found themselves backing up a talented and beautiful singer/songwriter/violinist, Helen Hooke, who had been one third of an all-girl rock trio, Deadly Nightshade, in the mid-'70s. We rocked hard with Helen at the legendary Folk City in the Village, and withstood some heavy verbal abuse from the mostly lesbian audiences, angered that Helen had chosen a backing band of all boys. No matter, it was fun backing her fiddle showcase, "Orange Blossom Special," as if we were the Ramones. Unfortunately, she declined our suggestion to call ourselves "Helen and the Trojans," which I still think would have been a good name.

Helen had access to her manager Bud Prager's small studio in midtown, where we rehearsed with her, and one day, she offered to record a demo for us. We laid down our first recordings of "Telephoto Lens" and "Glow in the Dark," a little bit herky-jerky and nervous, in the same studio that Prager's other act, Foreigner, made *their* demos. Thank you, Helen.

Very suddenly we found ourselves getting our own gigs in Manhattan, at the sacred temple of rock and sleaze, Max's Kansas City (opening for the wonderfully campy transsexual rocker, Jayne County), and later at Hurrah, the trendy rock disco where I first met David Bowie, then starring in *The Elephant Man* on Broadway. We spoke over the deafening music, which hopefully concealed my nervousness in meeting Ziggy Stardust himself.

One of our first New York shows was a double bill with the supremely original, but tragic New Wave opera icon, Klaus Nomi, at the Ukrainian Hall. Amid all the beautiful sloppiness of punk rock, Klaus's polished, stylized performance, zen-like concentration, and raw talent left a lasting impression on us.

We would start each show with "We're the Bongos . . . from *Hoboken*," and it always got a great response. Being from Hoboken seemed to set us apart. I mean, there were lots of groups from New York, and from everyplace else for that matter. But not many from Hoboken. That would soon change.

Rob used to say that our coming from Hoboken was like Jimmy Durante's nose: a trademark that made people smile and remember us. We were intent on making that little town of docks, factories, and taverns the new Liverpool. Now we were really starting to feel the buzz. Our first interview was for a gay monthly called *Christopher Street*. More press followed.

A young Englishman of twenty-one, Rod Pearce, had been bitten by the indie record label bug and, supposedly with earnings from a winning horse race, started Fetish Records in London. With just one 7" vinyl single release under his belt, but with big plans, he had come to New York and signed Dennis's group WKGB to release a single. It was Dennis who told Rod he should see the Bongos and handed him a copy of our demo. We happened to be playing at Maxwell's that weekend, and Pearce came to see us play. The next day we were offered a simple contract, which we signed together, seated at one of the tables in Maxwell's.

Lightning flashed as our pens touched the paper.

We re-recorded "Telephoto Lens" and "Glow in the Dark," this time at a "real" studio in Boonton, New Jersey, called Mixolydian, with engineer/owner Don Sternecker. In the good-sized live room, we were able to capture a fairly nice drum sound from Frank's gray pearl Ludwig kit. The Rolling Stones' recent album, *Some Girls*, was still dominating our turntable, and its thuddy snare sound was something we were interested in copping. To achieve this, Frank overdubbed a second snare on both songs, which was then compressed and gated with a Kepex Noise Gate, that clipped and punctuated the sound. Otherwise, both songs were recorded just as we had been performing them live, except that on "Glow," I doubled my Rickenbacker with a borrowed acoustic guitar, and on "Telephoto," I played a second electric guitar track with my Rick. The *aaahhhs* at the end of "Glow in the Dark" were sung by Frank and me, bussed to an Eventide Harmonizer, first in a new breed of sound processors. Tony Visconti had famously used one on *Low* and *Heroes*, saying in interviews that its pitch-shifter electronically "messed with the fabric of time." That was good enough endorsement for me.

Our first single had been recorded. Each side clocked in at *exactly* two minutes.

Now Rob and I began designing the all-important sleeve. The design we came up with, the hand-drawn and screened bongo drums making a pleasingly retro and slightly absurd background pattern, was soothing—both vintage and new. Consciously avoiding the current splashy, high-contrast or fluorescently colored graphics and fashions of the moment, our sleeve was in relatively austere black and white.

In the indie pop world, the seven-inch singles and their sleeves were the holy grail. For us, it was the perfect medium—small, compact, concise, like bongos themselves. We would have been happy releasing only singles. In fact, that was our plan. With Fetish Records being a one-man operation in London, it was left to us to deal with nearly every aspect of creating, releasing, and promoting the record. Now back in the U.K., Rod Pearce had made an arrangement with a broker in New York, who coordinated the mastering, disc manufacturing, and printing for the U.S. We brought them all the parts, and held our breath. . . .

The work began when the records arrived at 1118 Hudson Street. Rob and I sat at our kitchen table covered with its red-and-white-checked tablecloth, surrounded by thousands of copies of a little black-and-white squares. Our picture, with Rob's recently broken finger ridiculously splinted, looked back at us.

"Now what?" our photo seemed to be asking.

By hand, without computers, we personally sent copies to publications, radio stations, and distributors all over the country. With each record we sent, a press release was inserted, driving home the point that we were from Hoboken and hinting that our little port town was the new "American" Liverpool. Some of our meager first reviews were included. A rubber stamp marked our return address:

> The Bongos
> 1118 Hudson Street
> Hoboken, NJ 07030

As more reviews came in, we added them to press kits and recycled them to more publications, radio stations, and distributors with the disc. Soon, at the end of a review of our opening for the Teardrop Explodes, *The New York Rocker* was compelled to write: "A switch in billing was clearly in order. . . . Something major is brewing in the hometown of Frank Sinatra."

Now we began playing in other cities, driving in Rob's white 1966 Plymouth Valiant. All three of us in the front seat, and all of the equipment in the back. Like the Beverly Hillbillies might do, we would tie Frank's green wooden drum stool to the roof. Rob and Frank took turns driving. Wisely they never offered me the wheel. Not just then. Never.

Norfolk, Virginia, was one of our first destinations. The boys from the U.S. Navy base there assumed we were also in the Navy because of our buzzcuts and "white walls." We certainly didn't have enough originals yet to fill up the three sets that we were required to play, so we started playing Beatles covers. Not Beatles' *original* songs, but songs the Beatles *covered*, like "Boys" (with Frank singing lead, as Ringo had, we got all the Navy "squids" up and dancing) and "Slow Down," by Larry Williams (played real fast), and we would cover Velvet Underground songs, like "There She Goes." After our sets, soaking wet with sweat, I danced with the sailors for the rest of the night.

The 688 Club in Atlanta and the 40 Watt Club in Athens, Georgia, were early mainstays. And then, Boston. All in Rob's Valiant.

A circuit was developing. A network. College radio. Interviews. Clubs. Fanzines. "Alternative Rock" was being born. Our little 45 was in the shops in every town we visited. And if it wasn't, we made sure it soon was.

The shows on the road started getting wilder. Any inhibitions I had seemed to fall away like the remnants of a cocoon. I would hold my Rickenbacker so tight my sweat would penetrate the guitar's back, soaking the wood. Dropping to my knees to play solos, charging across the stage to Rob, playing Frank's tom-toms with my hands, diving into the audience . . . all fueled by a deadly cocktail of vodka and chlorophyll, the green substance found in plants and a natural oxygenator. An experiment from my days at the health food store, I'd mix it in a container and drink it onstage between songs like a kind of atomic Gatorade. Sometimes there was cocaine, which I was beginning to acquire a taste for.

Slowly we started to notice other groups forming in or moving to Hoboken . . . and playing in rotation at Maxwell's. Some were bands we'd met on the road, and had invited to play there. Others gravitated to the miracle mile, based on the press and radio play that had started to generate. Each band was unique; the only possible connecting thread was a slightly preppy look and a power pop sensibility. A kind of melodic adventurism, as opposed to the harder, more aggressive sounds and styles of the bands across the Hudson. The spirit among the Hoboken groups was far, far more supportive than competitive: we were all each other's biggest fans.

In May 1980, we were scheduled to open for one of our favorite groups, Joy Division, on the opening date of their first American tour, at our very own Maxwell's, followed by other dates in the area. We would clearly be on the right tour at the right time, as they were just about to explode in this country. This, we thought, was the break we had been waiting for.

Two days before the show, we got a phone call from England, telling us the dates and the entire U.S. tour, were cancelled. The group's frontman, Ian Curtis, had hung himself. He was only twenty-three. It was said the last thing he listened to was Iggy Pop.

How odd, I thought. . . . When I listened to Iggy, more than anything else, I wanted to *live*.

Rob and I went to see Captain Beefheart perform several shows during his "Shiny Beast" tour. At the Stanhope House in New Jersey, we had the chance to meet the Captain backstage, where we handed him a copy of "Telephoto Lens." "Bongos," he said in his gravelly but whimsical voice. "Cute." He looked us over and said, "Let me give you some advice. Whatever you do, never let the audience stand above you." Silence. In our minds, all the chattering in the room stopped for a moment, while the advice was absorbed. We thanked him, shook hands, and said good-bye, his remark tumbling in my mind over and over like laundry in a dryer.

I hadn't had a day job or any real income for a while, so I was happy to get a phone call from Jean telling me CBS was looking for extras on

As the World Turns. Jean, always resourceful, had recently landed a job working as production assistant on the CBS soap opera. "I can get you an appointment for Thursday."

I walked into the offices at CBS television studios with just a copy of the "Telephoto Lens"/"Glow in the Dark" single. The 7″ vinyl record served as my résumé and head shot. I wore my black jeans, a slightly baggy, black sweater from Lord & Taylor, and black Converse sneakers. I waited, arms crossed, in the reception area for three minutes, then I was called into the office of one of the show's casting directors.

As I walked into the office, I had one, momentary flash of terror. I mean, I wasn't an actor, I had no experience, no real résumé, no head-shot. And what the hell was I going to do for an audition, anyway?

She was one of those tall, beautiful, and powerful corporate women, fortyish, strong, and stylish. A perfect "female casting director" from Central Casting. She sat at her big desk as I walked in and sunk down in the classically lower-profile chair placed in front of her. I reached over to shake her hand, and in a moment she consumed and processed me with her eyes. It may have been my imagination, but in the movie of my life I was directing, I could feel her gaze penetrate my sweater, and I thought I could feel its heat on the button fly of my 501s. She asked for my résumé and head shot and I said, as plainly and deliberately as possible, that I was really a musician and all I had for her was my latest record. I stood and handed it her. She looked at it, amused that it was released on the *Fetish* label. I sat back down and she looked me in the eye: "Okay, son. Seduce me."

I thought about it for a moment, holding her stare. Then I stood up and leaned toward her on her desk and, speaking slowly and softly, told her a story about a boy coming in for an audition and seducing the show's producer right in her office. He had come from Florida to go to college here, and he was all alone in this big town. He was lookin' for a break, and would do anything to get a part on a television show. I walked around to her side of the desk, standing facing her with my body. The CBS eye watched knowingly and, apparently, approvingly.

The next day I was on the show.

Getting to makeup in Manhattan at 6:30 A.M. from Hoboken meant leaving the apartment at least an hour earlier. We had played a Bongos show the night before so, for fear of oversleeping and missing my call, I decided not to go to sleep at all. I just went home, changed out of my sweat-soaked stage clothes, showered, and got ready to go to work.

The *real* actors on the show were instantly suspicious of how and why I got the job, even though I was just an extra. Rumors were flying. Especially when I didn't know what "blocking" meant, and again, when I nearly knocked down one of the flimsy set walls, hitting it with a hospital stretcher I was pushing in one scene.

The actors who had been on the show the longest were exactly the same on or off the set; they had *become* their characters. In general, the scene on the set, and the relationships between all the actors on a soap opera, was like, well, a soap opera.

That evening when I got home to Hoboken, I called my mother to tell her to be sure to watch *As the World Turns* the next day, and she'd see her boy playing the part of an orderly in a hospital. Then, checking our answering machine, there was a message.

A concert was being organized to be held at the Rainbow Theatre in London to showcase five of the new breed of bands from New York. The Fleshtones, the Raybeats, the DBs, and the Bush Tetras were on board—all groups we liked—and they were interested in adding the Bongos. *Time Out London* was doing a special cover story on it for the week of the concert, and a live album would be recorded that night, to be released by Stiff Records. "Please call us back as soon as possible." We jumped at it.

So long to *As The World Turns*.

The reviews kept coming in and getting more effusive, and now we were going to London. Fetish wanted another single right away to tie in with the London concert.

We decided to record "In the Congo" and "Hunting" and this time put them out on a twelve-inch dance single. The trouble was, our songs were short, and how could we ever justify two- or three-minute songs on a twelve-inch record? We would need a third song, one that we could extend. But what?

The answer came the night before the session, while we rehearsed on the stage at Maxwell's. I was thinking of T.Rex and the *Electric Warrior* album, released ten years before, and the great opening track. I started playing the riff of "Mambo Sun," and soon we had our third song.

I knew we had something and was too hyped to go home just yet. Another all-nighter made me especially loose at the session the next day.

This time we brought in a producer, Mark Abel, who also lived in Hoboken. Mark had just co-produced the Feelies album, *Crazy Rhythms*, which was another staple on our turntable, and he helped us bring out a similar kind of subtlety to the recording. With a careful ear for EQ-ing and panning, he gave us the kind of stereo imagery we were looking for, and knew how to maximize our trio sound with minimal overdubbing. The on-and-off reverb on the kick drum on "Mambo Sun" was a nice touch, and Rob's butter-knife slide bass at the fade of that song was mysteriously cinematic. We had made our first record that would get us on the charts, and it had been effortless.

"Great American Rock 'n' Roll" —*Record World*

"The best in the field of new pop" —*Trouser Press*

"Pure celebration . . . seamless craftsmanship . . . A pop poetry" —*New York Rocker*

"Absolutely ingenious" —*New Musical Express*

Suddenly, the Bongos could do no wrong.

CHAPTER 6

NUMBERS WITH WINGS

HOW TO BECOME A CUDDLY POP STAR

The shooting death of John Lennon at the end of 1980 is what signaled the beginning of the new decade for me. That horrendous event symbolized the onset of a new, harsher era—one of the material over the spiritual, one that encouraged a new glorification of violence, and in music, one that praised commerciality above all else. In my mind, the murder of Beatle John Lennon was emblematic of a sort of killing of the sanctity of music. More and more it was seen as a commodity. The '60s dream was officially over.

I glanced at my Rickenbacker, like John's, leaning against the wall, and reels of childhood memories flickered in my mind. One of the first places I had visited when I arrived in New York was the Dakota, walking nonchalantly past the Gothic entrance where he was later shot, hoping to catch a glimpse. On that winter's day, I spotted John and Yoko walking across the street with Sean to Central Park. Waiting at the light a few feet away, I started to go over and speak to them, but their happy scene was such a perfect bubble, I chose not to puncture it.

The phone at 1118 Hudson Street, Apartment 5, Hoboken, New Jersey, rang off the hook the night of December 8, with friends from Florida asking me if I was okay. They knew what John had meant to me.

The next day was the deadline to bring the final artwork and master for our new single into Manhattan for printing and manufacturing. In a daze, I carried the oversized envelope with the graphics and master tape onto the harshly lit PATH train from Hoboken to 33rd Street, changing there to the F train to 57th. All around me on the train, rows of faces were buried in the death-gray and blood-red daily tabloids with the headline "Lennon Shot Dead" and those horrible photos. I thought about how, if not for John and the Beatles, I most likely would not have been on this subway carrying this artwork and this master tape, which would not exist. For that matter, I wondered, where and what *would* I be? It was odd to feel so elated and so sad at the same time. Strange days indeed. . . .

Still avoiding obvious New Wave graphics, the single sleeve for the *In the Congo* EP was based on one of my vintage shirts, a pastel pink flannel with a ridiculous diamond argyle pattern, photographed by Phil Marino. The color was then changed to a kind of '50s aqua (like a mid-century kitchen appliance) for the U.S. version, and back to pink for the U.K. version. We were also photographed throughout Hoboken: on the streets, at the PATH station, on the docks, in the backseat of Rob's Valiant, and on our rooftop, showing the Maxwell House factory and the Manhattan skyline beyond. The photos further promoted Hoboken as the new Liverpool, and the Bongos as members of a very affable *gang* as much as they did a *band*. Perhaps a gang that would rob thrift stores for their vintage clothing.

Through Rod Pearce of Fetish Records we met director Ed Steinberg, who had just launched the video distribution network RockAmerica. With MTV still in the future, Steinberg was remarkably prescient, and became one of the first New Wave millionaires by supplying monthly reels of video content to the new circuit of trendy rock discos around the country. He directed our first, primitive video for "In the Congo," and a more ambitious clip for "Mambo Sun," for which we created a desert scene with a truckload of sand in Phil Marino's otherwise pristine SoHo loft. Ed had simultaneously made videos for the mysterious girl we would often see dancing by herself in the dark near the DJ booth when we performed at the multifloored Danceteria, who went by the name *Madonna*.

The lyrics of "In the Congo" were an indication of my feelings about the major record labels at the time, particularly after witnessing the Laughing Dogs' regression since signing with Columbia:

Natural enemies/natural predators
In the Congo, In the Congo
I wanna go back home/I wanna row back home . . .

Stepping off the British Airways flight at London Heathrow, my first time out of the U.S., how could I *not* think of John and the Beatles and their domination of the '60s, and the brief but kick-ass reign of Marc Bolan and T.Rex the decade after? Who would the '80s belong to? These thoughts floated by in a distinctly British, jet-lagged haze as we proceeded through customs with our guitars and luggage and on to the Luna House hotel near Victoria Station. Miss Jean, referred to disparagingly by the hotel staff as "that blonde girl," arrived a few days later to join us, causing a series of whispers and innocent scandals.

The much-hyped Rainbow show was a bit of a letdown. The cavernous venue was unheated and frigid, giving the phrase "going on cold" a literal meaning. When I sang at the mic, I could see my own breath, and the sweat all over my body nearly froze as fast as it appeared. I'm sure I was visibly surrounded by a misty halo of evaporating frost. We arrived at the venue shivering and hungry. Ironically, the only food offered to us or to the audience that night was . . . ice cream. Backstage after *his* set with the DBs, Chris Stamey, disgusted, threw himself face down on the icy-cold concrete floor and lay as if dead. When he finally arose, his image remained in steaming frost for hours, like an eerie police outline of a murder victim on a sidewalk. For the rest of the night, everyone whispered about "the shroud of Stamey."

The Bongos opened the show of this new crop of New York pop, and our attempt to warm up the audience was, at least, noble. I broke a string on my Rickenbacker early on in our set, and had to borrow a rather flat-sounding Stratocaster from the Raybeats. Still, we rocked, as evidenced by the live album, *Start Swimming,* later released on Stiff Records. The highlight for me was being unexpectedly joined onstage by Genesis P-Orridge, Cosey Fanny Tutti, and Chris Carter from proto-industrial musical terrorists, Throbbing Gristle. P-Orridge, in military fatigues, played my Muson toy synthesizer and shouted, "We need some discipline in here!" (from their current single) between our refrains of "In the Congo, in the Congo." Cosey blew her cornet, which was treated with delays and electronic effects by Carter.

We had met TG in the days previous, just after our arrival in London, and even visited Genesis's home with its red and black walls, decorated with laminated headlines and articles about the Manson murders. He and Throbbing Gristle were genuine innovators, instigators, and visionaries who created an entire world—and genre—with their sound, image, and attitude. Like ours, their current singles were released on Fetish, making us label-mates. Others in the Fetish stable included darkly experimental groups, like avant-jazz expressionists Clock DVA and the Lydia Lunch–led Eight-Eyed Spy—all contrasted sharply with our wide-eyed innocence, giving the Bongos, without question, the distinction of being Fetish's house Pop Group. It is to Rod Pearce's credit that he was assembling such an eclectic roster.

Fortunately, the other London dates were warmer than the Rainbow in every way. It was at the legendary Dingwall's, on a bill with the much-heralded Au Pairs, that I overdid my intake of vodka + chlorophyll cocktails. Toward the end of our particularly hyperpaced set, and after spotting New Wave star Joe Jackson in the audience, everything began to get hazy. My heart was beating like crazy and I was sweating even more than usual. I wondered why I had chosen to wear a thick yellow sweatshirt, flannel-lined hunting pants, and steel-soled rubber work boots onstage. We completed the encore, just barely, and I pushed myself toward the backstage, not quite making it before collapsing to the concrete floor. At that point I blacked out, or more precisely, greened out. Through my closed eyelids, I was only aware of a deep emerald green. When I came to, I was surrounded, like Dorothy waking from her dream in *The Wizard of Oz*, by assorted Bongos, Au Pairs, and a Bush Tetra or two. Somebody must have carried me back to our hotel room that night, because I know I didn't make it on my own. To this day, all my contract riders for concerts contain the words "no green stage lights."

Another night had us performing at the trendy Cabaret Futura, a late-night Soho scene created by Richard Strange, a performance artist/

actor from the proto-punk group the Doctors of Madness. Strange's venue was the launching pad for Depeche Mode, the Pogues, and Soft Cell who, later, with producer Mike Thorne, would hit it big with Gloria Jones's "Tainted Love." On the night we played there, we were joined onstage by the brilliant and charming writer Paul Morley of the *New Musical Express*. Like Genesis P-Orridge had done at the Rainbow, Paul played my Muson, admittedly pretending to be Brian Eno.

The British press was remarkably supportive of the Bongos. The *NME* printed one of my favorite quotes from Frank about P-Orridge: "He's old, but he's a really nice guy," which made it to the gossip column, as did some rumors about me and Annabella Lwin, the often-nude lead singer of Bow Wow Wow, then fifteen years old. By the time this one got around, I received a rare transatlantic phone call from my mother, surprising me with her reprimanding tone and the use of the term "jail bait." Nonetheless, being sandwiched between Annabella and her libidinous drummer Dave Barbarossa in a crowded limo gave rise to a new song, "Barbarella."

In the midst of the London dates, a tour was booked for us through Germany, Holland, and Belgium, with Rotterdam as our base. We were paired with the Bush Tetras, a gritty, funky group of three gorgeously tough, streetwise girls up front and a wild man drummer in the back laying down the grooves. We rode together with our fellow travelers though the gray, austere towns of East Germany, during the days of Checkpoint Charlies, when jumping over the dividing Berlin Wall would trigger a shower of well-aimed bullets. One night, I woke up as the train screeched to an echoey stop in what appeared to be a deserted concentration camp. We were huddled asleep with the Bush Tetras, when we were confronted by an East German border security guard. One look at Rob, Frank, and me smiling innocently back at him caused his eyes to divert. Then, addressing the girls, in a disarray of leather jackets, bullet belts, and Doc Martens, he forcefully inquired, "Have you *heroin*?" A brief search of their bags followed, as I held my breath. Then a sigh of relief as the guard moved along. Luckily, the encore we performed together onstage with the Tetras each night was not a random choice: John Lennon's "Cold Turkey."

After the tour, we returned to London to record the next batch of songs for an eight-song EP and a new single. We were booked at Jacob's Studio, situated in a lovely stone house on a sheep farm in Surrey (the studio got its name from the rare breed of sheep bred there) and owned by John Foxx of art rockers Ultravox. Our co-producer and engineer on these sessions was Ken Thomas, one of Britain's hottest engineers; we already were fans of his work on Wire's *Pink Flag*, with producer Mike Thorne. Ken's studio etiquette, along with his agile maneuvering of the equipment, the pacing of the sessions, and our own delicate intraband dynamic, was unwavering. If I have good manners in the studio today, this is where I learned them. Thank you, Ken.

On our first night of recording, there was a thunderstorm. Lightning hit the studio, knocking the power out just as we were about to play our first note. We stood in the darkness, watching the storm through the studio's windows, waiting for the lights to come on and joking that we must have just been visited by Thunderclap Newman (the group that had the 1969 hit "Something in the Air"). Suddenly, in the darkness, a loud pounding on the glass of the front door caused another round of gasps. One of the studio staff answered the door to find, waiting there, none other than Andy (Thunderclap) Newman himself, who had come to pick up some master tapes. Thus began the recording sessions that would produce the bulk of our first album.

Knowing that we had a limited amount of time, we set up the studio like an assembly line, so we could swiftly go from cutting basic tracks to overdubs and doubling to vocals to backing vocals, with the least amount of changing over. To facilitate this, along one wall, a line of six or so guitar amps was set up for me, each with a distinctly different tone. A Fender Deluxe, a Twin, a Mesa Boogie, a Roland JC 120, a Marshall, a Vox AC 30, and other miscellaneous amps were included. Each was miked and most of them were tracked for each song. In this way, the appropriate sound for each song could be brought up during the mixing stage, and we avoided constant setting up and readjusting the amp for each song while tracking. This allowed us to record the songs with rapid-fire spontaneity, the vibe closer to a live performance.

Jacob's Studio was a particularly creative environment for us, large and spacious, with polished hardwood floors and large windows that allowed the sheep to peek in and watch us work. The control room was especially pleasant, larger and brighter than most. An Amek console was set near the center of the room, facing not the live room but a window to the outside. This was a nice reminder that there was a world beyond the studio, and, perhaps, affected our performance and mix choices. Most studios tend to be claustrophobic, creating tension, as well as mental shortsightedness, while the atmosphere at Jacob's was just the opposite. The two-inch Studer multitrack and half-inch stereo tape machines were to the right, along the wall in the control room, allowing easy access for manipulation. (When analog gear is present, I often don't think a session is complete until the reel is turned upside-down and something is recorded backwards at least *once!*)

More than any other aspect, the key to these sessions was the attitude within the group. While being our most focused recording experience yet, it was at the same time the loosest, most free-form, and adventurous. Rob grabbed the big double bass from the former hay loft of the stable (the main live room was a converted stable, an extension of the main building), and bowed it on "The Bulrushes." On "Burning Bush," he plucked out the melody on John Foxx's sitar, which lay in a corner. For percussion on "Automatic Doors," we all played toy Slinkys. Cosey Fanny Tutti came in to blow her cornet on "Three Wise Men," being picked up and shuttled to our session by Rob, after her midday strip gig. (Cosey was soon to appear nude in the British magazine *Legshow.*) Charlie Collins, the saxophonist from Clock DVA, sat in on "Certain Harbours." The sound of changing channels (BBC1, BBC2!), on the studio's television set, made its way onto "Video Eyes," buried in the mix like the song's topic of subliminal messages. For "Question Ball," all three of us were crammed tightly into a pantry to capture its peculiar, live ambience on Frank's bongo drums.

Being a residential studio, we all stayed overnight during the sessions, having breakfast and lunch served in the kitchen just off the control room. We worked well into the night, the vibe sustained, and the work flowed freely from the social atmosphere. This experience would be unconsciously missed when we returned to New York to record our next album.

But, by then, so much would have changed.

L ate one night, after dinner at a nearby pub, I sang all my lead vocals to nine songs in quick succession; to the basic tracks we had laid down over the past few days. After each vocal take, I would hear in a gentle and distinctly slurred British accent, "How was that for you, Richard?" in my headphones. The next day, Frank added his soaring, rocket booster harmonies, launching each chorus and sending it on its way. His lead on "Automatic Doors" and Rob's forceful performance on "Video Eyes" completed the tracking.

The crisp, clear sonic image created by the reflective surfaces of the walls and floors of the studio enhanced the directness and liveliness of our sound, and made the tracks easy to mix, which I would return to do on a solo trip several weeks later. But it was Ken Thomas's mastery and sensitivity that allowed us to move at such a fast clip during these sessions, and with such happy results. Later, we found out Ken's payment for the marathon Bongos sessions from Fetish Records: a Sony Walkman.

W e headed back to New York for some dates and found that, during the months we were away, things had changed. Word of the reviews and coverage we had gotten in the British press had made its way to the States and worked its magic. Suddenly, our name carried more weight. We were offered larger headlining slots. "Mambo Sun," from the new EP, had found itself on the *Billboard* Disco chart. Our booking agent, Bob Singerman, was now busy fielding offers from all over the country.

And other changes had taken place at home. The momentum at Maxwell's was picking up, with national and international acts eager to play there before their higher-profile New York City shows, and more bands had moved to Hoboken or made it their second home. The thriving music scene we had imagined and created in press releases was now materializing. Each time we returned home after a tour, we found this to be more and more true. The media was beginning to catch on, and soon "the Hoboken Sound" was a phrase that appeared in print often; first in the local, then in the national and international press. Rob and I would smile at each other, remembering how, just a few months prior, we said we were going to make Hoboken the new Liverpool.

After some East Coast dates that spring, I flew back to London to mix our new tracks with Ken Thomas. This time, traveling alone, the experience was markedly different than the trip several weeks prior. Yoko Ono's new, rush-released single, "Walking on Thin Ice," the one she and John were mixing the night he was shot, was in my head. I had played the record over and over until it was ingrained in my mind, loving the sound of the mix, the melody, and John's aggressive and amazing final guitar solo. As I walked the London streets alone, the song slowly began to mutate, morphing into another tune. A different melody. A different bassline. Something mine. A calmer vibe . . . like a view from the eye of storm. These words materialized as I walked:

> I spy
> I see through everything
> But I know
> I don't know anything
> And on cold nights
> My soul is like anyone's
> And on slow nights
> I'd forgive anyone. . . .

I had a new invention with me on that trip, a Casio VL-1, a small calculator/musical instrument with a tiny, push-button keyboard. I was able to program the bass line, which was the root of this new song, and a percussion loop, into the Casio on the spot. With headphones on, I walked along, singing what was becoming "Numbers with Wings."

Back at the Luna House hotel, I jotted down the words, scribbled another verse, figured out the chords on my Rickenbacker, then put the song away. The next day I was off the Surrey to start mixing our ten new tracks.

The mixes, as predicted, were a breeze. The tracks already sounded good, so all we had to do was pan things around to create the appropriate stereo image, choose which guitar amp tracks we needed and which we didn't, and experiment with some effects here and there. Mostly it was about balancing. Ken used *very* minimal (if any) EQing, and most of the ambiance of recordings were created with the room mics, not with added artificial reverbs, although, we did have a new Lexicon digital reverb unit and an EMT plate that we used to some degree on nearly every song.

The first mix we attempted was "Zebra Club," in some ways the most purely power pop-sounding song we ever recorded. The club referred to in the lyrics was the Peppermint Lounge in Times Square, which, along with Danceteria, had become our home club in Manhattan. Legendary nightclub and home of the Peppermint Twist, the dance craze of the early '60s, the Beatles famously hung out there on their first U.S. tour. Now, it was a New Wave hangout. The cascading arpeggios in "Zebra Club" that sound like they were played on a twelve-string were actually played on my six-string Rick, doubled, and the varispeed control on the tape machine to pitch the double slightly sharp to the original track. This created a natural chorusing, which simulated a twelve-string. The "flute" in the intro was played on my Casio VL-1, added at the mixing stage.

When it comes to mixing, the choices are literally endless. Especially now, with Logic, ProTools, and hard-drive recording in general. The infinite number of computer plug-ins and peripherals, each with their infinite choices of settings and combination, have further widened the field. But even then, with twenty-four plus tracks and myriad racks of outboard gear and effects that could be created manually, the possibilities were boundless. For me, the process of mixing is nearly identical to performing. The same kind of acute listening, the same control of dynamics, and blend of active and passive concentration are essential. I always prefer to mix on a traditional console, so I can "play" the faders, reverb and effects settings, and EQ knobs, while the track is running, just as I would be playing an instrument. Writing these moves into a computer simplifies the process, but reduces the chance for magic, and the results are never the same as hands-on.

Fetish wanted a new single from these sessions immediately. The original plan had been to release a track called "Nuts & Bolts," but the tempo of the final take was so impossibly fast and the length so brief, clocking in at under two minutes, that it was determined that it would whiz by on the radio without being noticed. The second choice was "The Bulrushes."

A session was booked with one the top mastering engineers in Britain, George Peckham, aka "Porky," famous for his run-off groove inscription, "A Porky Prime Cut," on all his vinyl handiwork. He was also noted for cutting some of the loudest, punchiest vinyl around and for the astonishing technical achievement of the "*three*-sided" 1973 Monty Python LP, *Matching Tie and Handkerchief.* Arriving on time for the session, I was greeted with a scrawled note, taped to his studio door: "Getting a haircut. Back in a few minutes." Apparently, this was Porky's code for "at the pub downstairs." A few minutes later, a smiling and ebullient Peckham stormed up the hallway, greeting me as if we were old friends.

Peckham's personality and attitude were in perfect sync with the Bongos ethos: a fine balance between giddy rock 'n' roll looseness and sober technical craft. However, in this instance, the word "sober" may not apply. At one point, a slight edit had to be made on our precious half-inch master tape. Already apprehensive at the thought of a razor blade being used to make the splice, I was absolutely appalled when Porky produced instead a pair of common scissors from a drawer. Smelling the beer on his breath, I held my *own* breath as he manually unreeled the tape, lifted it in the air toward to light, holding his thumb at the edit point, and proceeded to snip. I nearly greened out again, even without chlorophyll. He then taped the splice together. It was . . . perfect! As was the overall mastering of the disc, which resulted in the most satisfying-sounding vinyl product of any of the Bongos releases. To finish off his work, Peckham added the following inscription in the run-off groove: "Bongo Mania will rule U.K., okay?—Porky."

Back in the States, we continued crisscrossing the country nonstop, in a series of mini-tours, culminating in our first proper U.S. trek in the fall. To better represent the sound we were achieving in the studio with overdubbed guitars, we added a second guitarist, Steve Almaas from the Suicide Commandos. A passionate rock 'n' roll purist and a super talent in his own right, Almaas joined us for a series of dates that summer, bonding a friendship that would lead to me producing his first solo outing. The tour took us to Steve's hometown of Minneapolis for a two-night run at its premier rock venue, First Avenue. There was a distinct wildness in the air, bordering on the kind of Bongo Mania George Peckham had just predicted would "rule the U.K." With my guitar strapped on, I was making my way through the crowd to the stage when I was offered a powder to inhale from a cute young concert-goer. Thinking it was coke, I smiled and breathed it in. It is only when I tried to sing the opening song, "In the Congo," that I realized I had taken heroin. I was no longer there and neither was my voice. Even if I could have remembered the lyrics, not a sound would come out. The first quarter of the show that night was entirely instrumental. Finally getting my bearings, I got through the set, vowing "never again." In fact, I wouldn't have, had I known. No matter, the reviews continued to glow. "I can't remember the last time I heard a band this good!" wrote Eric Lindbom in the *Minneapolis Star*.

Before we got home from our summer tour, the fall tour was already booked. Almaas was planning his solo work, and we asked James Mastro, whom I had first met on my first nights out at CBGB when he was in Fast Car and who knew Rob and Frank, to join us on this, our first big U.S. tour.

Having recently been playing with Richard Lloyd, Tom Verlaine's excellent and inventive guitar foil in Television (they had recently released a fine debut on Elektra called *Alchemy*), had made James a formidable player himself, and his strong Keith Richards–style rhythm playing and Strat sound, was a perfect counterpoint to my own, more open strumming. While the feeling with Steve Almaas was that he was really a solo artist sitting in with us, Jim seemed to fit in as a Bongo.

The tour started in the San Francisco area, bringing back memories of the trip there with my family when I was fourteen. On the first day, a rare day off, we took the long drive to Stinson Beach outside the city. With a momentary unbridled feeling of freedom, like the Beatles escaping and frolicking in the field in *A Hard Day's Night*, we played volleyball on the uneven sand. If only slow motion photography worked in real life like it did in the film. Suddenly, landing hard and fast from a jump, my foot sank deep into a hole. A shriek of pain. With my ankle swelling to grapefruit dimensions, I had to be carried back to the flatbed pickup truck we came in. The next night onstage, at Berkeley Square, on a bill with the Lounge Lizards, was one of my more stationary performances; it hurt too much to move about. But although it seemingly started off on the wrong foot, the tour was a success with five shows in L.A. alone and stops in every major market on the way back east, then winding back and ending in Chicago.

Though our original plan was to only release singles and EPs, we knew, and labels knew, that the American market was geared to selling *albums*. In England, Fetish was preparing to release the remaining eight songs we recorded there as *Time and the River* (Rod Pearce's title suggestion was *Joyful Assault*, which, looking back, was a better title that we thought was too obvious). The "Bulrushes" single had done well for us in both countries and got us a good amount of airplay in New York on WNEW FM, where we found we had a great supporter in the influential and innovative Vin Scelsa, the first DJ to play us on the radio. Hearing ourselves on the airwaves for the first time had been a thrill I will never forget. I was startled at how the radio compression brought out the acoustic guitars, and expanded the subtle reverb on the lead vocal. It was the free-standing two- or three-minute single, packed with sound and energy like the holy grail templates "She Loves You" or "Can't Buy Me Love" by the Beatles that interested and satisfied me most. Just like when I pressed that little transistor radio to my ear.

But now it was time to make an album.

I remembered from my days at School Kids Records in Tampa how JEM Records in New Jersey was the major importer of albums from the U.K. They had also launched their own in-house labels, Passport and PVC. Maybe there was a way for them to license the Fetish tracks? A phone call or two between Marty Scott at JEM and Rod Pearce of Fetish, followed by a meeting in a London taxi, with the deal scrawled on a cocktail napkin, created the situation we were looking for, and *Drums Along the Hudson* was born.

When released in 1982 on the PVC label, it would include all of our Fetish singles and EP tracks, tightly sequenced and mastered by Greg Calbi, who impressed us with his personal mastering notes from John Lennon that were still pinned to the studio bulletin board. The process of cutting the acetate master on a lathe was fascinating to me, as I was able to watch the grooves containing our music being engraved, under a high-powered microscope. This was to check for possible skipping and distortion, because the grooves needed to be clean and even. The track "Three Wise Men," with its deep, insistent tom-toms, proved difficult to cut, as the drums were so aggressive and caused irregular patterns. For that reason, some of the low frequencies had to be rolled off, not to be heard again until the album would be painstakingly remastered in 2007 for an unimaginable (at the time) special-edition CD.

The cover was again designed with Phil Marino, who took a close-up photo of my hands playing bongo drums. To create the final image, the black-and-white photo was printed on clear plastic and laid over a canvas on which the outline of the image was drawn in pencil. Phil painted the main background colors, and Rob and I painted in the thousands of pointillistic dots (it was kind of a pop-ified homage to Georges Seurat) on the canvas. The clear plastic sheet with the original photo image printed on it was then laid over the painted canvas. The dotting took all night, and the paint was still wet when we delivered it to the label's art department the next day.

Even upon release, the album had the intentional feel of being archival. The poetic liner notes by *New Musical Express* writer Richard Grabel, set in the Bookman font face of children's schoolbooks, spoke of "all the Bongos' ages and stages," even though the group was barely two years old. The title lettering on the front and back was taken from a Tito Puente EP on RCA from the 1950s, *Mambo on Broadway*.

The reviews were, almost, unanimous raves. Only Robert Christgau, writing in the *Village Voice*, seemed to object: "Richard Barone's lyrics are so oblique you have to wonder what his angle is. Growing up isn't that confusing—or that personal. B+."

Ed Steinberg's videos for "In the Congo" and "Mambo Sun" were already in circulation. Now, with super-grainy black-and-white film footage shot live at the Peppermint Lounge, Phil Marino created a video for "Bulrushes," influencing the slew of grainy black-and-white videos that followed. Even R.E.M. called us to ask how we got the Super 8 film effect. ("We used super-eight film," we told them.) Suddenly all three videos were in distribution to clubs around the country and internationally. To accompany the *Drums* albums sent to radio station programmers, a radio special was created of us being interviewed by one of our favorite DJs and biggest fans, Matt Pinfield, later of MTV fame. Everything was in place.

We headed back out and stayed on the road, retracing our steps again and again, and building on our past tours. We could feel the familiarity now with the audiences, with the radio stations we visited, and with the journalists. The crowds were bigger and shows got wilder. Girls on the front row would try to rip the white Nike wrestling shoes off my feet. Boys would kiss me on the mouth as I made my way to the stage through the audience. Onstage, the shows were fluid, with more and more interplay. Jim and I would duel with our guitars, their necks and strings touching. I would slide across the stage on my knees, Rob would zoom over and change places with Jim, and Frank would attack the tom-toms with such force, the drum riser would nearly collapse.

We played our first show in Tampa at the Cuban Club in old Ybor City—the very neighborhood my grandmother and her family came to settle in over seventy years before. The audience was wild, but none wilder than my own mother, who stood on a table near the front, taking pictures with a disposable camera and, in a classic display of motherhood for all time, made sure to tell every pierced, leather-clad, Mohawk-headed punk in the mosh pit, "That's my son!" The audience the Snails needed so badly had finally materialized in Tampa, only it was five years too late.

By the time we got to New Orleans, the wildness was reaching a critical mass. We could feel it in the air. Walking past a park in the French Quarter after a spectacular Creole lunch, we spotted an old, apparently homeless, Creole woman on a bench. "Bongos. . . . Come here! I've been waiting for you. I want to talk to you. There's something I need to tell you," she croaked, gesturing with her crooked finger. Her eyes squinted, but were laserlike, making direct contact with each Bongo as we walked past. She sounded like she genuinely had some- thing to tell us. But we couldn't deal with it. Whatever it was, we didn't want to know. We kept walking. . . .

Celebrating after our show that night, we were taken to a crowded club with a dud DJ who was playing the worst of the current Top 40 hits. "Let's take over," I slurred to Jim, and the minute the DJ left his booth for a moment, I slipped in, looking for records to play. I found one by Pylon, another of our favorite groups from Athens, Georgia. I put on the twelve-inch dance mix of "Gyrate," and was looking for my next spin when the DJ returned, demanding I get out. By then, I couldn't: I was the Littlest DJ again, spinning records at *Beach Party*, and I wasn't budging. The DJ left again as I found a worn copy of *Electric Warrior* and cranked up "Get It On." The crowd on the dance floor was reaching a fever pitch when the DJ reappeared, this time with two cops, who physically removed me from the booth and rather ceremoniously ejected me from the club and onto the sidewalk. "No sense of humor," I thought to myself.

The next day we woke up early to drive to Austin in the Tioga, a small mobile home we were borrowing from Rob's father, to get us around the country. Rob was driving and Frank sitting up front in the passenger seat, while Jim and I were napping on the back couch, still hungover from the night before. We were on the highway, just out of town when suddenly the motor started puttering. Sputtering. Then stopping. Out of gas. We had been on our way to a station, and had underestimated the reserve tank. We were stuck in the middle lane of the interstate, on an upgrade, with traffic whizzing all around us. Someone suggested priming the carburetor with gasoline. The Tioga's design was based on a van, and the engine was accessible from the interior by just removing the fiberglass cover. I watched as the engine cover was removed, the carburetor primed with a little gasoline, the ignition switched on. *Pow*! Big blast. Fire breaks out. Frank and Rob go out their side doors, and I slide out the back door, scraping my wrists on the pavement, and rolling on the highway, as the Tioga started rolling back. Jim stayed inside, trying to put out the flames, and we all yelled, "Get out!" but he was already in the blaze. When he finally emerged, it was clear he had been severely burned and needed to get to the hospital right away. He had to have skin grafts on his leg, and remained in the hospital for several days.

Yet, while Jim recuperated from his awful initiation rite, the tour went on. Nothing, it seemed, could stop us. A day in the shop for repairs, and the Tioga hit the road again. We continued on again, as a trio. This time perhaps with a shade more caution. Later, we couldn't help but wonder if the fire was what the old Creole woman in the park had wanted to warn us about.

Other than the perils, touring was paying off. We had been building an extensive network of venues, radio and media contacts, and other bands that invisibly helped us along, and the album was selling. But I have never, before or since, met another band that networked better than R.E.M. At every radio station or publication stop on our tour circuit, there on the office bulletin board was invariably a friendly postcard sent from the road by Pete Buck or Mike Mills.

We had first met the group at one of our earliest out-of-town shows, when they and Mitch Easter were among the handful of people in attendance at an off-campus pizza parlor called Friday's in Greensboro, North Carolina. When they played in Hoboken the first time, the group stayed at our apartment, using it as a dressing room. I remember looking at Michael Stipe's shoes, held together with duct tape, thinking, but not saying, "This has got to go," and noticing the twigs and leaves in the frontman's dirty curly hair. Yes, he had hair then. I offered to wash it, and did, in a strange, almost biblical ritual over our kitchen sink. Later, Michael wrote out all of his famously indiscernible lyrics for *Chronic Town* for Rob, in his equally indecipherable handwriting.

Rejoined by Jim on the road, now as a full-fledged Bongo, we continued the endless tour. With the album making an impact on college radio, we got a call from our agent, telling us of an offer to open for the B-52's on their first big U.S. tour. Even though we were already in the midst of our own headlining club tour, this was too good to turn down. We *loved* the B-52's.

Not missing a beat, we were able to connect with them in Chicago, where we were already booked for two nights at a nightclub with our old friends the Raybeats. On the second night, we opened for the B-52's at the Aragon Ballroom, then rushed across town to do our club date. We continued with the B's for the next twenty shows.

Playing the larger ballrooms and theaters, our own stage show began to take on a more polished shape and a more expansive sound and look. Now with matching guitar amps (Jim and I both switched from Fender to Music Man fifty-watt combos in white cabinets set on black risers) and a simplified, uniform stage layout at each venue, we were able to command the space with more confidence.

It took a moment to adjust to being the "special guests" (translation: support act) on the bill, playing a trimmed-down half-hour set, without the luxury of our usual endless soundchecks. But the B-52's were gracious hosts and couldn't have been a better match for us. After the first "hellos" while crossing paths during changeover at soundcheck, our first social encounter was appropriately with Cindy Wilson, the one who had unknowingly inspired our name. She crawled into the Tioga with the friendliest "Howdy! What's up, boys!" that I have heard before or since. Soon we were pals with all the others. Kate Pierson would join us as guest vocalist on one of our future albums, Ricky Wilson inspired me to no end with his amazing open guitar tunings and technique, and my friendship and working relationship with Fred Schneider remains to this day. Although we rarely took days off, there were parties, occasionally "out of bounds," and trips to local beaches at every opportunity. Once, arriving at a party, we were greeted at the Tioga by Ricky, with drinks for us in hand, and his unforgettable smile. The B-52's were and are a gifted, talented, and supremely unique entity deserving all the success they've achieved and more.

The end-of-tour wrap party was at the B-52's communal house on Lake Mahopac, in upstate New York. Hanging out on the front porch, it appeared some psychedelics had been consumed, raising the level of intensity of the gathering. David Byrne of the Talking Heads, who had produced the B's current release, *Mesopotamia*, was there, seated quietly on the porch with a stoic upright posture. Byrne's larger-than-life giant-suited frontman parody in *Stop Making Sense* belied his own apparent introversion. He remained fully dressed, his black hair slicked back impeccably, observing, while the rest of us took all our clothes off and jumped in the lake; a torrent of loud laughing and splashing. The party only quieted down when someone from next door, the home of WNBC-TV's golden boy news anchor Chuck Scarborough, called the police.

Even before the tour was over, we knew it was time to plan our next recordings and to find a label that could take us to the next level.

Our brilliant attorney, Owen Epstein, elegantly shopped us to labels with an astonishingly concise two-sentence cover letter and copies of *Drums Along the Hudson*. The strongest bite came from Nancy Jeffries at RCA Records. Twelve years before, Nancy had been the singer in the Insect Trust, also from Hoboken, who had experimented with American roots music and released two major-label albums. She had then worked her way up the ranks at RCA over the past decade, landing in the A & R department as a talent scout. Nancy courted us, coming to our Hoboken rehearsals (which must have brought back memories and triggered mixed emotions), then finally made a formal offer.

When the contracts arrived at his office, Owen called us to tell us we had received a last-minute offer from Warner Bros. It was monetarily similar, so from a payphone on our way to a soundcheck in Long Island, we asked Owen what we should do. Pause. "Flip a coin," was his reply. We did. Warner Bros. won, but we still signed with RCA.

Maybe it was their past catalog with Elvis and Bowie or maybe it was their red neon corporate logo shining like a beacon high on the skyline across the river. Or maybe it was that Nancy was motherly. With her, we felt protected. We felt we had made an emotional bond. Perhaps it was the Hoboken connection. Maybe, we felt, she wanted to save us from the obscurity that had befallen the Insect Trust and, by doing so, vicariously ride out her own major-label ambitions that had been thwarted in the previous decade.

And she promised to stay at RCA at least long enough to get our record off the ground.

RCA wanted our label debut to launch a new format they had devised, the mini album. In actuality, it was simply a five-song Extended Play, but it gave the company the opportunity to get us out there at roughly half the cost of recording a whole album. They may not have figured that all the other costs (promotion, advertising, marketing, and even manufacturing) would be the same as producing a full album, so the plan was shortsighted. Regardless, we didn't complain. We had always liked the EP format anyway. For one thing, when cutting vinyl, the fewer songs allow you to cut larger grooves with more bass and more volume, allowing for a superior sound. Plus, I had five new songs that would go nicely together.

While plans were being made for our RCA debut, Jim and I flew down to Mitch Easter's Drive-In Studio in Greensboro, North Carolina, to record some songs we had written on tour. I had met Mitch with Chris Stamey and the DBs, back at the Rainbow in London. Then, I worked with him a few months later, when I produced Steve Almaas's solo debut, *Beat Rodeo*.

Mitch Easter was a kindred spirit, obsessed with sound recording. He played drums, while Jim and I handled most everything else, including the string parts, all recorded in the garage of Mitch's parents' house. The songs I brought to those sessions, I felt at the time, were too personal and acoustic-based to be Bongos songs. We weren't sure how or when we would release anything from those sessions, but the experience was magical, with experimentation and a straight-ahead singer/songwriter approach intermingling with each song. The feel was a combination of rough, folky garage pop, and a lo-fi approach to hi-fi production values. Now that we had signed with RCA, we considered this our last indie project for a while, and wanted to take full advantage of the freedom. Mitch would go on to produce R.E.M.'s first single and next two albums with Don Dixon.

The search for a producer for the Bongos' new recording started with a phone call I had been waiting to make since I was fifteen, to Tony Visconti. Phoning him at his Good Earth Studios in London, I was thrilled to find not only that he knew of the Bongos, but that he knew and loved our recording of "Mambo Sun." Schedules, budget, and geography prevailed, though. RCA wanted us to record in New York, where they could keep an eye on us, rather than London, which is where Tony wanted to record at his own studio. So the search continued. But we vowed to work together on something, someday.

RCA recommended Richard Gottehrer, a name that appeared as producer on an alarming number of albums during the New Wave era. Richard Hell and the Voidoids, Marshall Crenshaw, Blondie, and the Go-Gos had all made their debut releases under his direction. Our first fear was that his name appeared on *too many* records, and that his ubiquitous production credit would make our release less special.

But what appealed to us about Gottehrer was his earlier work as a songwriter ("My Boyfriend's Back" by the Angels in the early '60s) and as a writer/producer member of the mid-'60s garage hitmakers Strangeloves ("I Want Candy," which was at the time a hit by our friends Bow Wow Wow). He had the kind of history and spirit of creative reinvention that appealed strongly to us and, once we met with him in person, we signed him on. Richard worked closely with us to achieve a signature sound, perhaps spotting a similarity between us and his own former group. Particularly in how our song "Barbarella" used the same kind of tribal Bo Diddley beat as "I Want Candy."

Gottehrer was animated in the studio, gesturing wildly. At other times, apparently distracted with head buried in the latest issue of *Billboard*, he would suddenly spring into action. A tambourine hit in "Numbers with Wings" would need to become a panned, flanged image of a shooting star described to the engineer, John Jansen, with an arcing arm movement. Richard would join us in the live room, clapping, playing percussion, and singing along on "Barbarella" in his thick New York accent. Once, he glared at me momentarily, when I suggested we double a bass line with a cello, "the way *Tony Visconti* would do."

Although Skyline Studios in midtown Manhattan was an ocean away from a sheep farm in Surrey, we were thrilled with the power and precision of the atmosphere. Frank's drum kit was set up in the precipice of the door to the live room, facing into the center of the room, with a six-foot tunnel built in front of the kick drum to mic it close and far. The tunnel framed and contained the sound of the attack and the pushed air. The resulting drum sound was massive.

But changed from our sessions for *Drums Along the Hudson* was the sense of spontaneity. Now it seemed multiple takes were required to produce a master. "Barbarella" was the result of nearly fifty tries, before Gotterhrer was satisfied. To keep up the smiles and maintain the momentum, a small vial of white powder would emerge and make the rounds.

When I sang the lead vocal for "Numbers with Wings," Richard cleared the room of other band members and tech assistants, and worked with me one-on-one to achieve the kind of performance that had eluded me when I was aware of the crowded control room. He would direct me as a film or theatrical director would, using his gestures and facial expressions to pull out the most emotion and meaning from the minimal lyrics. When I heard the result, I couldn't believe it was me. But to me, the rest of the group seemed uneasy with me being singled out.

If you listen very closely to the final fade of the final track, "Sweet Blue Cage," on the *Numbers* mini album, you'll hear a dog barking. It was the final touch on the recording, representing Nipper, the RCA dog, listening for "his master's voice."

The recordings Jim and I made with Mitch Easter were released by Passport Records and entitled *Nuts & Bolts*, garnering some great press (*People* magazine later listed it as one of the top ten records that year) and radio play. Passport stickered every copy with the memorable tag line: "Half of the Bongos."

By the time *Numbers with Wings* came out, the network of college radio and other media that we had helped create was at last becoming a market to be taken seriously. With the help of a young firebrand, RCA radio promotion man, John Siegler, "Numbers with Wings" stayed number one on the college radio charts for six weeks.

One day, while playing Ms. PacMan in a dark corner of Mr. Big's Video Arcade in Hoboken, I was approached by two husky *GoodFella*-types in suits, spying their reflections in the glass of the machine, as I continued playing the game. "Bongos, right?" "Yes," I answered, looking up from the screen. "We can guarantee your records will be in every jukebox in Jersey," the tall one proclaimed. "We can make it happen." Just like in the movies. I stammered a response while squeezing past them, and out the front door. Also, around this time, Tommy Mottola, then-manager of Hall & Oates, phoned me on my private line in Hoboken, stating in a deep and commanding tone that he was interested in managing the Bongos. Suddenly everyone wanted a piece.

Nancy Jeffries had strongly recommended we acquire a manager. It was impossible for us to deal with the day-to-day record company issues while we were, for one thing, on the road. After being introduced to a string of potential managers, we settled on Vince Mauro. Vince had been a singer in his own right in the early '60s, then went into management and production, working with Dee Anthony to bring Peter Frampton to superstardom in the mid-'70s. He had also worked with Peter Allen, Morgana King, and Stan Getz, and was, like me, a fan of Peggy Lee, sharing the bill with her during his singing days. From now on, it was Vince who dealt with our RCA business. Obtaining a new booking agent for us (Barbara Skydel, at the powerful Premier Talent), suggesting we trade in our thrift-store outfits for something a little more . . . colorful, and helping us whip a show into shape, Vince sent us out on the road for our most successful tour yet.

Since the time we had made our first videos, MTV had been launched and instantly exploded, beaming music videos twenty-four hours a day into living rooms across the country. We were anxious to make a video for "Numbers with Wings," and RCA agreed. When asked who we wanted to direct it, we said Federico Fellini, the great Italian film director, whose films like *Juliet of the Spirits* and *Satyricon* were favorites of mine from college. RCA found that request impossible to comprehend (although Fellini later directed a hit video for Culture Club), but located in Juliano Waldman a director who had a great knowledge of the Italian master and had himself worked on a Fellini film as a cameraman. A storyboard was drawn up, describing a bizarre parade of sexual fetishes, fantasies, and perversions, some explicit, some implied. We flew to New York from the West Coast on a day off from our tour, staying at the Milford Plaza Hotel. There was no time even to go to our own apartments across the river in Hoboken. We shot the video, and got on the plane the next morning, and were back on stage in Los Angeles the next night.

The video got heavy play and support from MTV, getting us invited to all the MTV parties and events. At one such gathering, a shirtless Anthony Keidis of the Red Hot Chili Peppers lifted me up on his bare shoulders in mid-conversation, both of us mugging wildly for the cameras, giving me a bird's-eye view of the party and quite a rush at the same time. Too much was never enough.

In Los Angeles, a Beverly Hills Drive fountain at midday became a perfect wading pool for a couple of nude Bongos. With all the traffic zooming past, it's a miracle we weren't arrested. Later, we performed a concert at a gay S&M bar booked by its house DJ, Jim Vantyne, who had been present at our first meeting at the Laughing Dogs' loft. I was amused to finally see his virtual shrine to Nancy Sinatra, her LPs and singles decorating every corner of his apartment. As might be expected, the gig was more memorable for what was going on in the audience than what was happening onstage: California muscle and leather guys suspended from the ceiling on various straps and harnesses, performing acts to our music I didn't know were possible.

With "Numbers with Wings" in heavy rotation on KROQ, the next show, a concert at the Palace in Hollywood, was a triumph.

Wherever we went, record company reps and local promoters were always willing, and often insistent, in showing us a good time in every possible way. We met everyone. Everyone was introduced to us. It never occurred to us that it would ever end. The party was in full swing, and it wasn't always easy to see that it was as much for the benefit of those around us as it was for us. It was part of the job. To say that drugs were everywhere would be to understate to the point of sarcasm. In Texas, a particularly friendly regional rep from the record label invited us to lick cocaine from her various body parts in the dressing room. At one radio station we visited for an interview, I noted a fat little parcel of coke on a copy of *Numbers with Wings*. Airplay by any means necessary. The DJ emptied the packet on the album cover and, chopping it up with a razor blade, offered me a line. Once I was asked by one of our immediate team if Rob was taking drugs. "No," I answered. "He takes the least of all of us." "Perhaps he *should*," was the only half-kidding reply. Of course. It would be so much easier to control us if we were *all* always buzzed.

The party didn't stop. As we arrived at each new town, it merely changed players. During the next day, I couldn't fathom how I would go onstage again that night.

But I had to. I was the frontman. That was my job. Standing at the front of the ship, strapped to the nose of the 747, I felt the pressure against my body. I felt the wind. At night, I would have nightmares of standing onstage naked. I felt the eyes of all those people every night looking at me. Soaked in sweat and crawling on the stage, craving their reaction, the dreams turned inside out and blurred into existence. Diving out into the crowd with my long guitar cable to play solos to pull the audience into our show at all costs. Holding my guitar out to them like a sacrificial offering and letting them hit the strings. Luring them into our world. I felt a responsibility to get the reaction—not just for me, but for the band. I would push my voice to unnatural places way beyond my range. Rushing up to mic stands to sing with so much energy that once or twice I chipped my front teeth, and kept singing with chunks of broken teeth in my mouth. I didn't care. I had to win for us. I had to deliver the goods for the group . . . I had to bring home the bacon . . . and then write the song that would put us over the top. Six weeks at number one on college radio was not enough . . . I wanted us to be number one on *Billboard*'s Hot 100 for six *months*—or a year. Always, I had to write the song I hadn't written yet, the hit that was waiting to be written, and I had to perform a show after which everything would change and we would be legendary.

It was on the way to our next tour stop, Atlanta, that I started to feel I couldn't breathe. I remembered my childhood asthma, when I was six or seven, and my mother thought I would stop breathing during the night. She slept with me in my bed. She thought I was dying. Now here I am on a tour bus, not able to breathe in or out, heading toward a show. How will I perform? That thought made it even worse. I told Rob, and when we pulled into town, I went straight to the hospital. I was scared. I've avoided hospitals, then and now, associating them mostly with elderly, dying relatives. Sad places full of sickness.

I was examined, and the doctor was told of the situation: "He's on tour and he's performing in town tonight." I was left there alone. While the roadies and the band were setting up and checking the sound at the 688 Club, I was in the emergency room, given oxygen, and being shot up with human adrenaline to stimulate my breathing. It felt good. "Are you well enough to perform?" somebody asked, his voice coming through the haze. I nodded slowly. Six years old. I was six years old, still scared that I couldn't breathe. Trying to focus on that picture hanging on my bedroom wall. The one of the beautiful guardian angel helping those two little children—my sister and me—cross a rickety bridge of wood and rope over deep ravine. Praying. *Please* . . . please help me get to the other side. . . .

Almost showtime; I was driven to the venue in a white ambulance. Riding with me was a stringer for *Rolling Stone*, interviewing me the whole way. I had no idea what I was telling him. Arriving at the stage door, I was carried out by the crooks of my arms, my Rickenbacker was strapped onto me, and I was pointed in the direction of the center stage mic. Right up front, the lights in my eyes. Focusing, I looked down to a sea of arms, writhing and reaching, like the tentacles of giant anemone. Frank counted off, I stomped my overdrive pedal, and we slammed into "In the Congo." I didn't hold back one percent. I belted even more than usual. I jumped in the air and came crashing down to my knees for my guitar solos. I gave every ounce of energy my body could give. I mean, I had to. I was the frontman.

CHAPTER 7

BLOW UP

HOW TO SELF-DESTRUCT

O nce we had established that we were a viable commercial entity, we could begin the next important phase: total self-destruction. By mid-decade, we had finally succumbed to the indulgences and, occasionally, the questionable fluorescent fashions of the 1980s. Like Claudius, emperor of Rome, I watched with amusement the decadent decline of myself and my tiny empire, and allowed it all to happen. "It is the nature of things," I rationalized. Some friends privately referred to me as "Sluticus."

Like the never-ending feast scene in Fellini's *Satyricon*, *Beat Hotel* was a strange extravagance, recorded at no less than five different recording studios in New York and New Jersey, in long sessions, over a period of several months. While our demos of the songs made in a funky Hoboken rehearsal studio had been raw and noisy, Brazilian samba rhythms juxtaposed against power pop guitars and drums, the actual album was more refined, and defiantly overdubbed. Nearly everything was at least double- or tripletracked. For every guitar or vocal harmony that was recorded, another was conceived and added to the mix. On the song "Blow Up"—my favorite, which closes the album—Frank and I overdubbed our choirboy *ahhhhh*'s so many times to create the choral effect that the magnetic coating started to flake off the twenty-four-track master tape. I remember asking the engineer, "What is all that black powder on the tape machine?" "Oxides," he said. "The tape is falling apart." The months of playback, recording, and rewinding had taken their toll. You can hear this sound on the finished record, like fire crackling . . . black volcanic dust settling over Pompeii. . . .

> Blow up the house that owns you
> Blow up till you remain
> Blow up the gold that owns you
> Blow up your face and name.

While at Electric Lady Studios in the Village, I was amused to find that someone in the camp of our labelmates Hall & Oates, who were recording in the "A" room downstairs, had erected a holy shrine to Michael Jackson. Album jackets, book covers, photos of Michael, and candles were all arranged altarlike on a table against a studio wall. No doubt they were praying to the King of Pop for their next record to sell as many copies as *Thriller*. Actually, the prayers did not go completely unanswered; they enjoyed a sizable hit with their resulting album, *Big Bam Boom*.

For the producer of *Beat Hotel*, we chose John Jansen, who had beautifully engineered *Numbers with Wings* for our then-producer Richard Gottehrer the previous year. So beautifully, in fact, that it inspired a phone call from another labelmate and hero, Lou Reed, who said he loved the sound of our album and wanted to know more about the engineer. Jansen went on to produce Lou's next album, *New Sensations*. He had previously produced Television's *Adventure*, and worked on posthumous Hendrix tracks.

I spent many nights sleeping on a couch at that studio built by Hendrix, while my parents, who had suddenly decided to visit, occupied my apartment. I was sure then, and am sure now, that that studio is haunted. I could hear echoes of Jimi's feedback late into the night, long after all the sessions were over. I was told it was just residual sound in the reverb plates, but I knew better. I think Jimi, like that voodoo woman in New Orleans, was trying to tell me something.

I had personally wanted to continue working with Gottehrer, but was outnumbered. I had enjoyed the attention he gave me—especially during the recording of the lead vocals and my guitar overdubs. For the solos, he would conduct me as if I was a symphony orchestra, with a lot of humor and passion, stomping and waving his hands in the air. My bandmates were not quite as amused.

John Jansen was far more of a tech head, never displaying the kind of creative zeal that drove our sessions with Gottehrer. But during the many months of recording and mixing, Jansen, best known for his even more overblown work with Jim Steinman and Meatloaf, tried—and sometimes succeeded—in keeping up with our constant barrage of ideas. Regular swigs from a pasty pink bottle of Pepto Bismol, perpetually clutched in Jansen's right hand under the console, became more and more regular as the months progressed, and as we went increasingly over budget.

Going over budget was a favorite pastime in the '80s, led by Ronald Reagan as he drove up the national debt to outrageous heights. Shoppers heading uptown to Bloomingdale's were further motivated to push their own credit limits by the National Debt ticker on 42nd Street, counting off the trillions we owed as a nation. Recording budgets exploded, too. Fleetwood Mac was practically cheered for breaking the $1 million mark on their spending for *Tusk* as the decade began.

One night, during the *Beat Hotel* sessions, we stopped recording early to attend the first MTV Video Music Awards at Radio City Music Hall. Getting dressed in the studio bathroom, I wore a tuxedo shirt under a multicolor ribbon vest I had picked up in Cozumel, during a vacation there with Jim that had inspired some of *Beat Hotel*'s songs. With "Numbers with Wings" nominated for Best Direction, we sat in the hot seats on the aisle near the stage, surrounded by a who's who in pop for 1984. Our hearts sank slightly when we lost to ZZ Top (who had *two* videos in that category), but we were high from just being there. The afterparty raised that high to another level yet again, all televised live on MTV.

Diana Ross's white limousine pulled up next to ours, in the Tavern on the Green parking lot, when suddenly there was an intense rainstorm. Like the one that had recently devastated her Central Park concert, this one totally wiped out her giant blown-out hairstyle the second her car door was opened for her. Buzzed and laughing, we leaned out the window and gave her a thumbs-up, saying, "Looking great, Diana!" as she grimly smiled back. When we saw her inside, she had already reassembled herself for the cameras. "A true star," I thought.

Phil Marino's sleazy, hand-tinted back cover photo of *Beat Hotel* pictured the Bongos lounging around the fifth-floor hallway at 1118 Hudson Street like tarted-up male prostitutes. Finally, my junior high school ambition to be a hustler had come true! At least in pictures. The fact that the album's title came from the famous Paris hotel where William Burroughs and the other Beat writers lived—while we were portrayed on the jacket as whores—was a concept that did not escape Burroughs himself. At his seventy-second-birthday party, at the desanctified church-turned-nightclub, the Limelight, I sat with the great and legendary Beat—his rather frail hand tightly squeezing mine for most of the night, as the New York glitteratti lined up to pay their respects to the living myth. With the most potent sexual images of *The Wild Boys* and *Naked Lunch* flashing in my head, I handed him an RCA cassette of the Bongos' *Beat Hotel*, and, much to my delight, he wordlessly pulled a copy out of his own pocket to show me.

I had finally decided to take the plunge and leave the safe, economical nest of Hoboken. I moved into my own pristine and sunny little parlor floor studio apartment at 86 Perry Street—in the very same Greenwich Village neighborhood that Tiny Tim had lovingly described to me all those years ago in Tampa—with fourteen-foot ceilings, bright white enameled walls, and polished wooden floors. "Serpico's girlfriend lived in that apartment," I was often told by my new neighbors. Not really knowing much about Serpico, the whistle-blowing New York City cop of the 1970s, I rented the Al Pacino film and started to feel more like a real New Yorker.

It would be another year before I was able to actually unpack. Stacked boxes filled with all my earthly and unearthly possessions towered silently. With the *Beat Hotel* album in the stores and the Bongos back on MTV with a new video, it was time to get back on the road. After a two-week run to work out the sound and lights in a Nova Scotia club, the Beat Hotel Tour took us to every college town our agents could locate in a Rand McNally road atlas. Lots of bills like "The Bongos, The Bangles, and The English Beat." This was the mid-'80s, baby!

Besides the four Bongos, for the tour we added the excellent and exceptionally showy (an understatement) percussionist Steve Scales. Fresh from the hit Talking Heads film and tour, *Stop Making Sense*, Steve was a celebrity in his own right and added quite a lot to the madness onstage and off. In quieter moments, he would insert cassettes of Malcolm X and Reverend Jesse Jackson speeches into the bus's sound system, and we white boys would listen with him. It made it even more difficult to accept that while traveling through the deep South, Steve would refuse to get off the bus when we would pull up to truck stops. "Get me some chips. I ain't going out there!" I couldn't blame him. Some things hadn't changed—and still haven't.

Like a phantom train—through the cities and deserts—we rediscovered America over and over. Heading west on a particularly dark, spooky night, somewhere in Arizona, while watching Stephen King's film about a murderous car (*Christine*), our huge Silver Eagle tour bus suddenly broke down, puttering to a dead stop. Even the roadies, Mitch and Tommy, stopped their nonstop poker game with our soundman, Brendan. Stranded, we circled the tour bus in the blackness, as if it were a covered wagon until miraculously the boy band New Edition (with Bobby Brown) passed by in *their* bus and stopped for us. They had the next day off and, exemplifying perfect tour etiquette and Good Samaritanship, sent their bus back to pick us up and take us to our next stop.

My favorite snapshot memory of the summer of '85 was on the tour with Duran Duran offshoot, Power Station, then at the top of the charts with "Some Like It Hot," and their remake of my beloved T.Rex tune, "Get It On." After a show, we found our gleaming white tour bus smudged with hundreds of red lipstick teenage kisses. Were the kisses intended for us or for the Duran boys? Did it matter?

All the rock myths made sense to me now; my life itself was becoming a cliché. The hotels and college campuses all basically looked the same, so I never knew what city I was in until we got to a radio station for an interview. I couldn't laugh at *Spinal Tap* anymore. We watched it on the bus one evening before a show, and the rest of that night seemed like a continuation of the film.

I began to see myself as a cartoon rendering of a pop star. Like Astro Boy with a guitar.

Exhausted as the tour wore on, I'd sometimes wonder if I could even step out onstage, much less get through the ninety-minute set. Then, our entrance music—the theme from the film *How the West Was Won*—would blare over the P.A. My heart would race. We would pounce onto the stage as if taking possession of a foreign territory. "Ladies and gentlemen of the world, from Hoboken, *the Bongos.*" I'd pick up my Rickenbacker, stomp on the distortion pedal, and play the opening riff of "In the Congo" again, and then it all seemed to have a life of its own. A big machine. A big iron lung. The show breathed as much life into me as I breathed into it. Fueled by a sudden burst of adrenaline and the audience response . . . something would click . . . total abandon. . . .

Of course, during the course of the concert itself, I would turn my back to the audience for a second, and quickly inhale a measured line of coke from a small brown bottle with a special attachment. And there were many swigs of Rémy Martin VSOP (demanded in our contract rider), sucked from monogrammed pewter flask.

I was drenched in sweat by the second song . . . more like an expensive cognac-cocaine cocktail than human perspiration . . . shirt sticking to my skin . . . leather guitar strap leaving a permanent stripe, ruining yet another $250 Comme des Garçons shirt. A reviewer in St. Louis described me as "Paul McCartney from Hell," and that about said it all.

> There's a Roman circus,
> there's a Roman circus,
> there's a Roman circus
> in my mind, in my mind. . . .

Near the end of one particularly energized show, I fell, symbolically, off the edge—of a fourteen-foot-high stage, crashing hard on top of my still strapped-on guitar, as Jim followed and tumbled hard on top of me with a thud. The audience didn't seem to notice this happen on the darkened side of the stage—but they no doubt were aware of us both limping during the encore that night as I sang "This Is My Sin." There wasn't much pain until the next day, when it was time to do it all again. I feared I had a punctured lung, but the show, and tour, went on. And on.

Every show had to be great . . . no matter what. No matter how I felt, no matter how raw my voice was from belting every song every night. I couldn't consider holding back. I would recall the small sign that hung in the sacristy of the Roman Catholic church where I worked, way back home, just above the portal through which the priests would enter the altar:

> Say this Mass as if it is your first Mass.
> Say this Mass as if it is your last Mass.
> Say this Mass as if it is your only Mass.

Like a Mass, I began to think of the show as a sacrifice. Cocaine and Rémy were the bread and wine.

While we had mostly been away on tour for the past few years, Hoboken had become a true pop mecca. When we were first starting out, there may have been one other current band in Hoboken, the Individuals, led by our old friend Glenn Morrow. But by now, as a result of the press releases Rob and I wrote and sent around the country and world with comparisons to mid-'60s Liverpool, and the success of Maxwell's, Hoboken had drawn a whole crop of bands of varying degrees of distinction to make their mark. National magazines and local television stations produced specials on "the Hoboken Sound." I laughed at the thought of this, remembering how once upon a time, just a few years before, we had asked the restaurant's owners if we could use their unused storage room after hours to practice. Then was then. By the time Bruce Sprinsteen shot his "Glory Days" video at Maxwell's, I knew—for me—*its* glory days were over.

That summer, we performed an outdoor concert on the Hoboken waterfront along the Hudson, with the Manhattan skyline as the backdrop. We went on just before sunset, after a full day of the new Hoboken bands. The whole town came out. Even Jesus couldn't perform a miracle in his hometown, but it was, in our minds, a triumphant return. Hungover but happy, I wore the special fluorescent-painted shirt I wore on the front cover of *Beat Hotel,* and a T.Rex-ish, antique silk top hat borrowed from Natalie McDonald. (Years before, Natalie was the fourteen-year-old mistress of the T.Rex Fan Club. "Who do we know in Hackensack, New *Jersey?*" my mother would ask, eyeing the outrageous long distance bills incurred by calling Natalie to discuss T.Rex for hours. Now with her *Tribal Rhythms* newsletter, she provided the same service for the Bongos. We also became close friends, and I would soon take Natalie to the recording studio to produce her own over-the-top music.)

Ron Wood of the Rolling Stones was there in Hoboken that day and, after the show, came aboard our dressing room trailer bearing a big bag of white powder. The Stones were making an album (*Dirty Work*) at RPM studios in New York, not far from my new apartment, where we had recorded much of *Beat Hotel.* As Ron left, he looked back to me saying, "Come up to the studio, mate—and bring your *Rickenbacker!*" I did call the studio a few times to see how things were going, but tensions—or distractions—seemed to be running high in the Stones' world those days. I opted to steer clear.

Mick Jagger had also hung out with us one or two afternoons, while we were recording the drums for *Beat Hotel.* Yes, just the drums. It was the mid-'80s and that's how we did it: different studios for different instruments, and Power Station had the best drum sound in town. Mick was in the next room cutting his first solo album with Nile Rodgers there. He came in and sort of slunk around, leaning on the console with us, listening to Frank endlessly bash his snare drum. He sat for a while, impressively relaxed, talking about recording with and without the Stones. Then, silently as we continued tracking, he slunk out the door. *Slunk* is the operative word: when I first saw Mick, slumped and rumpled on the reception area couch, I discreetly alerted the studio receptionist that "a homeless man was sleeping in the lobby. Just so you know," I added. "I'm not saying you should kick him out or anything." The receptionist suggested I look closer, and it was then that I recognized that famous face. Later, I saw him spring to life and become Mick Jagger before my eyes. It was like *Star Wars*' C-3P0 shutting down and turning on again, but with lips.

It hadn't occurred to me yet that this ability to shut down may have been the way he has survived being the longest-running frontman.

One night, Jim and I sat with Mick and Jack Nicholson at a table in the VIP lounge at the Palladium on 14th Street. It was yet another vignette in a series of surreal situations. While Jack left the waitress a still-rolled-up $100 bill as a tip, Jagger elbowed me, pointing out Tom Jones standing alone at the bar, and urging me to "go talk to him." I threw myself at Tom, telling him he was my favorite singer, and understanding for a moment why girls throw their panties at him.

Another unholy night, this time at the the Limelight, saw the Bongos mingling in the suitably unholy circle of Duran Duran and Andy Warhol. While looking at Andy's slightly askew silver wig, I flashed back to Florida for a second—lying on the floor of my childhood bedroom thumbing through a copy of Warhol's *Interview* magazine, wanting to be a part of that paparazzied and Polaroided scene on the last page—and now realized I was there. A few frames flickered of my first meeting with Andy at the Factory five years before, when I was fresh off the train from Tampa. But things were moving fast. Hard to focus. There was no time to think about something as mundane as what I was *feeling* for very long. Andy's slightly askew silver wig, and the party went on. . . . The myth had become real.

Back in Hoboken to see the Feelies, I was leaning on the jukebox at Maxwell's when Anton Fier, the group's drummer, squinted at me from the bar. "So, what's it *really* like living in the fast lane?" he slurred, sarcastically. I wasn't sure how to answer him, so I didn't. Not everyone was enchanted by the Bongos' ascent.

Sitting in a huge, nearly empty movie theater with my friend Jon Klages to see Mikhail Baryshnikov in *White Nights*, Jon suddenly whispered to me, "Isn't that Tiny Tim up there?" Sure enough, it was Tiny, seated a few rows ahead, hair still hennaed bright red, with his new wife, Miss Jan. As he was leaving after the film, he spotted me and, with a smile as we made eye contact, came over. "Mr. Barone! I've been keeping an eye on you and your career with the Bongos! Congratulations!" He knew everything: Hoboken, England, RCA . . . I didn't tell him then how instrumental he was, giving me that first real push to leave Tampa. I sensed he knew that already. "Do you still

have those recordings we made? 'I've Never Seen a Straight Banana'?"
He remembered everything, every detail, though nine years had
passed. "Those must come out someday!" he reminded me. I nodded.
"Yes, they *will*." Then we were off on our separate ways again, into the
blinding glare of Times Square.

RCA, never the most nurturing record company, was by now far
removed, even from the company we had signed to just two years prior.
When we were first courted by the label, they were owned by General
Electric, who then also owned NBC. Next, they were purchased by
Hertz Rent-A-Car; then, Standard Foods took over. Suddenly we were
hearing phrases like "shelf life" with regard to our albums, like we
were breakfast cereals. Not much talk about music up there those days.
Nancy Jeffries was long gone, like a mother who went shopping and
never came home, and along with the sense of abandonment we felt,
our new team had no idea who or what the Bongos were. Except for a
few radio promotion guys with a lot of energy and humor, there wasn't
much for us at RCA anymore. It was like not knowing anyone at your
own party.

One day, our new A & R representative, a former journalist I had
respected a decade earlier, took me to lunch, bragging endlessly about
how he had worked with Jim Morrison and the Doors in the '60s, and
then suggested I write a song like the recent Denise Williams hit, "Let's
Hear It for the Boy." With those words, my hope and my lunch were
nearly lost.

It was just about then that Chris Blackwell came to the rescue.

Blackwell's Island Records had been my favorite record label since
high school. With most of my favorite artists on the roster: Roxy Music
and Eno, Sparks, John Cale, Nico. . . . This was *art*-rock. A world apart
from the lumbering corporate dinosaur, RCA (unaffectionately known
in the business as the Record Cemetery of America), Chris Blackwell
was, and is, a very wealthy, very handsome, smart, and stylish Brit who,
besides owning studios in the Bahamas and a label named Island, also
owned an actual private island or two. Several years before, Chris had
signed our friends the B-52's and had hit it big with U2 and others, as
well as controlling the Bob Marley catalog.

We met at his glamorous Essex House suite on Central Park South. We all seemed to like each other, so with a handshake, we began plans to go with Island. Our lawyer, Owen, whom we shared with Chris, would ease the transition from RCA, who had missed their deadline to pick up our option anyway. Chris suggested we co-produce our next album with Eric "E.T." Thorngren, the hot new engineer/producer who had just recorded our friends' Power Station's hits as well as the latest releases by the Eurythmics and the Talking Heads. His trademark was a particularly excessive drum sound, perhaps best exemplified by his massive hit with Robert Palmer, "Addicted to Love." I was thrilled. Now we would have a real hit! Recharged, I started writing a whole new batch of songs.

Finally moved into my new apartment, I sat on the big bed (which encompassed about 50 percent of the floor space) with my Rickenbacker, a Casio CZ 101 digital keyboard (a gift from Island), a Boss Dr. Rhythm drum machine, and a Fostex X-15 four-track portastudio, and started cranking out tune after tune. I told everyone who came over that I did my best work in bed, and I meant it.

Like almost all of the lyrics I wrote for the Bongos, these were like automatic writing. I would sit with the guitar and let the music tell me what I wanted to say. Only rarely would I interrupt and deliberately write anything narrative. Mostly telegraphic thoughts, I never questioned or rewrote them. The words would somehow fuse to the melody in my mind—and that was that.

> Nights of decadence then
> Days of recompense now
> Talking to myself, yeah
> It's no coincidence somehow
> I want you to hold me, make me see
> What my wildest dreams can be.

Like much of *Beat Hotel*, we started recording the new album back at RPM Studios, where the Stones had recently recorded. The sessions started out uneventfully. Our playing was tight from all the shows we had done. And E.T. was a sweet, swaggering, pony-tailed pirate with a friendly smile, a loud ready laugh, and a lovely girlfriend who would wheel a daiquiri cart into the studio each day at 5:00 P.M. Clearly, this producer could party. Maybe even *match* us. But damned if we would let him surpass us.

We were surrounded in the studio by dinosaurs—gifts from a studio employee with former ties to the Sinclair Oil Company, whose famous logo was the green brontosaurus, Dino. Cuddly but sober reminders of what can happen to you if you can't adapt to change. We had Dinos and tyrannosaurus's in all sizes. One giant inflatable dinosaur was kidnapped by Chris Blackwell's long-time assistant, Holly Ferguson, who would send daily ransom notes to the studio with Polaroids of the blindfolded Dino.

E.T. suggested we head down to Chris's studio in Nassau to complete the album, now tentatively titled *Phantom Train*. Vince, with his usual caution, warned us to stay and finish the record in New York—on our own turf. But it was winter now, and we loved the idea of recording in the Bahamas. With visions of Grace Jones, the Tom Tom Club, and other Compass Point regulars dancing in our heads, we never seriously considered any of our manager's warnings. There was never a question that we were going.

We didn't know it then, but the flight to Nassau was the beginning of the end of the Bongos.

We had been traveling constantly for the past five years. Yet that flight to Nassau seemed different. We were detaching from something . . . something umbilical.

New York had been our creative womb. Even though we had recorded much of our first album in a London suburb, it worked because we were basically recording our live repertoire, which we had been playing for a while. Now we were creating new material from scratch. Normally we would woodshed new songs in little private rehearsal studios where no one could see us. Like making sausage or politics, band rehearsals are better left unseen. At Compass Point, we would be in a fish bowl, under the microscope, through a backward telescope, darkly. How could I sense all this on that late-night flight to Nassau? Why were these thoughts in my head? It was a strange and surreal feeling—a mixed emotion of high expectation and impending doom.

The frontman at three.

Getting to first bass in high school.

Sherri Dodsworth

I was always listening for the perfect pop song.

Bored to destruction.

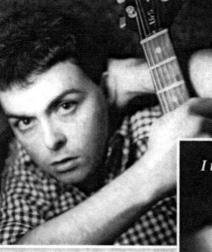

I practiced landing on the "one."

Snails publicity photo.

I was afraid I would have stage fright.

Jean Yuscavage

The Snails debut at the University of Tampa.

Recording Tiny Tim
in Tampa
(with Marla, center).

Photos by Richard Barone

"You must believe in your dreams, not in your fears."

Culture shock. The city digested us whole, and its stomach rumbled.

Arriving in the East Village.

"Can we practice in your backroom?"

Rob, Richard, and Frank at Maxwell's in Hoboken.

We found ourselves at the sacred temple of rock and sleaze, Max's Kansas City.

The BONGOS

MAX'S K.C. 213 Park Ave. S. N. Y. C.

TUESDAY, Dec. 18, 1979

"Paul McCartney from Hell."

Joyful assaults
in Hoboken, New York,
and London.

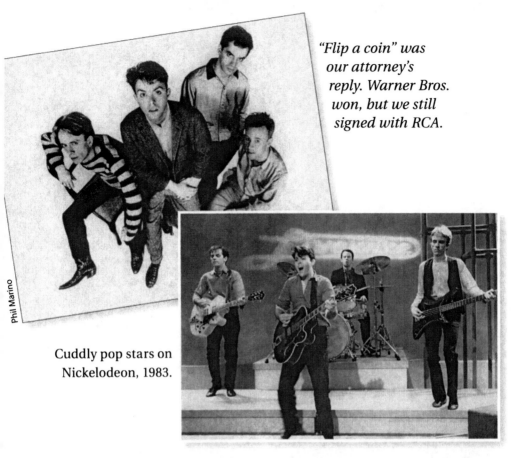

"Flip a coin" was our attorney's reply. Warner Bros. won, but we still signed with RCA.

Phil Marino

Cuddly pop stars on Nickelodeon, 1983.

With Fred Schneider and James (seated) at the Limelight.

Mei Mei Gillespie

Backstage at the Palladium, New York.

*Something would click . . .
total abandon. The show,
and the tour went on. And on.*

2 Part VI / Friday, May 3, 1985 ★

"We's hear stuff," Richard Barone, left, says about working at Jimi Hendrix's old studio. Behind him, from left, are fellow Bongos Frank Giannini, James Mastro, Rob Norris and Steve Seven.

RICHARD BARONE

*I could feel
myself slowly
becoming
sharper.*

"Barone fashions a kind of rock chamber music," wrote Anthony DeCurtis *in* Rolling Stone.

With Jane Scarpantoni.

Returning home for a visit. Tampa had changed. The quaint downtown was now completely gone.

Walking the little streets of the West Village, I wasn't looking for anything or anyone, but I was open to everything.

*Like Snakeskin,
the party boy in
The Fugitive Kind,
I wanted to shed
my own skin and
grow a new one.*

*The same night I got back
home to Perry Street,
I got a phone call from
my brother. "You'd better
get back down here."*

*"That's it!" Duane
shouted. "Hold that!"
It was all done in the
camera, by a master.*

*I always wanted to give the
Germans what they wanted.
No matter how much it hurt.*

Hamburg, 1992.

Florence Mazzone

"I was out on the edge,
a cat on the ledge,
before you were born."

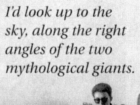

I'd look up to the
sky, along the right
angles of the two
mythological giants.

Phil Marino

"Richard, it's still not too late
to lower the key," whispered
David Johansen as I stepped
onstage to sing my aria.

With Johansen
and Jane Siberry
backstage at *The*
Downtown Messiah.

"... And we shall be changed."

Performing "The Trumpet Shall Sound" in *The Downtown Messiah*, 2001.

With George Wein and Debbie Harry at the JVC Jazz Festival press conference to announce the Peggy Lee Tribute at Carnegie Hall.

"Give the kid what he wants!"

"Where's he from?" I knew he meant "what planet."

Quincy Jones, backstage at the Bowl.

Directing Bea Arthur in Los Angeles.

"Richard, I'm going to kill you."

"Give me *eyes*, Richard," said Bea Arthur, just before showtime. I knew Nancy Sinatra's dressing room would have the biggest false eyelashes and best makeup, and Bea had me on my knees in no time. A producer's work is never done.

The Hollywood Bowl: July 14, 2004.

"I finally began to realize what makes a star."

With Nancy Sinatra, Petula Clark, and Jack Jones at the Hollywood Bowl tech rehearsal.

Mike Renzi

With Rita Moreno in New York . . .

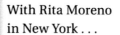

. . . and the Hollywood Bowl cast: Lorraine Feather, Jolie Jones, Freddy Cole, Petula Clark, Jack Jones, Sheryl Lee Ralphs, Bea Arthur, Maureen McGovern, Nicki Foster-Wells (Peggy Lee's daughter), Jane Monheit, Nancy Sinatra, Nnena Freelon, Rita Coolidge.

I strummed my guitar, while Paul paced the room with his notebook, singing and scribbling: "Silence is our song . . ."

With Paul Williams in Los Angeles.

An evening with Donovan . . .

Ellen Joy Voell

"You know, Richard, Allen Ginsberg always read Howl *in the nude."*

Ernie Black

. . . and a surprise while performing "Cosmic Wheels."

The sound gelled instantly, and Moby's contributions were perfect.

With Moby in the studio, 2006.

With Tony Visconti at his home studio . . .

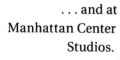

. . . and at Manhattan Center Studios.

"Richard, we can do anything."

Anything to shape the sound.

Getting aggressive onstage in New York, 2007.

"Richard is my mentor—and has influenced my musical path and destiny."

With Rolan Bolan, joining the reunited Bongos for "Mambo Sun" in 2007.

"I mean, I have to. I'm a frontma

New York, 20(

Arriving at Compass Point, we were hit by the warmth and shown to our charming little cottages on the beach, a little complex called Tip Top. I couldn't imagine getting any work done, but, hey, the rooms were decorated with some of my favorite Island album covers. My room had Roxy Music's *Stranded*, the one portraying a gorgeously made-up model in a wet torn dress—washed up on the shore in the tropics.

The next day we went to look at the studio and fell in love with it. It was a busy operation. During the day, Julio Iglesias was recording in one room and AC/DC—with Marshall stacks miked up and spread throughout the studio in hallways, lobby, and even the recreation room with the pool table—was in the other. It was impossible to find a quiet place, because, while AC/DC was recording basic tracks and guitar overdubs, all the amps throughout the building were turned up all the way.

I was immediately impressed and charmed that Julio seemed to sing his vocals while lying on a couch, which appeared to have been brought from his home and placed in the center of studio A. Relaxed and relaxing, this came through on the recordings, and since then, I have always tried to bring some element of "home" to the recording studio. One day, Julio's session extended overtime, ever so slightly, into our evening session. We went to the lounge to play pool and take some more Polaroids, no big deal. Soon we were back in session, when a huge basket of flowers arrived with a note:

> To the Bongos, sorry to have made you wait. Julio.

Stopping in to visit AC/DC, I was amazed to see Brian Johnson's lead vocal being recorded not in the live room, but in the control room, without headphones, facing the engineer, and sung in a kind of whisper. Hearing the hit song a few months later on the radio, the illusion was that he was belting at the top of his lungs in an arena. But then illusion is what it is all about, isn't it?

Only thing is, it's easy to forget that.

I remember Jim and I going to see Iggy Pop once, a couple of years before, at the Peppermint Lounge. At 2:00 or 2:30 A.M., he came out onstage looking wasted and hyped up, wearing only the skimpiest bikini briefs. He came straight out to center stage and pulled them down. "This is what you all want to see, so let's get it over with right now," he snarled in his Michigan drawl. As the legendary frontman of the Stooges, he had taken up where *his* frontman hero, Jim Morrison, had tragically left off, smearing peanut butter on his bare chest onstage or rolling in broken glass. Taking it to the edge. He proceeded to race through a rapid-fire muscular set made up of thirty-second versions of his most familiar songs, like "I Wanna Be Your Dog" and "Nightclubbing," crawling around the stage, posing outrageously and camping it up like, well, like Iggy Pop. David Lee Roth was in the audience, standing directly in front of us, yelling, "Faggot!" to Iggy, inciting him even more. Immediately after the show, Jim and I were invited backstage by the club owners to meet Iggy. Bracing ourselves, we expected to see the drugged-out madman we saw onstage: nude and wasted. Instead, he was sitting calmly and quietly on the couch, fully dressed, wearing nerdy horn-rimmed glasses, reading the *New York Times*. He stood to greet us graciously, shaking our hands. It occurred to me that we were meeting the real guy, James Osterberg. Just like Mick Jagger on the studio couch, I didn't recognize him at first, even though I had just seen him onstage. It was only years later that I could understand that, to survive, you have to separate the real person from the illusion. The *fan*tasy is for the *fan*s. But in 1985, at Compass Point, I hadn't quite grasped that.

"Never get high on your own supply," can be paraphrased: "Don't buy into the fantasy that you're supposed to be selling."

Another of the other denizens of Compass Point was Emil Schult, brilliant lyricist for Kraftwerk, also an extraordinary graphic artist and conceptualist. We immediately bonded. Emil contributed to our project by co-writing a lyric with me, shooting many, many photos, doing drawings of the Bongos, and designing some gorgeous retro-futuristic album cover graphics while we recorded and mixed.

The actual recording and mixing pace was surreal . . . slow, mostly, and often coming to a frustrating dead stop, just like our tour bus had done in the desert several months before. Only this time, New Edition was nowhere to be found. The SSL recording desk automation, which

E.T. used on every mix, had a nasty habit of breaking down and a repair team was hard to come by in the tropics. It seemed we were taking endless breaks—excursions to the beach, trips into town, excavations in search of pirate artifacts with Emil—when we needed to be recording. I was beginning to feel like the girl on the *Stranded* cover. And the party continued ... the powdered party favors that were constantly making the rounds were now *pink,* plentiful, and particularly lethal.

When the studio automation was working, the mixing was obsessive, E.T. spending sometimes four days or more on one mix. Listening repeatedly to the songs while mixing, the lyrics would pound at me, my own voice and words mocking me, over and over, day after day:

> Tangled in your web, baby, I am tangled in your web
> As a million things are said, baby, I'll be tangled in your web
> Nothing's really free, baby, nothing I can see
> Pictures on the wall distort a hanging mask of me
>
> Long night till tomorrow
> Time stops for a lifetime
> Dreams fall by the wayside
> Lay chained for a lifetime.

It was not only *like* listening to my inner dialogue, it *was* my inner dialogue.

> This train ain't bound for glory. . . .

There is a certain action that cartoon characters make. Wile E. Coyote on *Roadrunner* does it, and I believe Bugs Bunny and others do it, too. They can run off a cliff and, as long as they don't look down, they can stay suspended—or keep running—in midair. The second they look down and see there is nothing below them, they begin a swift descent, with a puff of smoke.

I looked down.

To survive, it is very important that you do not look down. There is no net, and if you stop, you're going to make like Wile E. Coyote and take a very bad fall. The Bongos had been forging ahead for six years on instinct and intuition. No matter what, we didn't look over our shoulders, we just kept going forward.

Now everything became blurry.

Fueled by cocaine, I grew paranoid and restless. I became hyper-aware of every nuance of everything. I was convinced the bathroom mirrors were two-way. I felt my every move was being scrutinized. Did I have what it takes?

And I sensed an undercurrent of violence surrounding the studio. I felt we were being watched all the time. Apparently, we were.

One day, returning from yet another excursion with Emil, during yet another SSL breakdown, something seemed terribly wrong. The studio was quiet, the staff was somber, some people were crying. It turns out that some local drug dealers had paid a visit to our producer at his apartment across the way from the studio. His girlfriend was home, and they demanded money. To make their point, the dealers shot and killed the couple's dog in front of her.

Now everything came to a complete stop.

Just before sunset that day, the four Bongos sat on the beach talking about the continental shelf and how at a certain point in the waters in front of us, the ocean floor drops from a few feet to several thousand. We were looking out to the sea when suddenly all four of us could clearly see the skyline of Manhattan on the horizon. The World Trade Center towers, the Empire State Building, the Statue of Liberty—all in perfect detail from this beach in the Bahamas. That was when we knew it was time to go home.

Always know when it's time to go home.

CHAPTER 8

I BELONG TO ME

HOW TO START OVER

Even self-destruction can leave you with a choice: Once you hit the wall, you can either scale it or slide down. I found the worst vantage point is in the middle. It's impossible to see where you are, where you've been, or where you're going. Everyone around you has the advantage. But, somewhere inside, your instincts and intuition lay intact. You've only misplaced them, like keys or sunglasses.

When we got back home from the Bahamas, we didn't speak to each other for weeks. It was as if we needed to digest the past five years. Five years that came crashing neatly down in the kind of controlled implosion you see on the six o'clock news. It seemed improbable that the dust would ever settle.

As if hit by a neutron bomb, we had been blown up, but the ghost image of the structure still stood, like a transparent shroud of *touring*. The hazy memory of the 300 shows a year we had just played, and the future dates that were being booked loomed like the monolith in *2001: A Space Odyssey*. Standing in its shadow, I wondered, "What is it? What does it mean?" like the shell-shocked astronaut in the film, while the indestructible machine of commerce continued to pump our records, cassettes, and videos into circulation. Business went on, but everything seemed different.

Phantom Train remained unfinished, another ghost, the reels of tape sitting in the Perry Street apartment I had moved into over a year before, joining the other boxes I had yet to unpack. The chorus we sang on the album's title song haunted me now: "This train ain't bound for glory / This train ain't bound for glory. . . ."

We had never actually signed a deal with Island Records, though we had prematurely squiggled our way out of our RCA contract to go to them. So now we found ourselves in that netherworld that is politely called "between labels."

Jim and I spent the early part of the day together before an afternoon band meeting at Vince's office at 57th and Broadway, the heart of the music industry in New York. We had become close friends, so all day I sensed something was up—something was not being said. At the meeting, he suddenly announced he was leaving the group. His words were followed by the requisite uneasy silence. "Well," I said finally, "if there is anything I can do to help . . . ," which sounded awkward. Soon he would be fronting his own band. I realized, for the first time, it was all about being the frontman, and I wondered if Jim knew that the frontman is usually the least enviable position of all.

I had been in training since before I could walk, sitting in my playpen, watching Ricky Ricardo fronting his band as he flickered in those reruns on the black-and-white screen. Sometimes I thought about how much easier it would have been to be one of the trombone players sitting behind his music stand, and remembered how it felt to be playing my guitar behind the singer in "a."

The frontman has nowhere to hide. The frontman is completely revealed. The frontman is naked.

And, who *is* the frontman, anyway? Is it me or some version of me? A mirage or just a front? Is it the guy looking in the mirror or his reflection?

Sometimes I was aware of being "off" or "on," but almost always I was "on." The electric version of me. The acoustic version had made himself scarce. When I'd pass by a mirror, if no one was looking, I would check to see if I was still there.

In my relationships with guys, and with women—even my family—who did they see? Who is it they think they know? Is *he* the frontman, too?

And worse, who did *I* see?

I wondered if I had to live up to my reviews when I was with someone socially. Was I fulfilling my role as "the cherubic choirboy" or "Paul McCartney from Hell"? Isn't that what they expected of me? Was it enough?

I didn't know anymore who I saw when I looked at myself. The more I wanted to be the simple guy who sat on the bed with his guitar, to whom, somehow, songs appeared, the more pressure I felt to be larger than life.

I thought of relationships I had let slip by. Guys and girls who had shown me true affection. I blamed it on band commitments, but was it because I couldn't relate to anyone unless I was on the stage? And I thought of Miss Jean, whom I seldom saw now.

My grandmother had died during the recording of *Beat Hotel*, taking with her my connection to the Old World she taught me about, and the compassion and complete acceptance that so few had ever offered me. I remembered the little shows I would perform for her as a boy. She had embraced even my most outrageous friends. In her last days, she was in and out of hospitals and nursing homes, while I was on the road performing, night after night. My visits to Florida had been rare.

Now, I thought about how I much I had wanted her to have seen me reach the kind of success she always told me I would achieve, for her to turn on the television and find me there, performing for her again in her living room. I wanted it more for her than for me. MTV had made that happen a little, but I wondered if she was proud enough of me. I went down to Battery Park to gaze across the Hudson at Ellis Island, and imagined her arrival there from Italy on an overcrowded immigrant ship at fourteen. Only then did I cry.

With a few more shows coming up here and there, we felt we needed reinforcements and recruited two friends, Ivan Julian from Richard Hell's Voidoids and multitalented George Usher on guitar and keyboards. Man, we rocked! But the momentum, drive, focus, and direction were all gone. Ran their course. Just as suddenly as we had arrived at our destination, the destination was suddenly no longer there. It wasn't the departure of a band member. It was the departure of the *desire*.

Now, as I walked the streets of New York, I felt as though every step was potentially a step off the edge of a cliff, off the continental shelf, into an abyss. Particularly in midtown, surrounded by the towers of the radiant city I'd dreamed of and loved. The town we would own. I felt the freedom of falling . . . falling . . . the frontman . . . falling . . . off . . . the stage. . . .

I started taking the subway, just so I could jump in front of an oncoming train. Deep inside the underground tunnel, every time a train would come speeding into the station, a voice in my head would say, "Jump!" just as it neared the spot where I stood. It was like a reflex. I could *feel* myself doing it. I could feel myself doing it like I bet Ian Curtis of Joy Division had the day before that first U.S. tour, on which we were booked to join them; and like frontmen Michael Hutchence of INXS and Kurt Cobain of Nirvana would.

But I didn't.

Instead, I went out. Every night. To the China Club to hang out with Julian Lennon, gentle and truly talented, who we had met on the *Beat Hotel* tour. (When he was to come over to my apartment one night, I had to remove the giant Richard Avedon portrait of his father that hung over my fireplace. . . . It was just too much to bear.) Or to the Pyramid Club in the East Village, where I would dance with the towering transvestite RuPaul until last call, losing my keys on the dance floor more than once. On these occasions, I had to stagger to the Sixth Precinct down the block and ask an NYPD cop to help me break into my own apartment as the sun came up.

It was at my favorite Mexican restaurant, Cactus Café in the East Village, that I discovered cocaine was much better than salt along the rim of a margarita glass. Other patrons, staring openly, were almost as amused as I was. I soon began adding cocaine to my Diet Cokes, rationalizing that I was bringing the beverage much closer to its original formula.

One night, at CBGB, a blonde, well-built, angel-faced, and underaged punk stood on his barstool when I entered and yelled at the top of this lungs: "I want to have a homosexual experience with Richard Barone!"

All the noise in the club came to a screeching stop. Being a frontman has its moments. But I wondered who it was that the kid really wanted to sleep with. Because even I saw myself as someone else.

> The road to excess leads to the palace of wisdom. . . . For we never know what is enough until we know what is more than enough.
>
> —William Blake

> Too much is never enough.
>
> —MTV motto

My connection to Marc Bolan, his music, and his family was and is psychologically and spiritually strong. Having heard the Bongos' recording of Marc's "Mambo Sun," Gloria Jones, his widow, wanted to know about my own music. Introduced through Natalie McDonald, we stayed up all night at my Perry Street apartment as she told us tearfully about the crash that killed Marc, just on the verge of his commercial rebirth, at the age of just twenty-nine. It was on September 16, 1977, during my last few months in Tampa, that I heard news on my car radio. The world was still mourning the sudden death of another king who had died exactly one month earlier: Elvis Presley. Gloria was driving the purple Austin Mini, and still carried the guilt, as well as having sustained her own injuries. Their beautiful son, Rolan, was not quite two years old at the time of Marc's death, and now eleven, lived with her in Los Angeles.

EMI had been talking about making a film bio of Marc's life and wanted Billy Idol to play Marc. Gloria wanted me. The film was never made, but Gloria and I, and later, Rolan, would stay in touch. I told Gloria how I had seen her onstage with T.Rex in Tampa all those years ago and how I went to the hotel afterwards. When she asked if I had met Marc, I told her that something in my mind had told me not to knock on the hotel room door. "Thank goodness you didn't, honey!" she said softly. As it turned out, that night in Tampa is when their relationship was consummated—with Sherri and me right outside their door, talking to Mickey Finn.

It was after a year of sporadic Bongos performances and constant nightclubbing that the pieces of me finally fell to earth, rearranging themselves in a different configuration. Rob's current New Age girlfriend, Lilly, had given me a small, unusually clear quartz crystal as a gift. Thanking her, I slipped it into my jeans pocket and forgot about it. I carried it around with me for several weeks, never giving it a second thought. Then one day on a NJ Transit train ride, on my way to produce a session for an excellent power pop group called In Color, I took it out of my pocket, admiring its clarity, distinct shape, and sharp lines. I thought about how it was naturally created and didn't have to do anything, yet was full of untapped energy—enough to run an electronic device or clock. I noticed how beautifully and uniquely it reflected and enhanced light passing through it.

The New Jersey towns were zooming past—just like on those long rides to Morristown, when it was all still so new to me—the sunlight coming through the windows and flickering through the trees and buildings and through the crystal. I rubbed the smooth glassy surfaces. In a strange and sudden flash, I felt it: what I needed to be was exactly like that crystal. I was scattered all over the place. I needed to crystallize.

Yeah, it was the late '80s, so it was a crystal. But it could have been any talisman—a rabbit's foot, gold coin, family ring—what is important is that it triggered a change. Lucky for me it *wasn't* a lucky rabbit's foot on a keychain or I might have felt I should have been covered with fur and dyed pink.

I had started to see myself like the character in Woody Allen's film *Deconstructing Harry*, who is out of focus, and I could feel myself slowly becoming sharper. I started working out with weights again and got my body in better shape. Controlling what I could. The years of touring had taken a toll, with far too much fast food and far too little exercise. I started meditating—very simply—but I could feel the effect and liked it.

I started writing new songs and revisited the ones I had written over the past years with different ears. I felt free to write songs that did not have to represent the group. I wanted to write about the man behind the front.

When the rain has stopped and everyone's out to play
I am a face in the window passing through another day
I've heard the cool, cool music of Mingus and Miles in the afternoon
I found the cold blue halo, forgotten by an angel in my room, but
I belong to me
Of course I love you, but
My life is mine to be
What I want to.

With the band in an ever more nebulous state, I started planning some solo shows. I didn't want to put together a band that in any way resembled or sounded like the Bongos. I didn't want to insult or offend the others by doing so, nor did I want to compete with the group or encourage comparisons. So no drum kit, no bass, i.e., no replacing Rob or Frank.

Besides, this is only a side project, I thought. Still, before going to sleep, I would imagine what a solo album might look and sound like, and would visualize the cover image blown up as an oversized poster on the walls of Tower Records.

Through Jim, I had met a brilliant cellist, Jane Scarpantoni, uniquely capable of rocking and even improvising—unusual for classically trained players. This was a sound I had always wanted to explore. The cello is considered to be the stringed instrument closest in timbre to the human voice, and I wanted to use it to reinforce the vocal harmonies, as well as covering bass, traditional bowed cello lines, and some solos. Nick Celeste, one of the members of In Color, had a high, clear, beautifully pure voice and a smooth touch on acoustic guitar.

The challenge was to frame the songs in classical, almost Baroque settings, yet give them grooves and room to rock. At first, I felt even more exposed and too free without the heavy bass and drums to anchor me and nail me down. Then I thought of Peggy Lee's gorgeous back-phrasing and how relaxed and playful her vocals were. Her *Black Coffee* album. Lee was a singer's singer, inspired by her contemporaries and the great jazz singers of her day: Billie Holiday, Ella, Nat King Cole. I started to loosen up and feel the songs take control. With the two musicians and a batch of old and new tunes, I started booking some dates.

The first show was not at a 10,000-seat arena, like the last Bongos tour with Power Station, but at a small Tex-Mex restaurant called Bandito's on Seventh Avenue, just a block down from my apartment. There was no stage, no roadies, no lighting designer. I even had to *tune my own guitar* for the first time in nearly five years. The audience was in my face, just like at the first Snails show I did at the University of Tampa. It all felt new again.

There that night was one of my future collaborators, songwriter Jules Shear, who, after our set, grilled me about how it felt to be playing without the support of a full electric band. He was especially intrigued that I had stripped down a number of Bongos songs and played them acoustically. I told him how free it felt to unplug. Little did I know that Jules would soon be hosting a series for MTV. The show would feature live performance of rock artists performing in intimate acoustic settings. They called it *Unplugged.*

Some other shows with the new trio followed, all low-key. The Speakeasy, a stalwart folk club in the Village, and trendy King Tut's Wah Wah Hut in the East Village, where our opening act consisted of two boys: a drummer with just a snare drum, and a dancer, totally nude, covered with thick, white cake icing. The drummer sat and started a slow drum roll and incrementally began speeding it up, while his buddy started spinning in time. As the beat and spinning got faster, cake icing flew off his body, spattering all over the audience, the walls, and completely covering our instruments, which were already on the stage. A hard act to follow.

Wherever we played, no matter how hardcore, punk, folk, jazz, or performance art-oriented the venues and audiences were, people seemed to like us. The music we were making seemed to cross lines. It was fragile. My voice sounded vulnerable, because it was scary to get up and sing, "Too many scared guys / too many scared guys / I want to kiss you but I'll go away" or "Love's an afterthought to you, a diamond piano stool / in your precious hiding place inside your mind. . . ." to a crowded room of mohawks, piercings, leather, and tattoos. We didn't sound like the Dead Kennedys, but something must have clicked.

With the Bongos, when we started to play the larger venues, the audience became a "concept" and not "people." I couldn't really see the audience at our larger shows, just a blur of distant faces. There was always a gap at least several yards wide between the front of the stage and the first row, which was a pit for security and photographers. Now, again, I was performing for people whose reactions I could immediately read. I could see the expression in their eyes. I could see their lips move if they knew the lyrics and hear their comments. I hadn't realized how much I'd missed that.

Vin Scelsa had moved to the top-rated K-ROCK radio station, and was hosting a series of shows at the Bottom Line, the premier 400 to 500-seat venue in New York, on Sunday nights. Hearing about my solo project, he invited me to perform on an upcoming show in his series.

It was Vince Mauro, still my manager and more involved than ever, who suggested we add percussion to the lineup to complete the sound for this larger setting. The search was on for the right player. I wanted to avoid using any drums that would emphasize the backbeat at all. I was looking for a combination of African, Latin, and symphonic percussion. Vince suggested finding someone who could also play mallet percussion, such as vibes or marimba add melodic elements. Through Mike Stoller of the legendary songwriting team Leiber and Stoller, we were referred to a raven-haired Native American, Valerie Naranjo.

We rehearsed only once in my tiny apartment on Perry Street: Valerie, with her vibes and marimba, log drum, and miscellaneous shakers and toys, knowing that for the show we would also rent two twenty-six-inch concert timpani with pedals; Jane played her two-hundred-year-old cello; Nick his Guild acoustic guitar; and I retired the Rickenbacker to break out my 1967 Guild X-500, which I had used as a prop guitar in the "Numbers with Wings" video, and had a fat, jazzy sound.

To compress and control the tone, I played first through a Rockman processor, set on chorus, and played through a Roland Jazz Chorus 120 amp. I used no distortion or effect pedals, only my E-Bow, which had become a signature since "Numbers." The E-Bow, or Energy Bow, is a device invented in the early '70s that vibrates the guitar string to act as a violin or cello bow with no "pluck" or attack on the string, producing a smooth and endless sustain.

When I heard the sound we made together, I knew we could make an album. And I wanted to do it fast. It had been nearly two years since *Beat Hotel* had been released, and *Phantom Train* was not scheduled for departure or arrival any time soon. It occurred to me to record the Bottom Line shows for a live album.

As quickly as the thought came, I called my old friend Marty Scott at JEM/Passport Records. He agreed to arrange for the mobile recording truck, and to release the album in the fall. To record the show, we chose Randy Ezratty, whose Effanel Music had recorded a Bongos concert two years before for an unreleased live album, and who was soon to work with Paul Simon and countless others on major live albums and videos. We would be performing two shows at the Bottom Line that night, so I felt sure that we would be covered, having two shots at each song in the show and having the capability of editing between the two.

Besides opening and closing the show with new arrangements of two Bongos covers, I chose three songs by three major influences: from the Beatles, I chose the lovely and obscure "Cry Baby Cry" from the *White Album*, a song I had wanted to record since childhood; from Marc Bolan, "The Visit," a song that depicts a love affair with an alien arriving on a UFO; and from David Bowie, "The Man Who Sold the World" with its haunting melody and Tony Visconti bass line that could be rendered so nicely on cello. In my mind, those songs stood as pillars, anchoring the set, giving me a framework and backdrop for my own tunes.

The big unmarked recording truck pulled up and parked on the Mercer Street side of the venue, and the crew proceeded to hang a network of thick black cables above the audience, all the way to the stage. Inside the truck was a complete studio facility and crew and several oversized gold-colored reels of 3M two-inch multitrack tape. The reels were oversized specifically for live recording, when the length of the song or performance is not precisely known, giving the engineer more leeway to just let it roll. Mics were carefully placed on the stage and throughout the venue, and the lines were split with the house system to take advantage of the Bottom Line's excellent acoustics.

The most difficult element to record was the percussion, since so much of it was improvised. Valerie was situated between her vibes and marimba, a table covered with shakers, log drums, and metallic percussion, and the two timpani. She also played piano on "Cry Baby Cry." Holding several sticks and mallets in each hand, it's no wonder she sometimes hit the mics, themselves becoming part of the percussion ensemble.

Watching all the preparations, I might have had second thoughts. I mean, we had only had one rehearsal with the full group. But I felt a strange calm and a kind of unreasonable confidence that all would go well. And I did *pray* before the show, just in case.

When we hit the stage that night, the first thing that struck me was the balance of male and female energies onstage. It may seem odd to say, but the give and take, push and pull of the two guys and the two women created a kind of floating sensation: the music was not particularly grounded—it was more like . . . levitating. I didn't feel like I was fronting as much as floating.

Adding to that sensation, forty or so sticks of incense were lit onstage, creating a blue cloud of smoke that hovered on the stage throughout the performance, capturing and giving movement to the beams of light.

Vin Scelsa's introduction was a beautiful and spontaneous twenty-minute speech (I was glad they were using those giant tape reels in the truck!). When he ended with, "Ladies and gentlemen, please welcome Richard *Barone*," I felt, maybe for the first time onstage, *relaxed*. We opened with "The Bulrushes," the first Bongos song Vin had played on the radio. Much slower than the original, the lyrics took on new meanings for me. When I sang, "Oh, Sally, let's look for baby Moses . . . ," I felt like I had found him.

The album was mixed during Fourth of July weekend, 1987, at Unique Recording Studios, in the middle of Times Square, more known for dance music than for what would soon be called chamber pop. The mix engineer was Jeff Lord-Alge, whose older brothers, Tom and Chris, were already two of the hottest engineers in the business. The ever-present budget restraints of an indie label were something I had nearly forgotten about after over four years with the majors. But after the weeklong mixes *of one song* that we had experienced at Compass Point, it was a relief to record the entire album in one evening, and then mix it in two days. After the overindulgence, discipline felt good.

We decided to mix the album as if we were in the venue, mixing the live performance. Choosing the best take of each song from the two shows, we assembled large reels with the edited twenty-four-track tapes, keeping the sequence exactly as it had been performed, and let it play as we mixed. The applause was left in after each song (faded at the ends, as each song was mixed), then a few seconds of leader tape between the songs. Going through the SSL console and using the onboard automation and compressor, we mixed one side each day. Yes, these were still the days of sides . . . we were cutting vinyl, as well as CDs and cassettes. This was to be my first release on CD, but in 1987, the CD was still a new format. Just as we were finishing side two, we could hear the Macy's Fourth of July fireworks rumbling in the East River. It was Independence Day.

The mastering was done by Greg Calbi at Sterling Sound, as had been nearly all my records, beginning with *Drums Along the Hudson*. The cover was photographed at sunset on the last block of Charles Lane next to the Hudson River—as I gazed toward Hoboken—by photographer William Duke, whose fashion work I had spotted in Italian *Vogue*. The image was inspired by Marlon Brando's character in Tennessee Williams's 1959 film, *The Fugitive Kind*, which was based on his play *Orpheus Descending*. Brando plays a drifter, a self-proclaimed party boy/entertainer who calls himself Snakeskin, wears a weathered, reptilian jacket, and strums an old acoustic guitar signed by, among others, Lead Belly. In one scene, Snakeskin describes a kind of bird that you can't see, that's transparent against the sky and that can't land because he has no feet. He spends his whole life on the wing and touches the earth only when he dies.

Like the party boy who was trying to make a change and do good, but somehow always ending up getting into trouble, I wanted to shed my own skin and grow a new one. If I had been "Paul McCartney from Hell," maybe now I would be "Iggy Pop from Heaven." I called my new album *Cool Blue Halo*.

To get through the performance and mixing, my nervousness and self-doubt were placed on hold as I forged ahead: business as usual. But suddenly, while walking the streets of New York, listening to the prerelease mastered cassette on my Sony Pro Walkman, I had second thoughts. I was devastated. *I hated it*!

I felt so *exposed* on the album. I sounded too *real* and so fucking fragile. "Nobody's going to like this," I thought to myself. "This is it. The critics are going to *kill* me."

But the label was excited about it. They had their publicist and radio promotion team fired up, going for major press and radio exposure. Well, as much as an indie label could generate, anyway, and more. I held my breath.

Taking a cue from my friends R.E.M., I was on the phone at the label's office in South Plainfield, New Jersey, calling and thanking every station that played a cut and doing impromptu radio interviews. *College Music Journal* (CMJ) made it a cover pick, and then the press started gushing in. The style and sound may have been difficult to categorize, but Anthony DeCurtis, reviewing the album in *Rolling Stone*, gave it a name: "Barone fashions a kind of rock chamber music," thus coining a new term. "Chamber pop" soon began appearing in reviews.

We were offered to tour as special guest with Suzanne Vega, who had been signed to A & M Records by Nancy Jeffries. (I was beginning to get used to the music industry's habit of playing musical chairs with executives, and since then, I have always acted accordingly. You never know who will end up where.) Suzanne was having a good measure of success with her song "Luka," and was musically a good match for us. Playing 2,000-seat theaters, we walked on the stage every night before Suzanne's set and, well, each show was magical. It got to a point where my voice was coming out so naturally and easily it sounded and felt to me like someone else was singing. Someone next to me. Once or twice, I looked to see if I could see him. I was listening more. It was completely effortless. That was the magic.

Cool Blue Halo got an unusual amount of radio play for a live album, and even though "Cry Baby Cry" was the track that we remixed, omitting the audience response, and serviced to radio, it seemed that different parts of the country chose different songs to play. In Seattle, for instance, we got heavy airplay on "The Man Who Sold the World," and so returned to that city's Backstage club several times. That's why, a few years later, I smiled when I heard Nirvana's *Unplugged* version of the tune, which was very close to our arrangement. Craig Overbay, our tireless road manager/sound mixer, played *Cool Blue Halo* constantly and toured with the Seattle boys right after us. So even if Kurt and company had missed it on their local radio, it was likely force-fed to them on their tour bus by Craig.

It was during this time that I met one of my closest friends, Nicholas Schaffner, author of *The Beatles Forever*, the best-selling fan's perspective of the Fab Four's Liverpool-to-legend saga, and its follow-up, *The British Invasion*. We became constant companions, and Nicholas was perhaps my biggest supporter during the *Cool Blue Halo* days. One night, after a return engagement at the Bottom Line, which was preceded by a full in-store concert performance at Tower Records in the Village, surrounded by the oversized posters I had visualized, I was scheduled for a late-night radio interview in Connecticut. Nicholas rode with me to the station in the back of a limo. On the way back into the city, late that night, we stopped to pick up the next day's edition of the *New York Times*. Gliding down Fifth Avenue in the hushed silence of the limo, it was as if the very air I had inhaled onstage that night had hallucinogenic powers. The city lights became like constellations shimmering all around us, as Nicholas read Robert Palmer's rave review of my show that night in the next day's paper. I felt like anything was possible again.

A trip to Germany followed, to perform at the first Berlin Independence Days Festival, where I fell in love with the still-divided city. Approached by several record labels interested in releasing *Cool Blue Halo* for the European market, we met and hit it off with Uwe Tessnow, signed with his Line Records, and planned a German tour to coincide with the release. Then a European deal with EMI Publishing. Now things were clicking. Gone were the green-outs on vodka-chlorophyll cocktails. Gone was the cocaine with Rémy Martin VSOP chasers. I was determined, like "Snakeskin," to stay on track and stay out of trouble, and I was feeling high enough from the success of this little album that took three days to make. One night in Berlin, late at night, I stood on my hotel room balcony, looked up, and saw one solitary star in the sky. And I made a wish.

By the time the album was licensed to New Rose Records in France— leading us to perform at the beautiful Rennes music festival, outside of Paris, with Bo Diddley and Lenny Kravitz—we had been touring behind *Cool Blue Halo* for well over a year. Not bad for a side project. Coming back to the States, though, there were more changes.

Passport Records, and its parent company, JEM, were going under. This would leave the album without a U.S. label (import copies would make it into the U.S. for many years to come.) But in the music industry, as in all businesses, one door closing often leads to another one opening. I was beginning to see how the companies, like their employees, also play a kind of musical chairs: moving, merging, or simply disappearing. It is the artists who remain. It's important to remember that.

On my mind, though, was something entirely different. Since working with Owen Epstein, the attorney who had so deftly maneuvered the piranha-infested major-label waters for us and sadly passed away suddenly in 1988 at age thirty-six, I had developed a keen interest in entertainment law. Wanting to have a firmer grip on the ever-changing lunar landscape of the music industry and realizing that more knowledge of the law would help me survive, as well as help me protect and develop other artists, I applied to Jesuit-run Fordham University to attend their School of Law, and was accepted.

Right on cue, the music industry came banging on my door. Only this time it was a telephone call. When the Panasonic speakerphone rang at 86 Perry Street, the call was picked up, as were 100 percent of my phone calls, by the answering machine. The voice of Marty Scott, former head of Passport Records, blasted through the apartment. He had been given his own label, Paradox, at MCA Records. Was I interested in making a new album for the label?

With the Fordham University literature and class descriptions spread out all over my bed, I interrupted the message being left, picked up the phone, and said simply, "Yes."

I knew I could take the chamber pop sound to a new level, and after checking out the latest crop of new bands in New York, I also wanted to rock again. With the decade ending, I wanted to make one last record with the *big* sound, one last goodbye to the '80s. Without realizing it at the time, I also wanted to record the orchestrated album the Bongos hadn't gotten around to making.

The solution was to combine a chamber ensemble and a rock band, and having them play together live in the studio at the same time to create a huge, orchestral rush of sound. For the players, I would start with the *Cool Blue Halo* team of Nick, Jane, and Valerie. To them I would add my friend Ivan Julian on electric guitar, Thaddeus Castanis (who I had recently seen in his group, World at a Glance) on bass, and Jay Dee Daugherty, of the Patti Smith Group, on drums. (The demos for the album featured the equally excellent drum-beating of Rick Solberg, who guested on the actual album.)

As I started work on the new album, Nicholas, with my enthusiastic encouragement, had begun writing his next book, a Pink Floyd biography. Conveniently, the group was on their first U.S. tour in years to promote their first album without bassist and founding member, Roger Waters. Through his publisher, Nicholas had arranged to meet and interview the three members still speaking to each other backstage, at a series of concerts. And when they came to the New York area, he invited me to join him. Sitting with the group and their families around a big dining table, just behind the stage at the Nassau Coliseum on Long Island, I was struck by their easy and relaxed mood. Like three successful British businessmen. While 18,000 fans waited in the stands, the group sat with Nicholas and me, having a very leisurely dinner just a few feet from the stage door.

The conversation, as had many of the best-known songs on their best-selling albums, centered around their original frontman, the famously LSD-ravaged Syd Barrett. They talked about how Syd had gone on television with pills crushed in his hair, so when he'd sweat from the heat of the lights, the toxic elixir would melt all over his face. "Remember when Syd taught *his cat* how to answer the phone?" drummer Nick Mason offered to Dave Gilmour, Barrett's friend and replacement in the group twenty years before. Dave looked wistfully into the airplane hangar–vast backstage loading area and added to keyboardist Rick Wright, "Yeah, then he tried to teach him how to make tea." Madcap laughs all around. Syd's condition became more and more erratic, onstage and off, to the point where he would play only one chord or note for an entire song or show.

Then one day, on their way to a gig in their van, the other members simply decided not to pick Syd up, and he never performed with them again. By the time Syd Barrett's permanent address changed to "the dark side of the Moon," Pink Floyd's image was no longer personality-driven. Their faces were rarely seen on the front of album covers, and onstage, the human members of the group were now dwarfed by the visual effects, inflatables, lights, and screen projections. "We didn't have a Roger Daltrey or Mick Jagger," Gilmour told Nicholas. At their peak, there was no longer a frontman.

Regardless, ego clashes ensued. As did lawsuits between Roger Waters and the rest of the group. Through Syd's sacrifice, the remaining members may have avoided the dangers of frontmandom, but not the pitfalls of power.

The three survivors stepped casually onstage and played a precision, immaculate set for their adoring, appreciative fans. When they played their frontman paean, "Comfortably Numb," I could think now only of Syd, a recluse at his mother's house in Cambridge, England. I thought about how close I had come to a similar fate, so close I could taste it, but realized in time that it was not my destiny. I felt a glorious rush of life as David Gilmour's brilliant, defining solo played through every nerve of my body.

Inspired, a bunch of new songs emerged in Brazil, during an extended trip to Rio De Janeiro and Manaus with Nicholas. To a constant soundtrack of Brazilian music, he and I explored rainforests or beaches by day and would return to our respective rooms to write our respective songs and manuscript at night. I had been reading Carl Jung's *Man and His Symbols*, especially his theories of the collective unconscious and primal man—how we all share the same archetypal dreams, even now. Jung's ideas pushed me to write the album almost entirely in symbols and dream images.

One trip down the Rio Negro to the mouth of the Amazon in a small boat inspired the song, "Native Tongue." I was just about to dip my hand into the milky water, when I noticed thousands of teeth just at the surface. Piranhas! My heart jumped and my hand jerked. Nonetheless, the song is about love and passion, not about being devoured by voraciously carnivorous freshwater fish. Back home, two other rivers, the East River and the Hudson, inspired another tune, "River to River," co-written with George Usher.

"Before You Were Born" came from the sudden realization that I was no longer always the youngest person in the room.

> I was out on the edge
> a cat on the ledge
> before you were born.

But it was "To the Pure . . . " that arrived most mysteriously. I just remembered turning the tape machine on late one winter night on Perry Street, and the next morning I played back the finished song.

> I woke up face down in the snow
> from a dream that started seven years ago
> I didn't know where I could be
> I can't believe I'd sold so many parts of me
>
> To the pure . . .
> From deep in the purest part of me.

Only later did I realize where the phrase came from. Hidden deep in my subconscious from my childhood Bible-reading must have been this passage from Titus 1:10–16: "To the pure all things are pure, but to those who are corrupted and do not believe, nothing is pure."

One day, shopping for a black long-sleeved T-shirt at the Gap store on Sixth Avenue and West 4th Street in the Village, I noticed that the friendly, handsome, and very young clerk was smiling at me. "Aren't you the guy in that video?"

"Yeah," I said and we chatted some more.

"Hey, could you take those off for a second?" he asked, gesturing to the mirrored aviator Ray Bans that I had been wearing in public almost constantly since the "blow-up" in the Bahamas.

"Sure . . . ," I stammered.

"Even better," he responded with a smile as I removed them, feeling exposed but somehow—suddenly—relieved. We exchanged phone numbers and talked that night.

We had lunch together a few days later. He was a student, just back from San Francisco, living in Hoboken, where he was born. When still in high school, he would see and hear me rehearse with the Bongos through the windows at Water Music recording studio across the courtyard from his family's apartment on Adams Street. A few nights after we had met for lunch, Valerie's marimba quartet was performing in a club in the West Village. "Wanna go?"

"Sure."

Later, he stayed over . . . for two weeks. His charm, creativity, joie de vivre, and love of music were irresistible, and throughout the following years, we would become inseparable.

Bernard was to have a profound influence on my musical taste—widening it with his own enthusiasm for artists I might have otherwise ignored, with his affinity for pop, dance and Latin rhythms, and with his openness as an avid listener and fan. I learned to experience my own music through his perspective. And visually my stage presentations were also colored by his style and fashion sense. Some of my most successful shows and major events were ones I would create at his suggestion. Most importantly, Bernard's support, encouragement, and companionship provided a kind of stability that had always eluded me—the "Help!" I needed to scale the wall I had hit. With the mirrored lenses off, I was beginning to see the view from just over the top of it.

I had wanted to work with Richard Gotterhrer again since "Numbers with Wings," and I also liked Don Dixon, who had recently produced the Smithereens. I had worked with Dixon on Marti Jones's first two A & M albums, for which I wrote songs and played, and I loved his strong style and personality. He later married Marti, a rare and wonderful artist in her own right. Dixon is an extremely hands-on producer and spends as much time in the live room, playing with the group and arranging, as he does in the control room. Instead of choosing one, I asked both Richard *and* Don to produce the new album—assigning specific songs to each.

Rehearsals took place at a studio located on and named after Charles Lane, the picturesque, cobblestone alleyway just a few blocks from my apartment, exactly where the cover of *Cool Blue Halo* had been shot. Downstairs from the studio was Richie Haven's place, and we could hear him practicing his passionate and uniquely aggressive acoustic guitar style each day when we'd arrive. What an inspiration. And he didn't even know.

Charles Lane had been in business since the '60s, and had been the rehearsal home of the heavy rock group, Mountain. We played through their seven-foot-tall monster Sunn amplifier stacks, the kind I would have drooled over in junior high. In fact, none of the equipment there was newer than 1973—but that was fine with me. Two beautiful white Mellotrons, the ambitious, analog tape-based keyboard that produced the gorgeous string and woodwind sounds heard on "Strawberry Fields Forever," "Nights in White Satin," and a multitude of art-rock classics, sat covered in a corner.

As we completed our rehearsals and entered the recording studio to begin laying tracks for *Primal Dream,* Charles Lane suddenly lost its lease of over twenty years and selling off all its vintage gear. They offered to sell me the previously unused, spare Mellotron.

The pristine instrument arrived at RPM Studios in its black padded vinyl road cover with rows and rows of buckles. A witty assistant engineer remarked that it looked like Michael Jackson's outfit on the cover of *Bad.* Taking its suit off, we found a message from its previous owner, Felix Pappalardi, Mountain's bassist/keyboardist/producer (who also produced Cream's *Disreali Gears* and was himself the victim of a violent, premature death, being shot by his wife/collaborator.) "Do Not

Even Fucking Touch!!!" was his ominous warning, written on dried yellowed masking tape with a black felt-tipped Sharpie.

We turned it on, its motor revved up, and it let out the sad, sweet sound of a violin section, like a ghost releasing a sigh. Or a genie finally escaping from his bottle, having been locked up in it for nearly two decades. It was spooky. "Haunted," the assistant engineer said. We put it to use immediately, adding the famous Mellotron flutes to "River to River," and the boys' choir to "Before You Were Born." On other songs, we used the cello samples, causing Jane Scarpantoni's brow to furrow. In the late '60s, British orchestral musicians were up in arms against the Mellotron and the BBC, fearing that these half-ton monsters would replace them entirely. There was no need for alarm, either from Jane or anyone else. The Mellotron was and is its own thing.

RPM's Neve recording console was a favorite of mine, as was its extensive microphone collection. Other than the Mellotron or E-Bow overdubs, most of the album was recorded live in the studio. The "layered" sound of *Primal Dream* is a natural one. The effect was created by the two drummer/percussionists Valerie and Jay Dee sharing the live room, Jane's cello and Nick's acoustic guitar in isolation booths, Ivan's overdriven electric in another isolation area, and my own live vocals and guitar in the main vocal booth—all playing together at the same time. Normally, these parts would be tracked separately, but the results would not have the spontaneity of a live performance, nor the necessary "bleeding" between tracks that produces a wall of sound.

The sessions were open, and a constant flow of guests came through to visit, often in the room while we cut tracks. Nicholas dropped by now and then, sometimes with Miss Jean, who was helping him transcribe the interviews for his Pink Floyd book. On my birthday, I was surprised by a male stripper dressed as Superman, who arrived to entertain me in the vocal booth while I sang "I Only Took What I Needed." I still don't know for sure who arranged for that, but, hey, thanks.

Techno wizard and Peter Gabriel cohort, Larry Fast, manually created an analog synth sequence for "Where the Truth Lies," and Fred Schneider of the B-52's laid down a cameo vocal appearance on "Mr. Used to Be." The title of that one came from an airline steward-ess who I had asked for some stationery to jot down lyrics on a flight from L.A. When she replied that they didn't have any, I countered that airlines always *used* to have stationery for passengers. She sassily retorted, "Honey, Mr. Used to Be is *dead* and *gone!*" Life is a musical: you must always be ready to break into a song!

The recording and mixing sessions were satisfying. There was now a difference in mixing an album primarily for CD (even though *Primal Dream* would also be issued on cassette and vinyl). We had entered the CD age and *very* soon those other formats would go the way of eight-track tapes, Edison wax cylinders, stone tablets, etc. In the past, when mixing primarily for vinyl, one had to exaggerate the effects a little. Tape or digital delay effects, and especially reverb, would often be eaten up by the vinyl surface noise. So we would always add a little extra. That's why, when you hear CDs of albums made pre-1987 or so, they sometimes sound a bit too "wet." Those mixes were intended to be heard on vinyl. Digital reproduction gives a much more "literal" reading of the mix when played back.

When mixing for a CD or any other digital format, we use the actual amount of effect that sounds right at the time of mixing. Paradoxically, when *recording* digitally, it is wise to add a little natural ambience or room sound when tracking, because the digital recording seems to eat up, or discard as unnecessary, much of the *natural* "air" in a recording (the way vinyl did with effects on playback). It seems to seek just the signal, ignoring the "space" as undesirable. The sound is often more "in your face" and, again, more "literal" than you would want. In my opinion, many current recordings are spoiled by this effect. For that reason, I make lavish use of room mics. Remember, when making a recording, we are creating an illusion. Use your ears and know the rules so you'll know when to ignore them.

The mastering, at the recommendation of Lou Reed during a lengthy and wonderful phone conversation about guitar tones, was by the legendary Bob Ludwig, and raised the end result to a new level for me. At one point, Bob even came downtown to my Perry Street apartment in the middle of a session uptown to hear how it sounded on my home system. That kind of dedication to one's work is what inspires me most.

By now I had learned that, when we finished making an album, the work had only begun. With the major label support of MCA, a tour was planned, opening for the Smithereens, booked by our shared agent.

Jay Dee Daugherty was committed to tour with the Church, so I recruited Tommy Goss, who had started out as the Bongos' roadie when he was barely legal, on drums. With the new big band, we hit the road, playing mostly universities and medium-sized venues and large clubs. Early on the tour, the Smithereens had a hit with their single, "A Girl Like You," which helped us sell out the remainder of the shows just after we left New York. We had to cancel one night as the 'Reens flew home to play *Saturday Night Live*: I was so happy for them, but wondered when it would be my turn.

Primal Dream was gaining ground on college radio, though, particularly with the track "River to River," Gottehrer's production tour de force on the album. With its sweeping, massed acoustic guitars, multi-tracked lead vocal (actually it wasn't intentional: when Richard heard my three vocal takes played back together, he liked the sound and used them *all*), cello, Mellotron, E-Bow, and layered harmonies, it had all my signature elements in one song. Yet for all its grandeur, there was resistance to release it as a single. My label informed me that "singles are never in minor keys. You can't have a hit song with minor chords." Reminded of all the minor-key opuses that crackled on the little transistor radio under my pillow as a kid, I rattled off a few examples. Still unconvinced, MCA wanted a video right away, and approved a budget of nearly one hundred thousand dollars.

I met with Australian director Michele Maher at the Cupping Room, in SoHo, and talked with her about Carl Jung, the shadowy, surrealistic paintings of Giorgio de Chirico, and the wrappings of Christo. All of these elements were used in the video for "River to River." It was a painting come to life.

The shoot was scheduled to coincide with our next tour stop in the New York area, which happened to be in Hoboken. A large vacant corner of a city block in a rough Jersey City neighborhood was rented for the evening, and Michele created the dreamscape that would be our stage. It seemed more like the set of a feature film, with its large crew and trucks and several camera operators (mostly women), massive catering, dressing room trailers, and extravagant lighting effects. A drive-in movie projector was used to project close-up images of me singing on the side of the building, the textured bricks and peeling paint of the wall showing through. Valerie had her timpani, Tommy used rented drums, and Jane, often wrapped Christo-like in black or white chiffon fabric, played a cheap prop cello. But I insisted on playing my *real* 1965 Rickenbacker, my "Bongo" guitar, which I had also posed with on the *Primal Dream* CD cover by Japanese artist Tak Kojima.

For the watery imagery of "River to River," two Jersey City fire trucks were standing by to hose us down as we performed the song. We used them for added effect, but they were not needed. Instead, the entire shoot took place in the middle of a torrential downpour. The rain was intense, pelting us with hard drops clearly visible in the video, lasting all night. Our clothing was drenched in minutes; the prop instruments were filled with water. As was the Rickenbacker, which was completely destroyed. I never played it again. A farewell to the '80s, indeed. It was just like when I left Florida all those years ago: I strangely didn't miss the guitar— or the decade.

The resulting video was a gorgeous visual accompaniment to the song, and MTV gave us a nice run with it. When they weren't playing it in its entirety, they were using bits of it in their logo collages, played between shows and other videos. Thank you, Michele, for those beautiful images. Radio play increased, giving us a sweet little radio hit. I wondered if some kid somewhere was listening to me under his pillow, living in my world for three minutes and forty seconds.

A short time later, R.E.M.'s minor-key, frontman anthem "Losing My Religion" ("That's me in the spot-light . . .") was released to become their biggest breakthrough hit, earning them a well-earned Grammy. So, enough about minor-key songs not being hit singles. There is no formula for a hit. The moment you try to impose one is the moment you close the door to the possibility.

The tour continued, up through New England. One night, after the concert, I went to my hotel room to read, as I seemed to do more and more now on the road. While I was lying in bed with a book, wearing my nerdy horn-rimmed glasses, I heard loud laughing and general racket in the hall outside my room. Looking through the little fish-eye peephole, I saw my band—distorted through the crystal looking-glass: Thaddeus in nothing but a pair of black bikini underwear, the girls, Nick, and some of the Smithereens cavorting, laughing, and rolling on the hallway floor. It was like viewing the Earth from far away, deep space—a perfect vantage point. My hand reflexively reached for the doorknob so I could go out there and join them. But I stopped. I didn't. Because for now, I was happy to be the observer.

Content that all was well, I turned off the lights, and went to sleep.

CHAPTER 9

CLOUDS OVER EDEN

KNOWING WHEN TO STOP

When everything seems to be going well, it seems life will invariably check in to remind you who's boss. As I'd struggled to build my world, lose my world, and regain my world, life had been going on around me. It's possible that while I was so caught up in becoming myself, I'd ignored the signs around me. The bigger picture I once glimpsed had shrunk down to the size of a peephole in a hotel room door. The distance between myself and those around me had grown distorted, as if viewed in a rearview mirror. I realized my isolation. Eventually, I looked around, saw the pain and plights of others, and came face to face with myself.

Back in New York, a recurring news item about a weeping icon inside a Greek Orthodox Church, in Astoria, Queens, had caught my eye. I visualized the scenes of mass religious hysteria portrayed in Fellini's films: the procession in *Nights of Cabiria* and the vignettes of wild Vatican fetishism that occur in nearly all his films. I imagined frenzied throngs of people, frantically pushing their way to the front of the line to glimpse the miracle—kneeling—for that one last, desperate shot at ... salvation. I imagined street vendors selling "weeping icon" mugs and mouse pads, and maybe even bottled tears from the icon herself.

I set aside a day to make the trek on the subway, descending once again into the depths of the city, to reemerge in its sanctified other self. When the N train rattled and roared into the station, the doors peeled open, and I got on board. Under the East River and into Queens, emerging from the underground tunnel into the light of day. Looking out the window at the rows of houses, just like the ones in the shaky film opening of *All in the Family*. Then looking back and seeing the still-breathtaking skyline of Manhattan from yet another new angle.

Arriving, I sensed, not the Roman Circus of bloodthirsty zeal I expected, but something resembling calm. There was a long, long line of people outside the church, lining the sidewalk for blocks, but it was orderly and quiet. I didn't see any vendors, except perhaps a souvlaki cart or two. And it was solemn. Even the smiles were solemn. I was completely surrounded by belief. I took my place in the line and took it all in. I listened for the conversations I could hear—the ones in English, at least—and it seemed the main topic was a question: not *if* she was really crying, but *why?*

"The war in the Persian Gulf." "AIDS." "The homeless." After a while, I could almost understand these muttered responses in Greek. I asked an elderly Greek woman why she thought the icon was crying. She looked me in the eye. "Everything," she answered.

When I finally got to see the icon for myself, the moment was almost too much to digest. The air inside the church was thick with incense, and the area lit only by candles. The small icon was painted and framed and she did appear to be crying. But it was the surrounding area that I wasn't prepared for. All around the icon, and shimmering along the entire altar area where it made its home, was gold jewelry and cash—gold Rolex watches, some embedded in the frame—all left as offerings by the pilgrims. What seemed like hundreds of thousands of dollars' worth. The juxtaposition was startling. I got a close look at the icon's eyes, and they *were* welled-up. I looked and tried to understand. Then I stepped out into the harsh afternoon light outside, as the line behind me continued endlessly.

The icon's mournful image still burned in my mind, visible when I closed my eyes, like a tattoo on the inside of my eyelids. I thought about it all the way home. When I got there, I picked up my acoustic guitar, plugged in my new Fostex four-track cassette recorder (a larger model that ran at twice the tape speed of my old X-15), set up a couple of mics, and started singing. I thought, oh, I'll fix and refine those lyrics later. But I never did. I never changed one word.

> For all the ladies standing in the line
> for all the people waiting for a sign
> you cry, you cry.
>
> And oh—how I need to believe
> But the devil deals with face cards up his sleeve—
> And oh—if your tears were a sign,
> I would put my life in your hands and stand in the line.

Of course, a few months later came the scandals: charges of insurance fraud at the church and excommunicated priests. But none of that changed my belief . . . and anyway I had the first song for my new album.

This time, instead of coming from symbols or concepts, the songs came out of the lives and loss around me. I didn't go looking for these songs. They came to me, insisting to be written. And while I often had thought of my songs as automatic writing, now even the conceptual thread seemed to have a life of its own. It was only later that I would see the connection.

What had started out as a nameless blip on the evening news had become a monumental quilt filled with names that covered the entire National Mall, in Washington, D.C. AIDS had already claimed several of the brightest lights in music, including some close to home. First, Klaus Nomi and the B-52's' Ricky Wilson, then the Patti Smith Group's Richard Sohl, whose delicate piano lattices had allowed Patti's punk poetry to transcend genre. In 1991, 37,106 people died of AIDS in the United States of America—more than ten times the number of lives lost on 9/11—just in that one year alone, and the worst years were yet to come. Still, little was said about it, except by "radical" groups like ACT UP, and even less was done about it.

I had known Nicholas was HIV positive. But a master of denial, I had never faced the inevitable. When he told me, "Richard, I've . . . joined the club," I couldn't speak. Only tears could follow those words. By the time I was finally able to muster up a barely audible, "We'll fight this together," the hopelessness in his eyes was all I could see. There were agonizing trips to Beth Israel Hospital on the East Side for tests and transfusions. One gorgeous spring afternoon, with the park outside the hospital as vibrant as those Technicolor days I remembered from childhood, I spotted in the corner of my eye the cornerstone of the building, inscribed with a phrase beginning, "Within these walls. . . ." Later that night, sitting with my guitar, the song appeared and became the cornerstone of the album.

I found myself feeling as if I was landing from a miraculous journey, yet not able to return home. Home had shifted. Home was now something that existed only inside myself. Only *there* was a kind of stability. Everything and everyone around me seemed to be in a state of flux. Nothing was lasting. Everything was temporary.

George Usher, listening while I sang "Within these Walls" to him a few nights later, contributed a poetic final verse. On another night, we discussed the prevalence of the word *verboten* in Germany. I had always found it interesting that in a country where, more than in others, it seems anything goes, the word "forbidden" seems to be posted everywhere. A book I was reading about tantric yoga further inspired the theme of "forbidden." "If you try to prune away your forbidden thoughts as you would branches of a tree, several new branches will appear." Also with George, the song "Clouds Over Eden" itself materialized, as the theme became clearer: Eden is here and now.

Miss Jean, more than a decade after the exuberance of our great train escape from Florida, had decided to move back to Tampa. I felt sad, thinking how rarely we had seen each other in the past few years. Yet I couldn't see how it could have been different.

> Ten years that seem
> A stranger's dream
> The subway map was misleading—
> She's leaving. . . .

One day while walking through the village, the cloud of songs circulating in my mind parted in an instant, as I heard a voice speaking, "Excuse me, aren't you *Richard Barone*?" When the voice introduced itself, I immediately knew Mark Johnson as the writer of one of my favorite songs recorded by the Roches, "Love Radiates Around." A magical composition; Mark definitely has the gift. One of us suggested we try collaborating on something and, within twenty-four hours, we were writing together—day and night, on the phone and in person—obsessively stringing images like beads on a rosary. One phrase came from a few words on a scrap of yellowed paper I spotted taped on the wall of his tiny Cornelia Street apartment, and became:

> . . . And in the eyes of God,
> where angels call our name,
> there is no right or wrong. . . .
> it all must be the same,
> the flaming streets of fame,
> the little yellow paper airplane. . . .

Another night, walking home in the snow together, a melody emerged—the notes themselves cascading like snowflakes, drifting slowly down to the ground, becoming, for me, a kind of joyful celebration of anonymity. And the freedom I once thought of as isolation.

> Nobody knows me
> Knows the way I feel
> Nobody sees that I'm
> Even here. . . .

The process is different with each of my writing partners. With Mark, it was around the clock. The phone would ring at 3:30 A.M.: "Richard! Richard! *The clock is clicking . . . !*" "*Keeping time!*" I'd answer, pen and bedside notepad always at the ready.

My home demos became more and more elaborate. With the Mellotron now at my fingertips (literally) in the Perry Street apartment, I could write out convincing string parts and other instrumental scoring as never before. I tapped out the beats on the little Boss Dr. Rhythm. And though the cassette multitrack was still lo-fi and primitive, the results were strangely satisfying. The question now was who would produce the actual album. Would this finally be my time to work with Tony Visconti?

A copy of *Cool Blue Halo* had gotten into the hands of an enigmatic, stylish British engineer/producer, Hugh Jones, who had a series of successes with groups like Echo and the Bunnymen and Modern English, and recently with Pale Saints and the Kitchens of Distinction. All were recordings I had admired, all with a decidedly British sensibility. He had been listening to my album and was interested in discussing working together. When Hugh contacted me to meet him for a drink at bar of the Mayflower Hotel on Central Park West, I had already decided he would be the one.

But I didn't let him know that. Yet.

The Mayflower itself had quite a rock 'n' roll reputation, as many of the groups passing through New York often stayed there—much like the Hyatt on Sunset in L.A., but without the scandals or *Spinal Tap*. I had met Dave Stewart and Annie Lennox there, when the Eurythmics had first come through town, along with numerous other groups. Hugh, a tall, lanky-limbed, denim-clad, chain-smoking bloke with a dangerously winning smile and short-cropped prematurely graying hair, greeted me with a drink in one hand and a cigarette in the other.

Immediately we began talking about recording and mixing techniques, and I was instantly aware that his passion matched mine. His politeness reminded me of Ken Thomas, the gracious engineer who had co-produced *Drums Along the Hudson*. Both had come up through the ranks of the English recording studio hierarchy—beginning as tea boys, graduating through the various levels of tape op, assistant engineer, finally engineer and producer. Along the way in that system, they learn the technology, as well as the delicate alchemy of keeping the artistic equilibrium of a recording session in balance. To my mind, what's missing in so many American engineers and producers is this kind of sensitivity. In the United States, engineering is often a kind of macho expression, all about the hardware. An overriding obsession with the equipment. Like boys trying to outbuild each other's hot rod in their garages. I'm not saying that's bad—it's fun—but the Brits have always seemed to keep it in balance. It took the Beatles years before they were even allowed into the control room at Abbey Road studios. That was for the gentlemen in lab coats.

Hugh and I started talking about the changes in recording over the past decade and how soon it was all going to be digital. It was inevitable, we both agreed, and nothing to fret over. But there were certain drawbacks. One was the emergence of numerous digital effects and racks with built-in, preset sounds that were being used on everyone's new albums. And with sampling, though the possibilities were endless, it seemed everyone was using the *same* samples and sounds.

That was when I realized how I wanted to approach recording my new album. Knowing that recording technology was changing so fast, I told Hugh I wanted to make one last album totally old school: no digital effects, no preset sounds or outside samples. I wanted to learn all the techniques that had gone down before and see how they worked. The sounds I had grown up with. In the past, when making an album, I would use whatever was at hand, no rules or restrictions. Now I wanted to adhere strictly to this plan of building the sound, brick by brick. I grandly thought of Picasso mastering his own form of realism and classical technique before he was able to truly render Cubism.

We would create all of our own effects, even down to chamber reverbs, such as those on early Beatles records. We could use plate reverb and tape delay, but no digital reverb (which is merely a *simulation* of the real thing). Of course, we would record twenty-four-track on two-inch analog tape. We would use vintage keyboards, including my Mellotron. (This didn't make Hugh too happy. As a young engineer in London, he had worked for the Mellotron company and recorded many of the sounds it held. The 'Tron sessions to record the original sounds apparently were tedious, rushed, and frustrating. "Oh, well," I smiled as he grimaced.) We would incorporate the ARP String Ensemble, an early string synthesizer with a pleasingly transparent sound also, by then, vintage. And besides Jane on cello, I wanted to use a full string quartet. If Hugh would agree to all that, then we were on.

Hugh was delighted with this manifesto, often referring to a specific Beatles session, and the dry, mono submix of the string quartet on "Eleanor Rigby" as templates. We left the Mayflower with a handshake and an embrace.

The next bit of business, after handing him a cassette of my ornate home demos for the album, was to decide on a studio. Hugh wanted to record in the U.K., which would have suited me just fine, but just like RCA, my current label wanted to keep me close to home, where they could keep an eye on me. After the blow-up in the Bahamas several years before, I was happy to record close enough to the real New York skyline that I wouldn't have to hallucinate it. Eventually we settled on recording at Mixolydian Studios in New Jersey, coming full-circle: I was beginning to see my new album as the end of a big cycle.

The rehearsals at Complete Music Services, with Bob Dylan in the next room, were smooth and joyful. A stylistic change was that this time not everyone would play on every song. Structured more like the Beatles' *White Album*, each song would dictate which instruments would be needed. So Hugh's first contribution was freeing me from the constraints of a *band*—and allowing this to truly be an album by a solo artist. I no longer felt like the frontman, it was now more like I was in the center, surrounded by these songs, each in their own musical vignette and setting.

With the musicians holed up in a townhouse in Morristown (another full circle), we carefully chose the time of day or night that each song's basic track was to be recorded. Before or after dinner was a big consideration, as the mood and performance would be affected. "Forbidden" was recorded late one night, after dinner and the pub, with the studio lights completely off. Hugh fed a slightly delayed click track to the drummer, Tommy, and a slightly less-delayed click to the bassist, Thaddeus. The rest of us were given the "actual" click, and when we all played together, it created the laid-back, in-the-pocket groove you hear on the finished album. On the recording console throughout the process was my copy of *The Beatles' Recording Sessions* by Mark Lewisohn, and any time we were stumped for a sound, we would refer to the book. One night, we drove all over New Jersey, looking for a British tea towel to lay over the snare drum, as Ringo had done at certain times. The result was well worth the scavenger hunt, and we used it on several songs.

Once the basic tracks for the bulk of the album were completed, the rhythm section went back to New York, while I stayed on with Hugh for the next several weeks to do the numerous overdubs of guitars, vocals, Mellotron, and the all-important miscellaneous experimentation. E. J. Rodriguez of the Lounge Lizards sat in on percussion.

Each night before dinner I would sneak into the studio's office and call Nicholas, whose condition had worsened. He was often in the hospital now. I'd play him bits of music we were working on over the phone, and I could sense his weakening smile through the long-distance connection.

With a limited work visa, Hugh's status in the U.S. was questionable, and as the months passed, I knew he was nervous about that. In one of my cruelest moments, I conspired with studio owner Don Sternecker to surprise Hugh on his birthday. A stripper was hired, asked to arrive dressed as a female United States Immigration Officer. We were in the middle of recording when she arrived, asking for Hugh by name, flashing some very legal-looking documents. His horrified dash to the basement dampened the sense of fun momentarily as I felt bad to have caused a near-heart attack. However, when the "officer" chased him downstairs, set up her boombox playing the Fine Young Cannibals' "She Drives Me Crazy," as she peeled off her badge and each article of her uniform to the music, Hugh's lethal smile returned (slightly) and his happy birthday was celebrated by all. Sorry, though, mate, I didn't mean to alarm you!

For the first time, it seemed I could be connected to people, places, and events, even when recording. The drug-fueled sense of isolation and paranoia I had felt making *Beat Hotel*, and at Compass Point had vanished, replaced with the sensation that making an album was part of something bigger.

With a refined knack for fine-tuning each sonic element, Hugh Jones was not only a superb engineer, he matched my enthusiasm for creating our own unique sounds and arrangements as we needed them. In his hands, "Within These Walls" had been transformed from a simple folky-pop song to a full-blown epic. On that track, we did not work with the rhythm section, but started instead with my acoustic guitar, which I played to an intricately programmed click track. Each section of the song was at a slightly different, accelerating tempo. Once we had that down and doubled, I played bass on the Hammond B-3's organ pedals, down on all fours as I played the pedals with my hands. For the bass drum, I played a large parade drum with a mallet. Inspired by the explosive "snare" sound on Simon and Garfunkel's "The Boxer," and after trying to hit nearly everything in the studio, I kicked a Fender Twin amp to rattle the spring reverb mechanism, and that gave us the backbeat sound we were looking for. Jane's memorable cello line was later augmented by the full string quartet.

The jangly pop sound of "Nobody Knows Me" was the result of listening repeatedly to the first album by the La's. With layers of Danelectro twelve- and six-string guitars, tea-toweled snare, and jaunty cello, Hugh would verbally punctuate the end of each playback by saying, "Ah . . . a shining pop moment!"

When my MCA labelmate Jill Sobule came to the studio to sing and play on our duet, "Waiting for the Train," she had just had back surgery and could not sit or stand to play a regular scale guitar. The solution was for her to play my ultralightweight Vagabond travel guitar, which she adopted as her main instrument, even today. She played the electric solo on the song lying flat on her back on the studio floor.

Our luckiest break at Mixolydian came when Borsalino, the famous Italian hat importer that occupied the massive basement (which ran the entire length and width of the building), had vacated, leaving us with a huge, empty, concrete space that became our echo chamber. We set up some amps, speakers, and microphones down there, and by adjusting the distance of the mics, we could create varying reverb environments. I played the long E-Bow solo at the end of "Miss Jean" down in the basement, the waves of reverb overlapping and hypnotizing me with endless sustain as I played alone in the dark underground chamber, as isolated as the song itself.

Every song on *Clouds Over Eden* has some sound or effect that was created especially for it. Much of the mixing was actually done while tracking, as instruments were balanced and bounced together as we recorded them. Most of the effects were also boldly printed to tape as we recorded, causing us to have to commit to the effects and balances we liked, as there was no reversing it later. One of my favorite effects on the album was the plate reverb (and occasionally chamber reverb) being sent through the rotating Leslie speakers attached to the

Hammond B-3. This was used most noticeably on the opening track, "Within These Walls."

For mixing, we moved to Sorcerer Sound near Chinatown in downtown Manhattan, which had the Neve console Hugh and I both preferred (the console at Mixolydian was an Amek, also one of my favorites, even now). There we added the string section that played the inspired arrangements written for us by Nicky Holland, who had recently collaborated and toured with Tears for Fears. The high vaulted ceiling in Studio B at Sorcerer was ideal for strings, which Hugh lovingly recorded, miked high above the musicians. It was a lifetime thrill to hear a living, breathing string quartet made up of some of New York's finest session players, play so solidly and with such passion on my songs. I phoned Nicholas and held the phone up to the speakers as they played.

Nicholas's Pink Floyd book, *Saucerful of Secrets,* had just been published. I was excited to see it, having lived through the process with him, having chased hundreds of red-marked, printed manuscript pages along the windy beach in San Juan, Puerto Rico, during a proofreading weekend, and having watched the galleys and graphics come together just as Nicholas had wanted. He was too ill to go out and celebrate, but I went to visit him at the beautiful mews home he had recently purchased in the secluded, gated Grove Court in the Village, where the great short-story writer O. Henry had written his famous short story, "The Last Leaf." Nicholas handed me my copy of his book, his eyes twinkling, though he was clearly frail, and I was again rendered speechless when he showed me the first page:

For Richard Barone: Friend, fan, musician, and star.

He smiled, signed, "What more can I say?" below the dedication, and I gave my best friend a big hug. Then we watched the Band's *The Last Waltz* on the large screen in his den. That night, I left Nicholas a cassette of my nearly completed album.

His working papers long expired, Hugh Jones finally had to go back to the U.K., leaving a few songs and the mastering unfinished. With Vince, I went back to the studio, to edit and complete "Law of the Jungle," which became a device to sum up the album, repeating key lines from all the previous songs in its long fadeout. Then we created the reprise of "Within These Walls," which closed the song cycle.

I had always loved the photography of Duane Michals, whose recent book, *Now Becoming Then*, was one of my favorites. Since the '50s and '60s, Duane's rich black-and-white pictures have had a particular look and style, which, like most of the greats, have allowed his work to cross the lines of art and commerce: his work hangs in museums, but he also shoots high fashion and commercial work. Duane is known for his photos taken in sequence, telling a story with his idiosyncratic and poetic handwritten text in the margin below each frame, and in the '80s, he created the cover for the Police album *Synchronicity*. I wanted him to shoot to cover for *Clouds Over Eden*.

Obtaining his home address, I wrote him a letter and sent a cassette of the music. I was thrilled when he called, agreeing to create the cover image. We shot a series of photos all over town—on subways, in restaurants, on sidewalks. In each image, a young hunk of an angel with silver wings was watching over me. We continued shooting the sequence, until one day, I was in Duane's townhouse kitchen, in the Gramercy Park neighborhood. I was standing, and, for a second, looked up at the recessed ceiling light. "That's it!" Duane shouted. "Hold that!" Then, he went into a small darkroom closet and photographed an image from the page of a book, a charcoal rendering of the New York skyline from the 1940s. He came back to the kitchen where I was still standing, and draped a black cloth over me; my head emerging from a hole cut in the center. Then he photographed me on the same frame. The unretouched image became the cover of *Clouds Over Eden*. It was all done in the camera by a master.

I came home from the studio late one night to hear a long message from Nicholas, sounding very calm. "Congratulations, Richard. You've made your best album yet. . . ." He went on to mention specific songs and moments. I had wanted so much for Nicholas to like this album; so having his approval made it already a success to me, even though it was months from being released. It was like being presented with several Grammys, a multiplatinum RIAA award, an Oscar, an Emmy and a Tony, all on the same day. At the root of any artist's motivation is the desire to be understood, especially by those they admire and love. Knowing Nicholas' honesty, it should have made me happy. But something in the tone of his voice on that message made me feel I would never see him again.

The next morning I got a phone call from his brother, telling me Nicholas had passed away during the night.

The tearful memorial service was held half a block from his new house. Streams of sunlight flooded in through the stained-glass windows of St. Luke's, on Hudson Street, that day, over Nicholas's friends and family, musicians, editors, and publishers. From high in the church's organ loft, with Jane Scarpantoni and her cello by my side and my acoustic guitar a shield across my heart, I sang John Lennon's "In My Life."

Time, and the music industry, waits for no one. There was no time to grieve. *Clouds Over Eden* was to be released first in Germany, and a trip to Hamburg was scheduled to finalize the cover and do advance press.

Back in the U.S.A., the Paradox label was dumped by MCA, leaving it without distribution, and requiring us to bring *Clouds* elsewhere. MESA/Bluemoon was a new entity being launched by Jim Snowdon, who had worked on the marketing of *Cool Blue Halo*. Distributed by Rhino/Warner Bros., and with an artistically eclectic roster, it seemed like a good place to be. So after some months of negotiating to gain control of the masters, the album was set for release there. In the meantime, I visited Florida, for the first time in a while.

As the doors of the plane opened, I felt the oppressive heat and humidity I had grown up with. But Tampa had changed. The quaint downtown was now completely gone, though a very few of the ornate buildings from the 1920s boom years still stood. Kress Department Store, the Tampa Theater. It was wonderful to see my parents, although my father seemed weaker. We went to the beach again, like old times, and visited with my sister and her husband and sons, and my brother, his wife and kids. His young son, Jason, sang and played "Miss Jean" perfectly for me on his acoustic guitar, which gave me an unexpected surge of love and pride.

I felt, maybe for the first time, the reality of what I had chosen to do with my own life. I had forfeited any chance of what was considered a traditional life. Instead of children, I had albums. Like children, each was different and each had a story to tell. Each was imbued with my DNA, my blood. But I couldn't fool myself that it was the same thing. Each was merely a crystallization of a moment, ephemeral. As much as I thought of my work as alive and human, it was not, and all I had given—on all those stages and in all those studios, the sweat and the sacrifice—was for something I couldn't quite understand. Yet I didn't—and couldn't—regret anything. I had sold my soul to the angels long ago.

The same night I got back home to Perry Street, I got a phone call from my brother. "You'd better get back down here." It was my father, suddenly diagnosed with lung cancer. I got back on a plane and went straight to the hospital, where I got to say good-bye.

Again, there was no time to grieve. Shows were booked and none were cancelled. I thought of a faded black-and-white picture of my father as a young man, playing percussion in a Latin big band in Tampa in the 1940s, looking happy and handsome. That was the image I held in my mind before each show, and did each performance for him.

We booked twelve consecutive "Guitar and Cello" shows at a new club called Fez in the Village, deep in the basement of the Time Café restaurant, where the rumbling subway train added sound effects on cue. The entire run was a sellout, and all the shows were recorded for future release. With ticketholders filed around the block, standing in line to hear me sing the songs of *Clouds Over Eden*, now *I* was the weeping icon.

Interview magazine did a feature on the series with the headline "Between Heaven and Cello." Eventually we released the simple DAT recordings of the shows in Germany, and used the headline as the CD title. Cellists of all stripes, most too young to remember ELO, would come up to me after performances, thanking me for bringing the cello into the rock mainstream. They were suddenly in demand.

Another tour of Europe, beginning in Hamburg, was rapidly booked to coincide with the release of the new, live CD. The day before we were to leave, I took a fall from atop the custom-made library ladder I used to reach the vinyl albums stored along the shelves built near the four-teen-foot ceiling at Perry Street. Like a slapstick comedy, the ladder fell in slow motion, diagonally across the room, and I came crashing down on my right hip. With luggage and instruments packed and waiting by the door, I couldn't move. Slowly, I broke through the pain and stood up. The tour went on as planned: the next morning Vince arrived in the car that took us to Kennedy Airport. And just like on the first West Coast Bongos tour, a decade earlier, I didn't have a leg to stand on. Still, I pushed myself just as hard as ever, though every step seemed impossible. I had always remembered reading about the Hamburg club owners and audiences yelling, *"Mach Shau*! Make Show!"* to the Beatles, and in their tradition, I always wanted to give the Germans what they wanted. No matter how much it hurt.

Needing more room, it was time to move into a larger apartment. Still in the Village, just a block and a half from its predecessor, soon it, too, was filled with towers of stacked boxes until there would be enough time to unpack. The *New York Times* came to photograph me for an article on the new album, and the fire escape of the turn-of-the-century building provided the only space for the photographer to shoot. It was a cold February morning, and I wore a handwoven raw-silk scarf that Nicholas had bought for me on my birthday. I left on tour later that same day.

With *Clouds Over Eden* released in the States, the "Guitar and Cello" shows headed west for a headlining tour of theaters and clubs. As a result of our work together, Jane had become busy with other session work and touring. So a new cellist, Lisa Haney, joined me this time, becoming my primary accompanist for the next several years and bringing her own sound, intensity, and humor to the stage. The grunge era was now in full swing, and we were often paired with these groups. Lisa and I, aware that our audiences' ears (especially in Seattle and Portland) were accustomed to the dense, grunge sound, would exaggerate our own dynamics (quieter sections became nearly inaudible, and on loud parts our acoustic instruments took a pounding). Lisa's long blonde hair whipped back in forth in time, while my own head and body moved in sync with hers. I would drop to my knees and face her while she played the solo on "Flew a Falcon," our eyes locked as my body followed the movement of her bow. There was enough sexual energy onstage that a record company rep pulled me aside at the Gavin radio convention in San Francisco, and said, "Man, whatever you do, don't lose the blonde!"

The songs from the new album, though intricately arranged in the studio with fuller instrumentation, lent themselves easily to the stripped-down treatment. I felt freer than ever onstage to take the songs and to be taken by the songs. But as far as recording another album, I felt I couldn't do it all again right away. I began to associate the recording studio with the kind of loss I experienced while making *Clouds*, and the album-tour-album-tour routine was beginning to feel a bit been-there-done-that-been-there-done-that.

Yet it was all I really knew.

Staring at the black sky out the window of the Airbus A300 with no indication as to where we were, I couldn't tell where I was headed. I had become like the little bird that Snakeskin talked about in *The Fugitive Kind*, invisible against the blue sky. Like I had been on the wing my whole life, with no legs to land. But I wasn't sure if I was ready yet to touch the earth and die.

CHAPTER 10

MUSICAL PROMISCUITY

HOW TO PLAY THE FIELD, AND WHY

The flight home was a reentry into the earth's atmosphere. I was coming down for a landing. Leaning over a passenger's shoulder in the business class cabin on the long flight from LAX, I saw the *New York Times* article about me and the photo on the fire escape. The woman reading looked up, startled, as she sensed me hovering over her shoulder, then recognized me from the photograph and asked me to sign her newspaper.

But even as I signed my name, there was something else on my mind. I wanted so much to break out of the claustrophobic holding pattern that had been my life for the past decade, orbiting over and over like a long lost stray satellite. This had been on my mind for the entire tour, even on the flight out west with Lisa, as we sat perfecting the set list for the show.

When I arrived back home, I finally started to unpack the boxes. And I started breathing, maybe for the first time. Walking the little streets of my West Village neighborhood on hot summer days with my shirt off, I wasn't looking for anything or anyone, but I was open to everything.

New collaborators found me. The first was Gary Lucas, the guitar genius who had come out of Captain Beefheart's Magic Band. He invited me to sing, co-write, and play my Mellotron with his group, Gods and Monsters, at downtown clubs like the Knitting Factory and the Cooler, a converted slaughterhouse in the newly up-and-coming

Meat Packing District. Jeff Buckley, who had been the previous lead vocalist of Gary's group, had just signed to Columbia Records, jumping onto the lopsided, out-of-control merry-go-round I had just hopped off.

When I was introduced to Jeff at the tiny club Sin-é on St. Mark's Place, he was standing at the bar, listening to the rough mixes for his album, *Grace*, on a Walkman. The moment we met, he boyishly took his headphones off himself and put them on me—excited for me to listen. Others had similarly made me listen to their music, but his joy and enthusiasm gave me the feeling that it was less about ego and more about his own genuine disbelief at how good he sounded. It was almost as if he needed me to hear it, too, to make it real. I gave him a hug, recalling for a moment his famous singer-songwriter father Tim, who had died of a drug overdose at the age of just twenty-eight, frustrated at a music industry that he felt had stifled his creativity. God, how I wished better for his son. I watched Jeff's star rise with my fingers crossed.

A few years later, I was standing at a corner waiting to cross Sixth Avenue on the way to a recording session, when someone I knew yelled out a taxi window to me that Jeff had drowned in Memphis, just as his band was arriving to begin work on his second album. For a second, the sound of the traffic stopped. Suspicions of suicide were quickly ruled out, but still I wondered about the timing and why he was wearing heavy boots to swim. It must have become difficult, whether he was aware of it or not—amidst all the sudden adulation and attention, while carrying around the weight of that heavy legacy and promise— to be Jeff Buckley.

Besides Gods and Monsters, I began performing with a ragtag consortium of downtown scenesters: the Loser's Lounge. Each show was a campy tribute to many of my favorites (Harry Nilsson, Paul McCartney, Roxy Music, Paul Williams, Donovan) with various singers—well-known and unknown—taking the stage to sing a song. A full-scale, live-band karaoke, the costumes and kitchiness (at the tribute to Nilsson, I sang "Everybody's Talking," dressed as hustler Joe

Buck, the *Midnight Cowboy*; at the Roxy Music tribute I sang "In Every Dream Home a Heartache" with an inflatable doll) helped me find the fun in performing again, and I produced three live CDs based on these shows. I hadn't realized how much I had missed "the scene"—the downtown scene particular to New York—that had drawn me here in the first place. My neighborhood. Oh, man, how I embraced it now.

I became a mad scientist, mixing people and projects furiously. Like Sir Isaac Newton working secretly in his lab, I looked for more and more combinations of human chemistries, and more and more different musical spheres to jump into. As photographer Mick Rock, in his book *Blood and Glitter*, discusses "the alchemy of image-making" and "the alchemical power of camera and film," I was finding the same mysteries and powers in performance and recording.

Though not quite a whore, I became musically promiscuous. I wanted in on *everything*. All the action. Every project. I felt I had to make up for all the time I had lost in the self-imposed exile of being strictly "a recording artist." I felt comfortable slipping into any musical setting: hosting a tribute to the Rat Pack (I sang Sinatra's "It Was a Very Good Year" with references to our shared Hoboken roots); then a live re-creation of the '60s pop television program, *Hullabaloo*; performing in a tribute to the delicate and doomed singer-songwriter Nick Drake at St. Ann's Church in Brooklyn Heights, where I sang, appropriately, his "Cello Song." And, of course, co-writing.

Returning her favor of sitting in on *Clouds*, I flew down to Nashville and sang on some tracks for Jill Sobule's Atlantic Records debut. That led to us writing numerous songs that found their way onto several hit television shows, including *The West Wing*. With the B-52's' consummate frontman, Fred Schneider, I also wrote several songs—including some on his solo album *Just Fred*—in a collaboration that continues to this day.

As I had learned in high school, the main ingredients for collaborating were still trust and love. Now I understood their power more than ever: without *trust*, you can't be totally free with your collaborator. For instance, when writing lyrics, to blurt out the line that may reveal too much about yourself. Without *love*, you have no interest in bringing out the best in your collaborator. Each should bring out the best in the other. Love + Trust. If I ever get a tattoo, it would be of those two words.

To get there, you have to enter a collaboration with an attitude of gratitude. It doesn't matter who you are. When Quincy Jones produced the session for the mega-superstar anthem "We Are the World" in 1985, he famously hung a sign outside the studio: "Check Your Egos at the Door." This applies to any true collaboration. If you cannot give yourself completely to the process, the process cannot give itself completely to you.

For me, collaborating serves several purposes. *Energy*: creative energy is enhanced when there are two or more people working and reacting together in trust and love. *Focus*: when writing with a partner, the natural process includes constant, spontaneous editing of one another, sharpening for clarity and checking for (unintentional) clichés. *Chops*: collaborating has the side effect of improving your writing and playing skills. The ante is upped with each great line or melodic idea from your partner. *Detachment*: Because it's not all *you*, collaborating allows an added detachment to your work, giving the freedom to step back and see the piece as a whole. *Fun*: Yeah, it's more fun than doing it alone.

Surely, there are many more examples, but those are my top five. The goal is always alchemical: to blend just the right portions of each other's personalities, talents, and styles to create something new and valuable, i.e., something that would not have existed without these particular collaborators coming together. Like your parents did when they created you.

Off the album/tour circuit, I now felt I could do anything. I parted ways with Vince, my respected manager of the past ten years, and the talented musicians I had been working with. I was now completely on my own. This time, I didn't feel as if I was stepping into the abyss. But it *was* a bit of a freefall.

For an artist, self-management is a near impossibility. Unless you are schizophrenic, it is difficult to have the kind of impassioned detachment, but undying faith, that a good manager possesses. (Think Brian Epstein, who continued to pitch the Beatles to every label in Britain, even after nearly every one had turned them down.) Not to mention the mentality necessary to maintain heightened right brain–left brain functions all the time. Managing is a twenty-four-seven job, leaving little time for creating music. Finally, the complementary roles of artist and manager are opposite. I did my best to keep my business on track. Without a representative it was frankly a mess.

But it didn't matter. This was my *Yes* period (not the group, thank God) and I was hungry to participate, perform, interact, and share. After participating in a songwriter's discussion circle at the Bottom Line (*In Their Own Words*), I was asked to host a variation there. I invited Jules Shear to co-host the series we called *Writers in the Round*, a more intimate, less-scripted format than the one in which I had just participated, that ran monthly for year. Our guests included established artists like Rosanne Cash, alongside up-and-comers like Ron Sexsmith and Joe Henry. We would gather to rehearse at my apartment a few blocks from the venue to learn each other's songs. Onstage, the spirit was all about collaboration, singing and playing backup for each other, each of us in awe of the magic of songwriting, trying to figure out the writing process for ourselves and sharing those thoughts and new material with each other and the audience. I wrote a new song for each show and found new writing partners in many of the guests. I learned so much from all of them.

Still, I rarely stepped foot in a studio to record my own material. The shroud of *Clouds* hung over me. On that album, themes I had avoided singing about before, because I was afraid they might come true, did. Of course, they already had. It wasn't as if I had *conjured them up*, but I was afraid of what nightmares I might create if I went into the studio now.

So I continued focusing almost entirely on live performance, and the occasional sitting-in with others. Always with an eye and ear out for artists I might want to produce. Because, even through all the frontman mania, I still saw myself as a producer: I truly enjoy bringing other artists' visions to life *as much as my own.*

In 1996, Hoboken friend and journalist Dawn Eden was on assignment from CompuServe's Internet music portal to interview Tiny Tim. This was to take place by telephone to a hotel room in Las Vegas where Tiny was performing and, knowing my history with the still-touring, ukulele-toting troubadour, Dawn suggested she do the interview from my apartment. It had been eleven years since I had bumped into him in the movie theater, and nearly two decades since we had first met. Yet his unlikely influence remained, as evidenced by the fact that Dawn and I were sitting cross-legged on the leopard-pattern-carpeted floor of an apartment in the heart of the very same West Village neighborhood Tiny had so lovingly described to me, as if he had known then that this was where I would make my home.

After Dawn had asked all her questions, she handed me the phone, and Tiny and I caught up like old friends. He remembered the date we met, and that it had been a leap year. This time, I thanked him for being an inspiration to me and for encouraging me to come to New York. "Mr. Barone, do you still have the recordings we made?" he asked, near the end of our conversation. "Of course, Tiny." "I'd like for you to put them out," he said, modulating his voice to a softer tone. "They're . . . *special*." Then he told me how to contact his new wife, Miss Sue, to take care of the formalities. I promised I would, sensing an unexpected urgency in his request. It was just a few months later that I heard on the news that Tiny had passed away, having suffered a heart attack onstage, while performing "Tip-Toe Thru the Tulips" for the very last time.

The music industry was changing rapidly. It was becoming as unstable as the asteroid in *The Empire Strikes Back*, where Han Solo, Princess Leia, and Chewbacca took refuge, only to find they had landed in the mouth of a serpent. Though the industry had always been in flux, the indulgences of the '80s and early '90s had taken a toll. Too many multimillion-dollar budgets, and superstar advances that never recouped, had burned the major labels badly—resulting in a head-spinning succession of roster-cuts, employee cutbacks, and mergers that reduced the number of majors again and again. I had seen this first-hand: at least five of the labels that had released my music, Fetish, Passport, Paradox, RCA, and now MESA/Bluemoon, had either bitten the dust completely or had been swallowed by another company. In the years to come, corporate mergers would further reduce the number of major labels.

Maybe the accumulated bad karma of decades of taking advantage of artists had come home to roost. In general, traditional recording contracts have always been notoriously disputed by artists, even those lucky enough to receive 10 to 12 percent of the net sale of their "own" recordings, which were really forever owned by the label. Encouraged to spend freely on studio time, touring, and lifestyle, those expenses were then recouped by the label before any royalties were paid to the artist who, as a result, may never have seen a dime. By the late '90s, artists would begin demanding better deals.

It's important to remember, when a major label contract is dangled, carrotlike, a few inches from your nose, that labels come and go, while *real,* committed artists remain. A good reason to heed the cliché, "Be true to yourself": You may be fooled, and remodel yourself to a label's specifications, only to have the label's interest—or the label itself— evaporate like a mirage on a hot desert highway, just before your tour bus breaks down in the middle of nowhere.

Perhaps the main reason for their failure has existed since the first hit records were made—on wax or wire or acetate—but is more true now than ever: the music industry is forever chasing its own tail. If an act on one label is successful, all the other labels try desperately to find a similar artist in an attempt to duplicate that success. The industry obviously sees music in terms of trends to be jumped on, seized, and copied. The problem is, by the time they have found their own versions of Norah Jones or Nirvana (artists who created *themselves* and became successful for their *individualism*), the trend is over. This, after spending million of dollars to market their "discoveries."

The brilliant label founders who built the music industry—creative, colorful, intuitive geniuses, like Seymour Stein of Sire Records, Ahmet Ertegan of Atlantic, Chris Blackwell of Island—were music *fans.* But, by the late '90s, they had become largely overshadowed by faceless conglomerates that had little to do with music, and even less to do with nurturing talent. Since the power shifted, the music industry has slipped more and more. The industry that once created trends was now *only* chasing them.

For me, creative survival came in the form of redefining: instead of thinking of *record companies* as "the industry," I began to think of it in terms of relationships—with passionate collaborators, musicians, agents, publishers, and *fans*—at its heart. Record companies had become, for the most part, mere distributors for artists, instead of creative partners. Not just for me, but for many. The do-it-yourself movement had foreshadowed a mentality that touched all levels of music creation and marketing. Sadly missed, though, is the screening process that occurred when musically astute people ran the record labels and signed the real, groundbreaking acts in the first place.

As digital technologies flourished, the threat of music downloading was hovering on the horizon, and the reactionary music industry was gearing up for a fight; just as it did when "home taping was killing music," a warning on records and in ads in the early '80s for a trend that instead invigorated record sales. The cassette-as-skull-and-crossbones logo you may find on a few artifacts from that time remains a comical reminder. The music industry spent more time, money, and creative energy fighting these imagined enemies than it did searching for and developing new, valid, long-lasting talent and putting exciting new technologies to good use.

By now, the digital revolution had succeeded. Bondi-blue Apple iMacs popped up on desktops everywhere, and music files were zipping around the globe and being shared—royalty-free—like flu germs from a sneeze. This Wild West, free-for-all file-sharing scared the record industry and had most musicians up in arms. Except, at least, one.

In 1997, one of the most-likely-to-succeed early Web sites selling CDs was Music Boulevard. Primarily an online retailer, like Amazon.com, it had an attractive interface that gave the sensation of browsing in a record store. In conjunction with their in-house record label, N2K, they had big plans to sell songs as downloads at ninety-nine cents a song.

I was one of the first artists included in their small catalog of downloadable music, and one of the few artists who agreed with the concept at all, which is why I was asked to become spokesman and advocate on behalf of legal music downloads. I appeared on the *Wall Street Journal Report* and other television and print media, extolling the virtues of music on demand. I was sincere and convinced it would catch on. I knew it was still too early then, but with the right set of wings, it would fly. No other musician I spoke with about it at the time agreed with me. Customers were few. It was a slow and painful process, learning to think out of the CD jewel box.

So for all of the inventiveness, most of the first crop of online music sellers failed. It would take forward-thinking Apple Computer—and a few more years of trial and error—to create a business model that would encompass hardware, software, and content worth getting excited about with iTunes and iPods, to finally change—and save—the music industry. Until the next revolution.

Checking the messages on my answering machine, I heard a startlingly low, gravelly voice, like a slightly more whiskey-tinged version of the octopus villain, Ursula, from Disney's *The Little Mermaid*, saying, "I-want-your-voice!" It was David Johansen. The New York Doll, who had morphed into Buster Poindexter and hit gold with "Hot Hot Hot." He was making a new album. Just as he had instigated androgynous Glam in the '70s with the Dolls and the Lounge revival in the '80s with his Buster persona, David was characteristically slightly ahead of the "La Vida Loca" trend with this album of authentic Latin grooves and styles, meshed with his uniquely twisted lyric sensibility. Would I sing on the album with him? "Yes! Send me the songs!" Although he didn't know it, these sessions brought me out from the under the cloud of *Clouds*, zapping me back into having fun in the studio again, as a *singer*. And it was an education in the genres I would put to the test a few years later, when I would produce and direct multitalented Mexican singer/actor Rubén Flores in *The Latin American Songbook*. The experience of making *Buster's Spanish Rocketship* was what making music is all about, and nobody throws a better party. Thank you, David.

Now, finally feeling embedded in New York City, I had found my special places around town to write. The medieval Cloisters, all the way uptown, on West 190th Street; the green of Rockefeller Park, all the way downtown, overlooking the Statue of Liberty; the Greek and Roman wing of the Metropolitan Museum of Art; and especially between the twin towers of the World Trade Center. On sunny days, I'd lie on my back on one of the benches around the circular fountain in the courtyard, the buzzing tourists blurring into the background as I'd look up to the sky, along the right angles of the two mythological giants. I imagined my thoughts and lyrics zooming to their tops, like elevators, breaking through the rooftops and dispersing like multicolored confetti snowflakes all over the city.

The end of the '90s also brought me two theatrical projects that I hadn't consciously realized how much I was looking for. Both were more or less continuous musical experiences, both roughly two hours long, performed with an intermission, and both had multiple singers and large casts. The similarities ended there.

Playwright Paul Scott Goodman had written a clever musical adaptation of Jay McInerney's best-selling first novel of '80s decadence, *Bright Lights, Big City*, and asked me to orchestrate and be musical director. It would be tremendously time-consuming to create the 900-page score and would even involve workshopping the play at Dartmouth College in Hanover, New Hampshire, for the summer. But when the shaggy-haired Goodman came over to my apartment to sing through the show for me on his Ovation twelve-string acoustic guitar, I was hooked. Through his thick Scottish accent and Yiddish humor, his songs, "I Like Drugs," "Coma Baby," and the others, along with McInerney's story, painted a picture of the previous decade that closely mirrored my own experiences. A little too closely sometimes. Of course I said yes.

The New York Theater Workshop in the East Village was staging the play, to be directed by Michael Greif, still riding high from his recent Broadway smash, also developed at NYTW, *Rent*. *Bright Lights* was their first big musical production since *Rent*, and the expectation that lightning would strike twice in the same place hung over the project with all the weight of a flickering marquee on the Great White Way. I was the odd man out: the only person onboard who had not been on *Rent*'s creative team.

For months I sat scoring arrangements for Paul's music, using as a guide the rough recording I made as he sang through the songs in my apartment. On my multitrack cassette deck, I added bass, electric guitar, keyboard, drumbeats, and strings played on my Mellotron. As rehearsals drew near, I gathered musicians stolen largely from the

Loser's Lounge band, including its leader, Joe McGinty, on piano, who meticulously transcribed and assembled the massive score and would conduct the band onstage, situated on a stylized scaffolding high above the action. I recruited Lisa Haney on cello, and old friend Ivan Julian on electric guitar.

Actor Patrick Wilson, also from Tampa, who would later star on Broadway in *The Full Monty,* on television in *Angels in America,* and in the film version of *The Phantom of the Opera,* among other high-profile roles, was set for the lead as Jamie. The rehearsals with the cast were more than I bargained for, as, under Greif's sometimes heavy-handed direction, endless, miniscule cuts and changes were made to the music to fit the dramatic movement, cutting some of my favorite passages. This humbling process was tedious, but the discipline was priceless training. What became evident to me, more than ever was that in theater, each note and beat must have meaning and purpose. I had always known this in a general sense. But now I was experiencing first-hand how music and action serve each other.

We all knew that, like the novel, it is a bold play that may offend some people. Its opening scene, for example, was of snorting cocaine on the floor of the bathroom at the Limelight, the very place I where had hung out with Andy Warhol and Run DMC and all the others. I couldn't help thinking it was still a bit soon to look back at the decade this way and to see ourselves under such a bright light on such a big stage. Plus, Michael Greif's rainbow cast was not in keeping with McKinerney's original concept of white upper-middle-class kids being reckless and cavalier with their fortunate lives—changing the dynamic of the story.

The anticipation for opening night had all our hearts pounding and breaths held. Unfortunately it was nothing like the pounding the show took from the press, including brutal coverage in *Time* magazine. The music, though, got off easy and was praised by the *New York Times* as being "some of the most appealing new theater music in town" in a review that panned nearly every other aspect. I exhaled. Though it continued its run for several more weeks, the show, for the time being, was doomed. It will come around again, though, and probably succeed—when the memory of the '80s has receded far enough into the past that we can no longer believe it really happened.

While I was arriving at the New York Theater Workshop before 9:00 A.M. every morning for rehearsal (the theater world, unlike the music world, gets up early), another project was brewing just up the block on West 4th Street.

I was coming off stage from a performance at the Bottom Line one night, when the club's super-smart, silver-haired, omnipresent co-owner, Allan Pepper, pulled me aside and brought me over to the bar, his hand on my shoulder. The question he asked came completely from out of the blue. "Richard," he said slowly in his familiar soft voice and signature New York accent. "If we were to stage Handel's *Messiah* here at Christmastime, how would we do it?"

"Here? In the club?" I asked.

He nodded, holding my gaze. Silence.

"Give me twenty-four hours and I'll tell you," was my reply.

I had a worn, vinyl boxed set of the venerable Baroque masterpiece at home and, firing up the old turntable, put it on. Through the distraction of the superb but densely overenunciated operatic voices, I could hear pop tunes, blues, funk, folky melodies. The arias all seemed to be strung together like bejeweled charms on a gold bracelet of gorgeous choruses. It occurred to me to have each aria done in a completely different musical genre, each representing the music drifting or blasting through the clubs and streets of Greenwich Village. Handel's hallowed arrangements would be rewritten in these styles, and each sung by a star in that genre in their own way. For the choruses, a more or less traditional—but suitably bohemian—choir would be assembled to perform them more or less traditionally. That was the thread. And to tell the story—of prophecy, arrival, and rejection, and ultimate redemption—a narrator, reciting the normally sung Old and New Testament passages in Handel's original.

I furiously made some notes and some phone calls, notably to friend and Messiah aficionado Jeanne Stahlman. The next day I called Allan and told him I had it, and I told him what it was. What did he think? He already had a title, *The Downtown Messiah*. So while still working on *Bright Lights Big City* down the block, we started putting together the creative team and cast for the massive undertaking of staging the world's most famous Baroque oratorio—in a rock club.

Peter Kiesewalter (later of the East Village Opera Company) did the arrangements and conducted the band and string quartet, and Margaret Dorn led the choir, which included the members of her downtown vocal group, the Accidentals. Vin Scelsa provided the narration; his familiar voice comforting and passionate. Later, DJ Meg Griffin joined the cast, adding her own personality to the narrative.

The show ran for six consecutive Decembers, until the Bottom Line lost its lease in 2003 after thirty years to landlord, NYU. It featured soloists like my friend David Johansen, as well as Jane Siberry, Maggie and Terre Roche, Vernon Reid, Dan Bern, Don Byron, Randy Brecker, Howlin' Wolf's legendary guitarist, Hubert Sumlin, and many others. (Always the prankster, Johansen once tried to psych me out at one of the performances, after watching me struggle with my aria's stratospheric high notes at rehearsal. "It's not too late to lower the key," he whispered to me with an ear-to-ear grin, just as I was opening my mouth to sing.) Each performed their aria in a unique arrangement that allowed their personalities to shine through. Ann Powers, in the *New York Times*, wrote: "Mr. Barone has stated the desire to keep Handel's sacred cow alive through respectful modernization. He has done so less by forcing in cutting-edge sounds than by letting his vibrant cast show off its humanity through this treasured work." For me, just to have the lead singer of the New York Dolls sing an aria in Handel's *Messiah* was in itself worthy of a *Hallelujah*!

The concert was broadcast nationally each year on over 200 public radio stations and televised locally, reaching a wider audience than any of us had first imagined. While racing through the main concourse of Grand Central Station, one afternoon in mid December, a backward-baseball-capped homeboy gave me a ghetto high sign and called out, "Yo, *Messiah*!"

Beginning in 2002, at the invitation of the city, a free concert was added at the end of the Bottom Line run, held in the glass-domed World Financial Center facing Ground Zero, in the phantom shadow of the missing Twin Towers. As at each concert, I would sing the final aria. With all of the other soloists having already performed, and my directorial duties temporarily complete, I would take a deep breath and, hearing Randy Brecker's heralding trumpet intro, enter the stage. I was the frontman again, but transformed.

Wearing silver jeans and shirt reflecting the lights, with hair bleached platinum blonde, and the choir standing behind him, the frontman looked out at the galaxy of two thousand faces before him, then up at the open, empty sky and sang:

> The trumpet shall sound,
> and the dead shall be raised,
> incorruptible.
> And we shall be changed. . . .

CHAPTER 11

I'LL BE YOUR MIRROR

HOW TO BE A PRODUCER

The days of September 2001 were some of the most perfect I had ever experienced. The Village shimmered in ridiculously delicate fall breezes, sunlight streaming on the cobblestone streets and brownstones like the yellow-gold in Van Gogh's paintings of Provence. With a seemingly endless supply of production projects to get involved with, I was doing what I loved and felt none of the pressure that used to keep me on the edge of the stage or subway platform, ready to jump. Maybe as a result, I noticed in myself an odd kind of complacency had begun to set in.

In fact, I still wasn't performing much at all lately, except for the occasional, multi-artist variety show or benefit. I preferred the sanctuary of the recording studio, where I would lock myself in and go unshaven for days, while producing new artists and associates, like Lach from the emerging Antifolk scene, and puckish, punkish outsiders, like Jenni Muldaur's Angry Elves.

Gloria Jones had been in touch again, too. Rolan Bolan had recently graduated from college and had been recording some demos. Would I be interested in producing some tracks for him? Thus began a lovely, ongoing friendship and collaboration, which seemed destined. Rolan's music combines the rock guitar textures of his father with the Motown soul of his mother, in a hybrid sound that is fully his own.

I had met the brilliant songwriter, actor, and humanitarian Paul Williams, when I performed his "Fill Your Heart" at his Loser's Lounge tribute, at the Westbeth Theater in the Village. The song was a favorite of mine, having appeared on Tiny Tim's debut album and later on David Bowie's *Hunky Dory*. When we spoke afterwards, Paul expressed interest in writing something for me. With the gorgeous lyrics of his I had just sung and the guilty pleasures of his Carpenters hits lushly swirling in my brain, I could barely contain my excitement.

On September 10, after yet another perfect day, I packed a couple pairs of jeans and black T-shirts, my Vagabond travel guitar, and notebook, and stayed up late installing the brand-new Mac OS X on my iMac. I was to leave the next day from JFK to meet with Paul in Los Angeles to write our song. Having booked myself at the Hyatt on Sunset ("the *Riot* House," for old time's sake), I prepared some musical ideas, some chord progressions and melody fragments, and recorded them for him on my computer.

The morning began even more perfectly than the days before. "Severe clear," they call it in the airport control towers. A tree was being planted in front of my building, and the sprinkling of sunlight on the leaves was silvery. It was a day so perfectly beautiful, it could make you sad. I stayed in bed and went back to sleep.

My wake-up calls were a rapid-fire series of friends' voices, alarmed and a little breathless, crackling on the speakerphone: "Go outside and look at the World Trade Center. A plane hit it." "A plane just crashed into one of the Trade Towers—go outside and check it out."

How could that happen, I wondered, still half asleep. Throwing on a T-shirt and camouflage shorts, and not bothering to tie the laces on my sneakers, I stumbled noisily down the one flight of stairs, outside past the guys planting the tree, and walked the partial block to Seventh Avenue and 11th Street, where I would have a clear view of the towers. Traffic had already stopped, and I found most of my neighbors—those I knew and those I had never met—gathered on the corner, transfixed by the black smoke billowing from a gaping hole in one of the buildings.

We were standing in the middle of the surreally silent intersection, when a second plane made a sharp turn and melted high into the other tower, almost like a computer-generated image. It couldn't be real.

From that point on, everything was a flickering series of images, a made-for-TV movie. . . .

Flashing back to my childhood, in grainy Super 8, like my father's old projector, I remembered the recurring nightmare of watching a plane crashing into flames into Tampa International Airport, about the same distance as ground zero was to me now. Flashing forward again, in all-too-sharp HD, I tingled with the sudden déjà vu and felt, along with the suddenly familiar strangers all around me, a communal sense of confusion.

After a gasp, hardly anyone spoke for a few minutes. St. Vincent's Hospital staff, in white, began to line the sidewalk with stretchers. They were to wait there all day, for victims who would never arrive. A line of blood donors quickly formed at the hospital and from across the street, I saw David Byrne, now completely white-haired, hustling across 11th Street to get in line.

I stood silent and watched for what seemed like a second and a lifetime, until a thin bright red line formed on the floor of impact, like the lit end of a cigarette, while what first appeared to be debris—but were actually people—fell from the upper floors, near the top. A big football-player-type nearby, in shorts like mine, but with tree trunk legs, watched as the building began to collapse and suddenly came tumbling straight down in slow motion: a silent moving holographic implosion, which I was to continue to see for weeks, every time I closed my eyes and tried to sleep. He broke the silence with a childlike *"Oh no!"* His knees buckled, and he fell hard to the pavement . . . the ghost image of the fallen building still lingering in the blue sky.

I couldn't watch anymore and went home. CNN had already added theme music to the images. Before the phone went dead, I had gotten a single message on my answering machine, a wrong number: "I just wanted to make sure you got out okay? *I* barely did . . . the stairs . . . *crackle.* . . . Call me when you get this and let me know you're all right," said the breathless voice. The message haunts me still. I stood motionless at the kitchen sink, by the window, soon hearing the F-16s—a little too late, I thought—and numerous military and police helicopters circling overhead, smelling the particular odor of that day, a combination of jet fuel and death, that lingered for weeks, feeling an odd culmination of some kind. It was as if everything—*everything*—to this point had been the orchestral crescendo of the Beatles' "A Day in the Life," and now we were in that breath just before the final chord. It was the glitter apocalypse of David Bowie's *Ziggy Stardust* and *Diamond Dogs*—but without the glitter.

By the time the second tower fell, the air was thick with a dust I knew would never really settle. Everything below 14th Street, just a few blocks above my own, was quickly cut off from all traffic and barricaded. Even pedestrians were restricted for several days: residents had to show ID. I thought of David Byrne in the blood donor line and recalled his song "Life During Wartime": "This ain't no party, this ain't no disco / this ain't no fooling around / This ain't no Mudd Club, or CBGB / I don't have time for that now." It played over and over in my head.

It seemed selfish to cry. Instead, standing at my kitchen window, I made a vow to myself at that moment to make every moment matter. To make everything count: all the music I make or facilitate, everything I say to those I love.

I couldn't wait to get back to work. There was so much I wanted to do, now more than ever. My mind raced. But first, along with everyone who had just experienced the unthinkable, I needed to acknowledge what had just happened.

Under the shadow of the fallen towers, my beloved Village, and all of downtown Manhattan, was darkening. Businesses, clubs, studios, and restaurants closed, many never to reopen their doors. The legendary Bottom Line nightclub that had launched the careers of Bruce Springsteen and countless others, and the home of so many of my own projects, was itself suffering from slow nights and cancellations. I phoned Allan Pepper. "Can we do something?" I asked. "A . . . special night . . . free admission?" At first silence, then, I got excited when he replied, "And we could stay open all night! An all-night jam session. . . ." We both started making calls, rounding up artists and producers to bring in others, inviting them to be part of the all-night marathon. A little act of defiance. The date was set for October 1, 2001. My birthday.

Opening the evening was Jackie DeShannon, singing "What the World Needs Now" ("is love, sweet love") followed by the most colossal collage of colorfuls one could imagine. Like the television variety shows I had loved as a child, and with some of the same performers. John Sebastian took to the stage to sing "Welcome Back," the Beatles' sound-alikes, the Fab Faux, sang "Because" from *Abbey Road*, and even the four Bongos got together for the first time in years to bash out "Numbers with Wings" and "Barbarella." The entire event was broadcast live on the local college radio station, WFUV, so people, tuned in on their car radios, drove in from all around the area, bringing a constant influx of listeners to the overflowing crowd all night long. Firemen from the NYFD stood on their chairs between acts, to be heard in the jam-packed club, tearfully sharing their experiences of loss on *that day*, just over two weeks earlier.

And yet, it was a happy night, and, perhaps strangely, my happiest birthday. Maybe because it was the kind of night that proves the power we deal with when a guitar is strummed, when a voice sings. There was a glimmer of something hopeful that night. Like we might actually survive.

Tony Visconti had closed down his London studio, Good Earth, and moved back to New York with his wife, May Pang and their two kids, Sebastian and Lara. We had met often socially at parties and music industry events. When a three-day tribute to T.Rex was planned at the downtown club Fez, Tony and I were both asked to perform.

At the cramped little rehearsal studio on West 28th Street, we were seated on a raised, thronelike viewing area, watching the other acts attempt to re-create the T.Rex sound that Tony had masterminded nearly thirty years before. Now handsomely graying and dignified, with a boyish gleam in his eye, he was asked questions like, "Did Marc play an A major or A minor on the chorus?" It was while sitting, watching, and listening together to Marc's music—the songs that had inspired me more than anything to pick up a guitar and play—that I said to Tony, "You know, we still need to make that album someday."

He smiled, and said, "Yes, I know." The shows were a big success, and we continued our conversation via e-mail.

Joining Ringo Starr, Stevie Nicks, Brian Wilson, and others, I had contributed a track of my own ("I Guess the Lord Must Be in New York City") for the Harry Nilsson tribute CD, *For the Love of Harry*. I worked this time with longtime Lou Reed collaborator, Mike Rathke, and producer/engineer Steve Rosenthal at his Magic Shop studios in SoHo. Phil Spector, Andrew Loog Oldham, the Rolling Stones, Reed, and other discriminating clients had made it their home for recent projects, and I, too, felt particularly at home there. Being a Nilsson fan, I offered to produce another track, by Fred Schneider, for the tribute album—a madcap, psycho-psychedelic-grunge reworking of Harry's classic "Coconut," which was to become the single and land us both on *Late Night with Conan O'Brien* to perform live, in a glorious and messy explosion of energy. The unlikely hard-core approach to the familiar little neo-reggae tune came about when Fred came over to my apartment to discuss the arrangement, and I happened to be listening to Iggy Pop's *Raw Power* album.

"That's what I want!" said Fred.

"What?" I replied. "That sound. That's what I want for 'Coconut.'"

"O . . . *kay*," I smiled.

At first it seemed like I was agreeing to attempt the impossible. But that is often what a producer must agree to do. The challenge, the *job* of every producer is to bring into existence the fantasy—the passing thought, the dream, the wish, the . . . impossible—and often to do this on a level that must remain unspoken. If it becomes an obvious kind of power or if it is driven by ego, the creative spell is broken. The producer must get into the artist's head and then get out in the nick of time, so he can step back and see the result.

The record producer's role is the *most* like an alchemist's. Because he's able to stand back and experience it, he's in the best position to mix the chemistries and the personalities—as well as the sounds—to produce something rare and valuable. When the situation is right, a producer can simply let it happen, becoming almost transparent. Seeming to do nothing is the best way of controlling a creative situation.

In actuality, though, there are many tools that are useful to have on hand, and no one has to know you're using them. One is *history*. For me, it's essential to have a broad knowledge of what's gone down before. Then you can decide what to use or choose *not* to use from the past, depending on what you want the listener's experience to be. I always feel it's an embarrassment to sound like you're referencing or mimicking something you've never even heard.

Another is the (raw) power of *suggestion*. Once you're in the producer's chair, and the artist trusts you, *everything* you say will find its way into the finished product. Bring up topics and references that bring about the result you want in the artist's performance; e.g., just listening to Iggy Pop triggered a whole new direction for Fred's "Coconut."

And you can always rely on your own *experience*. Whatever your experience, use it to understand the pressure an artist feels, and let it guide you to be patient and wise.

Amen.

Producing records is mysterious business. The first Velvet Underground album, undisputedly one of the most influential rock albums ever made, was "produced" by their manager, who happened to be pop artist Andy Warhol. While it is common knowledge that the majority of the work was done by Lou Reed and engineer Tom Wilson, it was Warhol's encouragement and advice—and clout—that brought the album into existence. That album launched multiple solo careers, as well as several genres of rock, including alternative, glam, punk, and Goth, and, as legend has it, thousands of bands. A visual artist, Warhol was concerned with the Big Picture, and this position gave him the perspective and detachment that drew out those songs and performances. All of the arts are interchangeable.

A track on that album may have been written by Reed as a love song, but can also stand to represent Andy's role as producer: "I'll be your mirror / Reflect what you are / In case you don't know."

Honesty is startling. No one expects it, especially from a recording artist. I think a producer's fundamental job is to bring out the undeniable truth.

The first Rolling Stones albums, similarly, were produced by *their* colorful manager, former publicist Andrew Loog Oldham. Again, he did so by bringing out the rawness that made the Stones unique and keeping the emphasis on the *result* and its *perception*: the big picture.

I believe, in one sense, that the artist's duty is to himself and the producer's duty is to the public. The artist should be able to express himself absolutely freely, knowing that the producer is keeping an eye on how the overall experience will be perceived by the listener. The producer is like a translator at the United Nations, but instead of translating propaganda, he is translating dreams and thoughts and emotions into tangible expressions, sonic experiences, and entertainment.

I finally felt that the emotional cycle of *Clouds Over Eden*, recorded nearly a decade before, was complete. I had been writing and slowly recording new songs. While producing Fred Schneider's Nilsson track at the Magic Shop, I became friends with Steve Rosenthal, who owned the studio. Boasting an early '70s, broadcast Neve console from the BBC, blessed by Rupert Neve himself, and tons of analog and digital gear, the sound was impeccable. Steve began coming over to my apartment, where we mapped out ideas for a few tunes.

"Guru" is the song that was born fully grown, the minute I took the "TV Yellow" Les Paul Special I had been waiting for out of the box. I instinctively began strumming the A-major-7 chord that opens the tune. At the Magic Shop, I played guitar, bass, and Mellotron, and Steve handled the programming, engineering, and the MiniMoog. Lisa Haney returned on cello, and Steve brought in a hot young Indian tabla player, Deep Singh, who would soon be featured in the Broadway show *Bombay Dreams*.

Just as Rolan Bolan had come so gracefully into my life, suddenly Sean Lennon similarly materialized for a brief cameo appearance at the session for "Guru." One of the most Beatlesque recordings I had ever made, I was tracking the Mellotron string overdubs when Sean, who had also been recording at the studio, arrived and sat on the couch to watch. He was full of questions about the instrument, and it was a special thrill for me to explain the inner workings of the

Mellotron to him, particularly since it was his father's band that had brought the instrument into the pop mainstream with the intro of John's "Strawberry Fields Forever."

I had written "Odd Girl Out," its title coming from an iconic, early '60s lesbian pulp novel, with Jill Sobule, who came by the studio to add harmonies in a feisty late-night session. For the recording, Steve set up an intricate double drum kit: a small dampened kit for the verses and a big, full, open rock kit for the chorus. Tommy Goss, alumnus from the *Clouds* album, sat in the middle, swiveling between the two as he played. Tony Shanahan from the Patti Smith group played a Hofner bass, meticulously recorded according to the descriptions provided in the *Beatles Recording Sessions* book. With a couple of new songs down on tape (yes, *analog tape*), I had finally jumped back in the game of being a recording artist. But there was so much more I wanted to do.

I had first seen the great Miss Peggy Lee perform in her Broadway show, *Peg*, in the mid-'80s. A decade later, I met her after a performance in the intimate lounge of the New York Hilton, where Madonna also sat in the audience. (The next week, I happened to be at Platinum Island recording studios when I heard a house version of "Fever" pumping from the studio down the hall, where Madonna was recording it for her *Erotica* album. Never have I seen an artist harder on herself to achieve the phrasing and performance she was looking for. Her determination was awe-inspiring.)

Even at seventy-five, after six decades of performing, Peggy Lee was a singer's singer. Watching from the first-tier box at Carnegie Hall in 1995, I knew I wanted to produce a tribute to her. But where? And how? The idea lingered, then flickered away, while other projects came and went. It was several years later, while listening to "Let's Love," a song Paul McCartney had written for Peggy in the '70s, I heard a voice from another room—or was it a voice in my head?—saying, "Why don't you produce a tribute to Peggy Lee?" After producing and directing large-scale shows like *The Downtown Messiah*, and my work on *Bright Lights Big City*, it seemed possible. When she died in January 2002, I was saddened, but more determined than ever. I started phoning her favorite musicians, beginning with jazz bassist Jay Leonhart. I told him my vision.

"Have you called George Wein?" he asked. "He might be able to help."

I knew George Wein had invented the jazz festival as we know it, in Newport, Rhode Island, in the '50s, but wasn't sure how he would react to a bleached-blonde post-punk rocker hell-bent on producing a tribute to Peggy Lee. I called Wein's office and through his associate Dan Melnick, set up a meeting to present my idea. At the long conference table with Wein at its head, and lined on either side with his associates, I stated my case: My idea was to combine some of the variety show elements I had been working with, with lots of glamour, and a focus on the many great songs that Lee had *written*. I wanted to use Peggy's own favorite rhythm section, comprised of some of the top jazzmen—musical director–pianist Mike Renzi, drummer Grady Tate, guitarist Bucky Pizzarelli, and bassist Leonhart—backed by a traditional jazz big band, approximately eighteen guest vocalists, and several speakers, many who would have to be flown in from various parts of the country and Europe. There would be an overture and a video screen on which to project film and still images as backdrops. It wouldn't be cheap. Oh, *and* I wanted to do it at Carnegie Hall.

I held my breath, as questions and concerns were bandied about. Then abruptly Wein stood up, noisily pushing his chair out of the way. "Give the kid what he wants," he barked and walked back to his office.

On the way home, I felt as if Peggy were riding with me on the 1 train. Later that evening, I started making calls and writing a script for the show. I was thrilled at how many of the stars agreed to perform—Debbie Harry and Nancy Sinatra were two of the first—then Rita Moreno (she had recorded "New York City Blues," a tune Peggy had co-written with Quincy Jones) who would turn in a show-stopping performance. Newcomers Jane Monheit and Peter Cincotti, and legends Shirley Horn, Chris Connor, and Marian McPartland . . . Petula Clark, Freddie Cole, Dee Dee Bridgewater, Maria Muldaur—all agreed to perform. Mike Stoller—who, with Jerry Lieber, had penned Peggy's 1969 hit "Is That All There Is?"—agreed to speak. Quincy and I had hit it off on some lengthy phone conversations about Peggy, and he invited me to his house in Bel Air to talk more and have our conversation filmed for use in the show.

I had recently seen comedienne Bea Arthur in her one-woman Broadway show and was knocked out. Finding out that she was a fan and friend of Peggy Lee, I invited her to sing. *Every* artist who hit the stage that night was a star of the highest magnitude. And I was to find the bigger the star, the more gracious and grateful they were to be asked.

This was a bit of a revelation: I finally began to realize what makes a star and that artists who are *not* gracious and grateful—as well as being relentlessly hard-working—are either not stars or stars of a much lower magnitude. Semi-stars. There may even be a sliding scale: the less of those two ingredients, the less of a star one is. It seems, in reality, there are not as many *true* stars as we are led to believe. Happily, I have only been let down a very few times. Thanks to my intensive childhood training, along with my mother's scrapbook and newfound knowledge, I usually know my stars!

Like me, the cast was anxious to collaborate. My cell phone would ring while I was shopping in a drugstore and it would be Nancy Sinatra or Bea Arthur, asking my opinion, and open to my direction. At first, I was startled by the trust and love. I had failed to notice, in all the years since "The Littlest DJ," that I had grown up. That I was no longer the chubby kid with the striped T-shirt and flip-flops. Along the uncharted path I'd taken—driven by a desire that even I couldn't define—I must have acquired *experience* because, now, even putting on a show of this scale seemed to come naturally to me.

The tech rehearsal/soundcheck that afternoon of June 23, 2003, was chaotic, with endless union rules and regulations stifling the oversized cast, and creating headaches for the crew to deal with. Bea had taken ill, and I had to convince legendary composer Cy Coleman to perform one of her numbers, his classic "Big Spender," from *Sweet Charity*.

I remained remarkably calm. As each artist came out onstage for a final practice run-through of their number, I went out to the empty seats of Carnegie Hall to take it in as the audience would do a few hours later. I felt I was home. Maybe for the first time.

My mother had flown in from Tampa for the show that night and, in a sleek evening gown, attended the after party given by the Society of Singers, Peggy Lee's favorite charity and the beneficiary of the night's proceeds. The star-studded room atop Shelley's on 57th Street was a scene far removed from the punk rock club in Tampa, where she had told everyone who would listen (or not), "That's my son!" Now, breaking the sophisticated air of the party at Shelley's, I heard from across the room, "Richard Barone, you crazy muthafucka," shouted by alternative-rock journalist J. R. Taylor. "What are you gonna do to top this?"

Wein's scouts from Los Angeles were at Carnegie Hall that night and, during the second act, came backstage to ask me if I could bring the show to the Hollywood Bowl. Naturally I said yes. Even before the curtain had closed on the Carnegie event, I began thinking of ways to expand the show for the West Coast. A date in Chicago at the historic Ravinia Festival was also booked for 2004.

I promised Peggy Lee's granddaughter Holly and daughter Nicki, who had both been hugely supportive, that the Bowl concert would be an even bigger celebration than in New York. And it was, with the full string section of the L.A. Philharmonic and an expanded cast. Rat Pack protégé Jack Jones joined the cast, turning in a high-tech virtual duet with Peggy. Rita Coolidge and Maureen McGovern were also added. Quincy's lovely daughter, former model Jolie Jones, sang the lullaby, "Angels on Your Pillow," Grady Tate supplying the gentle echoing vocal, just as he had done with Peggy on Broadway. Nancy Sinatra (with whom I spent some unforgettable times in L.A. and in Chicago, where we discussed at length many of the performing and show-pacing techniques she learned from her father while on a tour of his favorite Italian restaurants) knocked out the crowd of nearly 20,000 with her opening number. Bea Arthur was back and in fine form, turning in a spectacular performance. "Richard!" she said onstage when a lighting cue came late. "I am going to *kill* you!" I moved a few soloists to different, more appropriate songs to match their presence and personalities, and this caused some questions and flared tempers. "I don't know *what* your relationship is with *that woman*!" snapped an angry Petula Clark when I assigned an additional song *she* had wanted to sing to jazz ingénue Monheit.

But I stood in the wings of the Hollywood Bowl, beaming like a proud parent as each artist received their thunderous ovation and in the end the critics agreed with my song assignments; each soloist received great notice. Most importantly, Peggy and her music were as alive and lively as ever, and I was honored to be able to let the world know with these shows.

For the first time in years, I started to think about how I *felt*, how my life had changed since I had stepped out of the limelight. The frontman I had been was now the distant memory of another life. He was a ghost. An alien. I began to recall feelings I had supressed when I fronted the Bongos. The resentment, for instance, that I felt from my bandmates when I would attempt to take charge, and the resentment I felt toward them when I bore all the pressure to create. Perhaps these feelings were irrational and harsh, but they were profound. They had become a part of me. Finally, I was able to let them go. I thought about other frontmen, my brothers in a fraternity of which I had once been a member. I thought about those who hadn't survived.

The saddest story of all was that of Badfinger. Full of promise as the '70s began, they were the group most likely to succeed. Signed to the Beatles' Apple label and with a hit debut single written and produced by Paul McCartney (who also played on the track), a debut album produced by Tony Visconti, and a follow-up by George Harrison, they were the chosen ones, the "new Beatles." With their patrons freshly broken up, they would carry the mantle. In the process, they invented '70s power pop, with the guitar crunch of "No Matter What" and the Beatlesque "Baby Blue." But by 1975, financially broken and in despair after being ripped off by an unscrupulous manager, the group's leader, Pete Ham, hanged himself in his garage studio in Surrey, leaving behind a suicide note as concise as his song lyrics. "I will not be allowed to *love and trust* everybody," he wrote. "This is better." A few years later, another member of the group, Tom Evans, also hanged himself in a similar way. Together they had written "Without You," a smash hit for Harry Nilsson (and, years later, Mariah Carey). Whenever I hear the song's chorus—"I can't live, if living is without you / I can't give, I can't give anymore. . . ." I think of those two words, Love + Trust. Without them. . . .

From the sublime to the ridiculous. In New York, I was making final preparations for my Central Park event, "The (Not-So) Great American Songbook." The idea was developed with the park's director of SummerStage, Alexa Birdsong, and it was another variety-format concert. This time, the focus was on songs "we love to hate," radio hits from the '70s and '80s. The one-hit wonders, guilty pleasures, and the songs that, intentionally or not, crossed the fine line from pop to kitsch. Simultaneously with this concert, *Blender* magazine had published their "one hundred worst records of all time," and we were amused by how many were in our list. But our show was a loving tribute—these were songs that musicians love to play and singers love to sing. We never said they were bad . . . they just were not great. Marshall Crenshaw, Kiki and Herb, Moby, and others performed, as I hosted and sang a medley of Barry Manilow's "Mandy" and Looking Glass's "Brandy." It was exhilarating to tackle these tunes, and the backdrop of Central Park was magical, especially as the wind gently billowed Kiki's (played by drag performance artist Justin Bond) green chiffon gown, as she sang "You Light Up My Life" to the crowd; and as the entire cast took the stage—and the whole audience stood and sang along—for the show's raucous finale, "We Built This City on Rock and Roll."

I had met Donovan, one of my earliest musical heroes, through our mutual friend, Ellen Joy Voell, after they were erroneously turned away at the door from one of my sold-out solo performances at Joe's Pub. That embarrassing mishap at the jewel-like music venue of New York's historic Public Theater was later reported in the *New York Times* in an article entitled "A Night Out with Richard Barone." At a conciliatory dinner the next night, Donovan invited me to perform as special guest on a bill with him one magical fall evening at the Tabernacle in woodsy Mt. Tabor, New Jersey. While closing my set with his underappreciated mystical folk-rock anthem "Cosmic Wheels," the Scottish troubadour surprised me by creeping up from behind the stage and joining me at the mic, turning the finale into an impromptu duet. Later, we jammed until the sun came up, playing every Beatles tune we could think of, while he shared his personal stories of his friends, the Fab Four.

When Donovan returned to the U.S. the following year—from his idyllic medieval castle in Ireland—it was to perform his conceptual piece, *Beat Café*, at my own stomping ground, Joe's Pub. Again, he asked me to join him. This time, however, it was as a scripted part of his show. For nine performances, I was the beatnik MC, the poet called up from the audience to read Allen Ginsberg's *Howl*, and the singer joining him for the final reprise of the title song.

"You know, Richard, Ginsberg always read *Howl* in the nude," Donovan told me in his soft brogue during one of the rehearsals. "To make it authentic, you'll have to. . . ."

"I don't think so," I grinned, interrupting, and went back to memorizing my lines.

Of all the artists I work with, Donovan may be most humble about his deep influence on pop music and culture. It's this purity, combined with his brilliance and talent, that inspires me still. His creative journey is truly timeless . . . and mythic.

I had also recently met Les Paul backstage at of one his regular Monday night shows at the Iridium jazz club. Besides pioneering the solid-body electric guitar and inventing multitrack recording—the two primary tools of my trade—Les is a remarkable musician, witty performer, and producer with legions of devotees, including Jimmy Page, Jeff Beck, and Paul McCartney. We had a lengthy discussion about the new, *digital* Les Paul guitar that Gibson would be launching a year later. I had already been working with a prototype, using it as my main guitar on recording sessions. Plugging directly into the computer using its ethernet interface, it allowed me to create stereo and surround images.

The conversation was becoming more and more heated, as Les aggressively interrogated me on what I liked about the digital instrument and what I could do with it. Suddenly, I realized there was a Fox News television camera over my shoulder. "This man is my hero!" I offered for the camera as Les smiled, making it on the next morning's news.

Tony Visconti and I had begun meeting at his studio, writing and recording songs together, with no deadline, no label, and no overall project in mind. Not since I sat, as a seven-year-old, on the floor of my parents' house in Tampa, with a reel-to-reel tape recorder, had I recorded so purely, just for the sheer joy of it. Apple's Logic software had made the writing, arranging, and recording process as seamless as our imagining. Tony and I both feel and "hear" the arrangement and production of each song as we write it, so working in this way allowed us to instantly capture the initial inspiration of each of these elements, as we had conceived them. It was the kind of recording process that I had always dreamed of, the nondestructive aspect encouraging us to try every option. Once I asked Tony if we could turn a solo backwards. He looked at me eye to eye, and in a serious tone with a smile said, "Richard, we can do *anything*." I had been waiting all my life to hear a producer say that.

Typically, I would come to Tony with a title, phrase, or general lyric idea. "Tony, I feel *sanctified*." Or, "Okay, I know it sounds odd, but I'm really aware of *gravity's pull* today." We would discuss it, then go to separate corners to write for a bit, Tony on a couch, me typically on the floor, both with notepads. Coming back together, we would combine our efforts and begin tracking. Recording a "master" for a song so freshly written was new to me, but exciting. We were capturing the spirit of creating, instead of *re*-creating an inspiration.

Sometimes I'd bring him a riff or a bit of melody. In one instance, Tony had constructed a drum part from miscellaneous beats he had accumulated from a recent session. He edited them together, handed it to me, and it became a song, "Candied Babes."

Since we were recording as we wrote, we played most of the instruments ourselves, with occasional guests coming by, some unexpected. One day, recording in Tony's apartment, I was playing a guitar solo, using his early Roland guitar synthesizer. The liquid tone and melodic style of the solo reminded me of Marc Bolan, but I didn't say so, I just played. Suddenly, there was a great gust of wind in the kitchen, even though all the windows were closed, knocking over some glasses and blowing papers around. Just like at my first apartment on Hamilton Heath. "Oh, hello, Marc," Tony said, barely looking up, and we continued tracking.

As I got busy with shows, often with Tony accompanying me on bass, he got busy with his other production work. I was at his apartment one day, when the phone rang. "Can you get that for me?" he asked, while playing bass on one of our songs. I picked it up. "Tony, it's *David*." I knew Tony and David Bowie hadn't worked together for over fourteen years, so, handing him the phone, I was certain Bowie was calling to ask Tony to produce his next project. They ended up making two albums back-to-back, *Heathen* and *Reality*. Likewise, I produced several albums for other artists, including a talented newcomer named Johnny Rodgers. I also wrote and recorded a song with Mike Thorne, the groundbreaking producer of Soft Cell, Wire, 'Til Tuesday, and Bronski Beat. Tony and I reconvened, and soon, we had accumulated nine or ten completed songs.

Paul Williams and I were finally able to meet again and write *our* song. Back on September 11, 2001, en route to meet me in L.A., Paul's flight had been redirected to Houston, where he was grounded until the national airspace was reopened two days later. Then scheduling, circumstances, and the general climate of those post-9/11 days kept us from being able to be in the same place at the same time. Finally, it was in the charming living room of his magical home in West Hollywood, surrounded by awards, mementos of Streisand, the Carpenters, and framed black-and-white photos of his acting roles. Speaking very little, I strummed my Vagabond travel guitar, while Paul paced the room with his notebook, singing and scribbling: "Beyond the season of goodbyes and of times we could trust / We write our names and trace a heart in the ashes and dust."

On September 11, 2006, I found myself in a small Italian restaurant near Ground Zero, having dinner with Tony, my music publisher,

Lionel Conway (who had worked the Bongos catalog when he headed Chris Blackwell's Island Publishing), and my new manager, Alexandra. It was a beautiful, clear night, and after dinner, we walked for a bit, Lionel and Tony walking ahead, talking about old times in the music business and how it's changed since they both began in the mid-'60s. *So many* changes.

Alexandra and I lagged behind, watching them reminisce about the acts they had both worked with—my heroes. We smiled and chatted about how the industry may have "gone south," but for those passionate about music and still making it, it doesn't matter. They survive, creative and energized, in a state of youthful timelessness.

We stopped to snap a picture on a Tribeca street corner, with the 9/11 tribute, two shafts of blue light reaching to the stars against the dark sky, shooting upwards, directly behind us. After the camera flashed, Lionel jumped, frowning. "Wait! Is it appropriate that we were all *smiling* in front of the memorial?"

"Yes," I smiled.

CHAPTER 12

YET ANOTHER MIDNIGHT

FINDING HAPPINESS

Not so long ago I received a phone call from a friend at Gibson Guitars, asking me if I would be interested in smashing a guitar at the christening ceremony of the new Hard Rock Café in Times Square. At first, I was hesitant. Destroying a guitar—on purpose—didn't seem like something I would want to do. But then they told me that the guitars were factory seconds that would never be sold anyway, and that Gibson was donating a number of guitars to schools, equivalent to the number of instruments destroyed. When I was informed of some of the other ninety-nine guitar smashers, it started to sound like fun, so I agreed.

On a sunny fall morning, holding a black Les Paul Special, I found myself right next to erstwhile Beach Boy Brian Wilson, as we stood on Broadway facing a firing line of network television cameras. Brian, looking like a happy, oversized twelve-year-old, was ready to bust a Gibson acoustic. On the count of one-two-three, everyone, with a great crashing sound and showers of splintered wood, smashed their guitars on the cinder blocks that had been placed in front of us. I glanced over at Brian, who, gleeful in the destruction, was left with just the neck, some stray, tangled strings, and a ridiculous, mischievous grin.

Immediately after the ceremony, some of us were invited to breakfast downstairs. I was seated across from Brian, and seeing him up close is when it finally, *really*, hit me. His history: the pain, pressure, and responsibility he must have felt as the spiritual and creative frontman of a group that included his brothers and was managed by his father. I thought about his crack-up. Like an American Syd Barrett, his creative and chemical indulgences led to a mutiny within the group, and Brian was left high and dry without a surfboard. I remembered the rumors of his vegetative state, the surreal image of him sitting at a piano in a sandbox in his house, waiting for inspiration. The agony he must have gone through, not only in executing his intricate arrangements—with one deaf ear—but in the constant demands to deliver the hits. I recalled a Beach Boys concert I had attended in Florida in the '70s, where a ghostly Brian was led slowly and carefully out mid-show, without an introduction, to play bass. The boy genius, on display for the world to see. A rare specimen. He looked like a frightened deer in the headlights of the audience's glare, then walked off the stage mid-song.

Over breakfast, we talked a little about his upcoming show later that night at the Performing Arts Center, across the river in New Jersey. The concert would be a live presentation of his lost masterpiece, *SMiLE*, the Beach Boys album he had begun, scheduled for release, and then abandoned nearly forty years before. Now it was finally finished, in the stores, and Brian was on tour performing it live, as a solo artist. I was excited and happy for his happiness and full of congratulations. When I got up to leave, Brian stood. All his years and pain fell away with his genuine "smile," as he waved good-bye. Though I was less than two feet away, he stood and waved, as if to salute me.

It seems happiness is a choice you make. As the producer of your own life, you decide what makes you happy. Happiness exists only when you let it. Even doing what you love can make you happy or unhappy. But, any time you look for happiness from outside of yourself, you are destined never to find it. It has to come from you, because you decide.

Meeting Brian Wilson got me thinking about my own unfinished business, especially with the Bongos. The group had "blown up," but had never actually *broken* up. There had been no conclusion. They were the past, yes, and I had moved on. But, it was like watching a movie and not staying until the end. We blew up too soon. Our peers went on to sign multimillion dollar deals, while I was starting over from scratch as a solo artist. And now, new groups like the Killers were topping the charts with a sound and image that mirrored ours. The nagging "what if's" lingered, and probably always will.

Though bootleg and pirate copies were being sold around the world, legitimate Bongos albums had become hard to find in the United States, and *Drums Along the Hudson* had been out of print for over a decade. Original vinyl copies were going for over two hundred dollars in auctions on eBay. Although we did not control the rights to our RCA albums, we *did* control *Drums,* the ownership given to us as a generous gift by Rod Pearce when he folded the Fetish label in the late '80s. It was time to reissue it, with some live and bonus material. So while finishing songs for my solo album, I started looking around for a label to re-release *Drums.* We finally settled on Cooking Vinyl, a feisty British-based indie that was starting a U.S. division. It reminded us of our happy beginnings with Fetish.

On the very morning the contracts were due to arrive, I got an e-mail from Moby. "I'm just listening to *Drums Along the Hudson,*" he wrote. "What a remarkable album." I wrote back instantly to tell him of his uncanny timing and suggested that *he* produce a bonus track for us. "Sure!" was his equally instant reply. The year before, when we had worked together on the show in Central Park, Moby told me that "The Bulrushes" was one the first songs he had ever performed in public, so I suggested we remake that song now, with the original three Bongos and him as producer.

Time has a way of expanding and contracting with memory and emotions. It was as if the years that had passed since Rob, Frank, and I were last in a studio together had never happened. It felt exactly like the next day of a tour. At Dubway Studios, the sound gelled instantly, and Moby's contributions (he played acoustic guitar, electric twelve-string, piano, and Juno 106 synthesizer) were perfect textures. The Juno, in particular, was a welcome addition, as it recalled the electronic accents that Dennis Kelley added to our earliest recordings with his EMS Synthi. In fact, the spirit of the session was as open and free-flowing as those of *Drums* had been, and, in some small way, the Bongos' story seemed more complete.

Jolie Jones was in New York, and called me to say hello. We had become friends while working on the Peggy Lee tribute at the Bowl and stayed in touch. Chita Rivera was playing that night at Feinstein's at the Regency, and I thought it might be fun to check her out. I was interested in producing a tribute to Cy Coleman, who had recently passed away, and I wanted to ask Chita to be involved. As we chatted in the rarified air of one of the city's top intimate nightclubs, Jolie told me about her children's book, *Little Kisses*, which was being published through Julie Andrews's imprint at HarperCollins. "Wow. Why don't we make a companion CD?" I blurted. After all these years, I still blurt. Even if I'm already overbooked with sessions and projects, I can't resist a good blurt.

She loved the idea and soon started making a list of children's songs that could be included. Then it occurred to me, "Why don't we *write* the songs," I offered, "based on the book?" Another day, another blurt. Thus began one of the loveliest writing and recording projects I'd done, one that included Johnny Rodgers and Jolie's son, Sunny Levine, who would e-mail and instant message rhythm and percussion loops from L.A. to us at the former Hit Factory in New York. The legendary recording studio complex had now been taken over by Gibson Guitars as their showroom and rehearsal studios. We wrote the entire album there, at an incredible clip. The creative spirits that inhabited those rooms seemed to be holding our hands and walking us through each melody and lyric, because we were able to complete a song on each visit. One day, I went into the studio reading a *Q Magazine* article on John Lennon, when, looking at the photos, I suddenly realized that we were in the very room where John Lennon's final sessions, with Yoko, had taken place. Where they had recorded and mixed "Walking on Thin Ice" the night John was killed. I got chills for a second, then relaxed into a kind of semi-understanding of why I felt so connected to the place. Ironically, one of the first things we had worked on for Jolie's album was an arrangement of Lennon's "I'm Only Sleeping."

The challenge was to make the album innocent and pure, but not infantile or boring. The melodies and rhythms, we felt, should appeal equally to parents, who would most likely be hearing it with their kids. We invited the great jazz saxophonist David Sanborn (who

I first became aware of from Bowie's *Young Americans* album and was a friend of Jolie's) to play on the title track, giving him the direction to play as if he were seven years old. In fact, all of us maintained an attitude of childhood in our playing and singing on the album, and the atmosphere was more like a playground than a recording studio. Even the engineer, Jason Marcucci, not only understood, but helped maintain the spirit of fun. There was an entirely unprofessional amount of hugging and giggling going on while making *Little Kisses* that is delightfully audible on the finished product.

With some of the recording being done in L.A., at Sunny's home studio, Jolie and I stopped in to visit her dad late one evening after a session to let him hear some of the tunes. When I had visited Quincy Jones before, it was at his former residence, which was gorgeous, with spectacular views of Hollywood. But directly across the street, his new estate, which had taken five years to build, was—*literally*—stunning, and I told him so. "It's my dream home, man," he said to me very softly.

In his screening room, its walls decorated with the posters from the movies he had scored, Quincy was entertaining guests, including the heirs of the Ebony/Jet publishing empire. In the corner was a strange and futuristic musical device that, Quincy noticed, I immediately gravitated towards. It was made mostly of clear Plexiglas, and had the general appearance of a stylized Theramin, the early electronic instrument used primarily for sound effects. However, this apparatus had multiple terminals that was connected to a laptop computer and used lasers.

"Everyone," Quincy announced, "this is *Richard Barone* and he is going to perform for us." I knew this trick. It was akin to the "Army training" that Tiny Tim talked about. Putting me on the spot. "This is what mentors do," I thought to myself. So I said brightly, "Okay. How does this thing work?" Q explained that each of the six horizontal laser beams is a MIDI controller, which triggers a sample in the software loaded into the computer. Besides being a solo instrument, it's capable of playing rhythm tracks, like a sophisticated karaoke machine, to which you can not only sing, but play the lead instruments. A full-body version was being developed, I was told, which would read the movements of a dancer to trigger sounds. "And the *booty* is the *bass*," Quincy added with a smile. He asked me what I wanted to play, and for some reason the song that came to mind was Stevie Wonder's "Isn't She Lovely?" A few clicks on the laptop assigned the instruments to corresponding lasers, the harmonica on the top right, the string section middle left, the bass on the middle right, keyboards and drum fills in the others. By placing a hand in one of the beams, you could play that instrument sample, as if on an invisible keyboard of light. Quincy started the rhythm track playing.

"Whatever you do, don't put your hand in this one," he warned, gesturing to the laser on the lower left." "You mean . . . *this* one?" I retorted like a sassy third-grader, putting my hand directly in the light he warned about. The rhythm track stopped dead, and Quincy glared silently. Then he started it up again. Now I had gotten the picture, and, with my right hand, lightly began riffing on the melody in the light beam that triggered the harmonica. I placed my left hand slightly over the beam controlling the string section, but moved my hand too fast. Quincy grabbed it by the wrist and slowed me down. "Play it like *strings*," he directed, guiding me to make smoother motions, more closely resembling the bowing action of a violinist or cellist. Now I was playing the song and sang a verse. My body moved with the music, as if the beams of light were, in turn, controlling *my* movements, and I made no effort to restrain myself. When the song was over, I accepted the applause with a quick bow. Quincy turned to Jolie and asked, "Where's he *from*?" "New York," she replied. "I know *that*," he answered. I know what he meant was "What planet?"

Back in New York, I continued producing, spending almost an entire year in the studio, one project after another, and rarely coming up for air. I was perpetually in an altered state of studio mind, as if I *were* on another planet, one where eight hours of studio planet time equals ten minutes in Earth time. I was reaching out to a now-invisible audience from the isolated silence of the recording studio. "Normal" human activities were secondary.

In December, at my suggestion, I produced a duet for Johnny Rodgers and Liza Minelli, with whom Johnny had been touring as accompanist. Liza had always intrigued me. Although she perpetually kept one foot in the door of the old school, showbiz world of Sinatra and the Rat Packers (with whom she toured in the '90s), she also seemed to pop up, literally, in the modern pop world. Whichever one she happened to find herself in. In the '70s, at the height of her *Cabaret* success, she appeared on Alice Cooper's *Muscle of Love* album, and was a favorite in the Warhol crowd. In the late '80s, she made an album produced by the Pet Shop Boys. And in 2006, she appeared on the alt-rock album of the year by My Chemical Romance, *The Black Parade*. The ability to straddle the decades and survive is one of the traits I admire most in an artist, so, working with her was an honor.

We had an arranger write a chart for six horns, a rhythm section of guitar, bass, and two drummers; piano and two lead vocals. And, to capture the energy of the performance, I wanted to record the whole thing *live*. Because of its accommodating size and equipment, I again chose the Magic Shop studio, asking Steve Rosenthal to engineer. I constantly looked to Liza, studying her facial reactions and body movements to set the tempo and feel for the track, so when she and Johnny were ready to sing, and *swing*, the vibe was already there. Liza was an absolute pro, and so endlessly *giving*. A true star. It was a magical session.

One rainy winter night, my friend Alex, nineteen years old, took me to see his favorite band, Placebo, when they came through New York. I had seen the British group a few years before at Irving Plaza, seated in the lofty VIP box high above the crowd along with Tony Visconti, David Bowie, and Iman. This time, though, I was right in the thick of it—in front of the stage with the fans, standing in the suddenly amassing mosh pit of the new Nokia Theater in Times Square, pressed and tossed between bodies, in an unsteady ocean of black denim, leather, tattoos, and mascara, whiffing the scents of patchouli oil, pot, and Heineken. I hadn't watched a band from this vantage point since seeing the Ramones at CBGB.

Placebo reached out to the audience with same glam rock echoes of T.Rex and Bowie as I had—and just as Marc and David had echoed the icons, myths, and legends before them—creating wave after wave of energized reactions. The frontman, Brian Molko, shortish but stylish in a black shirt and yellow striped tie, had all the right moves, androgynous and excessive, as he shared his duties with his taller punkish counterpart, bassist Stefan Olsdal. At one point, for an extended moment mid-song, the frontman and I made eye contact. I was pulled to the other side of the mirror and saw myself.

I had met photographer Mick Rock through Tony, and we had become friends over the past few years, meeting for tea to look over contact sheets and discuss art, rock, and the great images he had created that meant so much to me. Exchanging ideas and images, we talked about possibilities for photo shoots all the time, and with my CD almost finished, it was time to do one. I felt strongly that I wanted to be clothes-free in these new images for many reasons. Mick and I began talking about the role of frontman, about how naked, how vulnerable, the frontman is. The frontman is allowed little or no privacy. Everything is revealed. The challenge was, I didn't want the shot to seem "posey" or "show-offy," egotistical, or even sexual. I wanted instead something masculine, determined. We discussed this, but I still wasn't satisfied. Until, one day, I visited Alexandra at her apartment, high above Manhattan and right there, as I entered, was the image I had been looking for.

On the wall in the entryway was a large framed black-and-white photograph of a World War II gunner, wearing headphones, and bringing two Navy airmen to safety after a heroic water rescue (during which the gunner had to remove his flight suit), while being shot at by Japanese warships. He looked strong and confidently nonchalant, doing his job, in the nude, under the most adverse conditions possible. The photograph had been taken by Horace Bristol, on assignment for the Navy, in 1944.

This is what I wanted.

I met Mick for tea the next day, showed him the photo, and he agreed we had our reference image. The shoot would take place, courtesy of Gibson Guitars, at my beloved former Hit Factory in the basement, the very place where the previous year I had met Alexandra at Les Paul's ninetieth-birthday party. The party had been a wild, all night affair, attended by some of the most famous guitarists in the world, who had performed earlier that evening with Les at Carnegie Hall. Alexandra and I danced all night, not knowing that the next year she would become my manager.

Working out at the gym on a daily basis, I showed my trainers the "Gunner" photo, and other classical male images, including statues by Michelangelo, paintings by Caravaggio, and of Greek and Roman deities and heroes, on my video iPod. "This is what I want to look like." They would smile and push me to work with weights like I had never done before. It was actually *without* supervision that I pushed myself too far. Once, I ended up in the hospital, the first time since that time on tour. "Never have we seen such abuse to the soft tissue," snickered the doctor at St. Vincent's, as she brought in the other MDs to take a look. I lightened up my routine after that and, by the time the hot summer day of the shoot arrived, I felt ready to strip.

A few days before it was to take place, Syd Barrett died. He had been out the public eye for so long, the news came through like a transmission from outer space. Mick Rock, as one of Syd's closest friends and trusted collaborators since their days in Cambridge and one of the few photographers allowed to snap Barrett in his later years, was deluged with interview and photo requests. I phoned Mick the night before our session. "Let's dedicate the shoot to Syd," I suggested.

I had always been inherently shy. So to do a shoot that would require me to be completely nude for the good part of day, in front of technical people (including Mick's assistants and video crew, Gibson's staff, and representatives from Apple Computer, who were cataloging the frames for Mick in their new program, Aperture) was a big deal. But it turned out to be the most relaxed and productive day of shooting I had ever experienced. To a soundtrack of Iggy, the Modern Lovers, and the Velvet Underground, I sang along at the top of my lungs as Mick snapped frame after frame. It is a true testament to the magic of Love + Trust in collaboration that I felt so at ease, and not nearly as vulnerable as the character I was portraying. And strangely I felt that I lost any remaining inhibitions that day. Now, I believed, I could truly do *anything*.

I wonder if there is such a thing as free will. I mean, I was born the year rock and roll was born. I was born on the night James Dean died. I was on Top 40 radio before I could ride a bike. And even before I was born, my mother had herself wanted to be a singer. A star. It was in her blood, and flowed in mine. From my playpen, it had been reinforced, over and over. I wanted to face the audience again, on my own terms. Me, as I am *now*. I didn't care that I'd have to put myself back out into the line of fire, dodging the equally dangerous bullets of criticism or adulation. I wanted to stand, like Tommy in the Who's rock opera, and scream, "See me . . . Feel me . . . Touch me . . . *Heal* me . . . !" I wanted to raise Ziggy Stardust, the sacrificial rock messiah, up from the dead, reaching out to a new audience, "Give me your hands! You're *not* alone!" I wanted to go out onstage with all the raw power of Iggy, with all the intensity of Lou, with all the boundless energy of Jagger. I wanted to go out there again, knowing what I know now, and sing it for Kurt, Jim, Ian, Freddie Mercury, Pete, Michael, Brian, Sid, and Syd, Janis and Jimi . . . for Marc . . . and for you. And for me. I mean, I *have* to. I'm a frontman.

I began to feel less and less attached to time. Sure, appointments must be kept, and studio clocks tick dollars and cents, but in general, I am younger as I write this now than when I was touring, touring, touring, or stumbling home drunk, having lost my keys on the dance floor again. Time can move in different directions. History may repeat itself, but changes can be made the second or third time around. This is how we tie up loose ends and move forward.

Life is the perfect pop song.

On New Year's Eve, Tony Visconti invited me to his apartment, a few blocks from mine, where he was entertaining some guests, mostly from his t'ai chi master class. Just as I entered, before I had even removed my coat, Tony announced me to his guests. "Ah," he said, "here's Richard. Ladies and gentlemen, Richard *Barone*. He's going to sing for us!" By now, I knew the drill. Smiling to everyone seated, I walked over to Tony and gave him a hug, whispering, "Okay, but will you play bass?" "Sure." So, strapping on and plugging in a Les Paul Goldtop, I sang the song we had written together a New Year's Eve before:

> We could live, we could die
> we could crash, we could fly
> we could laugh, we could try
> yet another midnight
>
> Comes,
> and it goes
> And the cup
> overflows
> Where it ends
> no one knows
> yet another midnight . . . .

Time is a myth. It exists only as much as you let it. It is a continuum that loops around like a double helix. Like strands of DNA. It twists and turns and goes inside out. Time, like happiness, can mean whatever you let it. Midnight is the end of the day, and another new beginning.

ACKNOWLEDGMENTS

A special thanks to my friend and literary agent Janet Rosen for popping the question; to my first editor Richard Johnston; to John Cerullo, Belinda Yong, Mike Edison, Carol Flannery, Kevin Becketti, Jenna Young, and all at Backbeat and Hal Leonard; and to Mick Rock. I am indebted to my family and friends, including all the artists and musicians I am honored to know and work with, and to those who have inspired me; to my friend and mentor Tony Visconti; to the record labels that allowed my dreams to have a place to go; to the photographers whose work appears in this book; to Alex Rudenok and Ellen Joy Voell for their invaluable assistance; to my friends at Gibson Guitars and Apple Inc.; to my Angel; to all the frontmen and frontresses—past, present and future. . . .

And especially to Alexandra Parent, my friend and manager, who encouraged me to get to know the Frontman, look him in the eye, and tell his story.

The cover image of *FRONTMAN* was inspired by *Rescue at Rabaul: PBY Blister Gunner, 1944* by Horace Bristol (1908–97), one of the original *Time/LIFE* photographers. Digitally restored by rock musician and photographer, Graham Nash, and R. Mac Holbert for Nash Editions, Bristol's images of World War II are some of the most potent war photographs of the twentieth century. The "Gunner," described on page 194, is reproduced here with kind permission. © The Horace and Masako Bristol Estate.

SELECTED DISCOGRAPHY

Solo Albums

Glow (2007)
Collection: An Embarrassment of Richard (RBM Special Editions, 2004)
The Big Three—Boxed Set (Line, Germany 2000)
Between Heaven and Cello (Line, Germany 1997)
Clouds Over Eden (MESA Bluemoon/Rhino, 1993)
Primal Dream (MCA/Paradox, 1990)
Cool Blue Halo (Passport, 1987)

With The Bongos

Drums Along the Hudson — Special Edition (Cooking Vinyl, 2007)
Phantom Train (Unreleased, 1985)
The Shroud of Touring — Live (Unreleased, 1985)
Beat Hotel (RCA, 1985)
Numbers with Wings (RCA, 1983)
Drums Along the Hudson (PVC, 1982)

Solo Singles and EPs

"1, 2, 3 . . . Infinity" (RBM Special Editions, 2006)
"Forbidden"/"Standing in the Line"/"Law of the Jungle" (MESA, 1993)
"Nobody Knows Me"/"Standing in the Line"/"Native Tongue"
    (Line, Germany 1992)
Primal Cuts E.P. (Line, Germany, 1991)
"I Only Took What I Needed" (MCA/Paradox, 1991)
"River to River" (MCA/Paradox, 1990)
"Cry Baby Cry"/"I Belong to Me" (Passport, 1987)

Bongos Singles, EPs, and Compilations

"Brave New World"—Radio Edit 12" (RCA, 1985)
"Brave New World"/"Totem Pole" (RCA, 1985)
Last Testament (Fetish, 1985)
"Numbers with Wings"/"Barbarella" 12" (RCA, 1983)
"Numbers with Wings"/"Skydiving" (RCA Sweden, 1983)
"Barbarella"—Live at Columbia University (Trouser Press Flexi-disc, 1983)
Time and the River E.P. (Fetish, 1981)
"Mambo Sun" (Edit)/"Hunting" (Fetish, 1982)
"Zebra Club"/"Certain Harbours" (Fetish, 1981)
"The Bulrushes"/"Automatic Doors" (Fetish, 1981)
Start Swimming (Stiff, 1981)
"In the Congo"/"Mambo Sun" (Fetish, 1980)
"In the Congo"/"Hunting"/"Mambo Sun" 12" (Fetish, 1980)
"Telephoto Lens"/"Glow in the Dark" (Fetish, 1980)

Miscellaneous Guest Appearances and Compilations

October Project: Covered (October Project, 2006)
Sudden Sunsets: Highlights of the Benson AIDS Series (Downtown Music
    Productions, 2006)
Gary Lucas, Gods & Monsters, *Coming Clean* (Mighty Quinn, 2006)
Little Noises: Poems by Marcia Pelletiere (Saf'lini 2004)
Hit the Hay: Volume #7 (Sound Asleep, Sweden 2004)
The Baskervilles (Secret Crush, 2003)
Lynne Me Your Ears: A Tribute to Jeff Lynne (Not Lame, 2002)
Gary Lucas, *Improve the Shining Hour* (Knitting Factory Works, 2000)
Steve Almaas, *Kingo a Wild One* (Parasol, 2000)
Leif Arntzen, *I Love You* (Gwendoline, 2000)
Simply Mad, Mad, Mad, Mad About the Loser's Lounge (Zilcho, 1999)
Refuge: A Benefit for the People of Kosova (Orchard, 1999)
Our Favorite Texan: Bobby Fuller Four-Ever! (#9, Japan 1999)
George Usher, *Dutch April* (Parasol, 1998)
Buster Poindexter, *Spanish Rocket Ship* (Island, 1997)
Yellow Pills: Volume 4 (Big Deal, 1997)
It's Only a Dream (Medulla, 1996)
For the Love of Harry: Everybody Sings Nilsson (BMG/MusicMasters, 1995)
Jill Sobule (Atlantic, 1994)
The Windbreakers, *Any Monkey with a Typewriter* (Big Monkey, 1983)
Nuts and Bolts—with James Mastro (Passport, 1983)

Production Credits

Johnny Rodgers and Liza Minelli, "Let's Make a Date" (TBR, 2007)
Jolie Jones, *Little Kisses* (2006)
The Analogues (2006)
Tracy Stark, *Feast for the Heart* (2006)
Klaus Nomi, *The Nomi Song Remixes* (Palm Pictures, 2005)
Johnny Rodgers, *Box of Photographs* (PS Classics, 2005)
Lach, *Today* (Fortified, 2004)
Amy Rigby, *Till the Wheels Fall Off* (Signature Sounds, 2003)
Rolan Bolan, "Operator" (2001)
Angry Elves, *Make a World* (Stump Rock, 2001)
Lach, *Kids Fly Free* (Fortified, 2001)
Loser's Lounge, *How Can a Loser Ever Win?* (Zilcho, 2001)
Loser's Lounge, *Simply Mad, Mad, Mad, Mad About the Loser's Lounge*
    (Zilcho, 1999)
Lach, *Blang!* (Fortified, 1999)
Fred Schneider, "Coconut" (BMG/MusicMasters, 1995)
Natalie McDonald, "Sequins in Excelsis Deo" (Barracuda Blue, 1991)
The Fundamentals, *Feelin' Strange* (P.O.S./Paradox, 1989)
Natalie McDonald, "The Third Degree" (Pinnacle, 1988)
Phosphenes (Coyote, 1983)
Steve Almaas, *Beat Rodeo* (Coyote, 1983)
Tiny Tim (Unreleased, 1976)
Snails (Unreleased, 1976)

Selected Songwriting Credits

Jill Sobule
    I Never Learned to Swim (Beyond, 2001)
    Pink Pearl (Beyond, 2000)
    Happy Town (Atlantic, 1997)
Johnny Rodgers
    Box of Photographs (PS Classics, 2005)
Marti Jones
    My Tidy Doily Dream (DAR, 2002)
    Match Game (A & M, 1986)
    Unsophisticated Time (A & M, 1985)
Fred Schneider
    Just Fred (Reprise, 1996)

George Usher
    Fire Garden (Parasol, 2003)
    Somewhere Down the Road (Lazy Cat, Japan 1998)
    Miracle School (Massa, 1996)
    Neptune (Lonesome Whippoorwill, Sweden 1990)
Sally Timms
    Cowboy Sally's Twilight Laments for Lost Buckaroos (Bloodshot, 1999)
Deni Bonet
    Last Girl on Earth (2007)

Continue the *Frontman* journey with music playlists, iMixes, and special features at www.FrontmanBook.com.

PERMISSIONS

"Before You Were Born"
Richard Barone
© 1990 Miniature Music (ASCAP)

"To the Pure . . . "
Richard Barone
© 1990 Miniature Music (ASCAP)

"Standing in the Line"
Richard Barone
©1992 Miniature Music (ASCAP)

"Miss Jean"
Lyrics by Richard Barone
© 1993 Miniature Music (ASCAP)/Juters Music (BMI)

"Paper Airplane"
Richard Barone & Mark Johnson
© 1993 Miniature Music (ASCAP)/Cold Weather Music (BMI)

"Life During Wartime"
David Byrne, Chris Franz, Tina Weymouth, Jerry Harrison
© 1979 Bleu Disque Music Co., Inc.

"I'll Be Your Mirror"
Lou Reed
© 1966 Oakfield Avenue Music (BMI)
All rights controlled and administered by Screen Gems/EMI, Inc.

"Yet Another Midnight"
Richard Barone & Tony Visconti
© 2007 Richard Barone Music/Pneumatic Music (BMI)

INDEX

SONG INDEX

To experience the soundtrack to *FRONTMAN*, along with videos and related album tracks, please visit www.FrontmanBook.com.